SHAPING THE GLOBAL LEADER

Considering behavioral norms in their cultural contexts, this book arrives at a fully operational international leadership theory – and makes it accessible to academic and professional readers alike.

Shaping the Global Leader fundamentally covers eight cultural dimensions gleaned from acclaimed international leadership scholars such as Geert Hofstede and the GLOBE study authors. Each cultural dimension is followed by interviews of renowned organizational leaders who relate their experiences in that area and each section underscores strategies for moving forward. The authors highlight critical lessons from classic behavioral psychology experiments and apply these findings to the international organizational context.

This book serves as an eminently readable and enlightening handbook for those working, leading or studying interculturally. Both students and professionals in international leadership or business will be provided with clear and actionable organizational insights for an increasingly complex global landscape.

Henry P. Biggs, PhD, JD, MBA, serves currently as CEO of Course Scheduling and Eusabian Technologies – software development companies with locations in the United States, Europe, and Asia. Formerly the Chair of the Foreign Language Department at Houghton College, Biggs served as the Assistant then Associate Dean in the College of Arts and Sciences at Washington University in St. Louis, where he also taught International Leadership with co-author Lenny Ramsey. He is a dual citizen of the United States and Italy, and currently resides in Paris, France.

Tom Bussen, JD, MBA, formerly served as a Peace Corps Volunteer in Asia and as an Assistant Professor of Business at the American University of Central Asia, Bishkek, Kyrgyzstan. Bussen taught courses there in Leadership, International Business, and Ethics. More recently, Bussen served as Visiting Researcher at the Central European University in Budapest, Hungary, and is now a doctoral student in Organizational Behavior Management at the University of Florida.

Lenny Ramsey, PhD, is an Assistant Professor of Physical Therapy at Carroll University. She earned her PhD in Neuroscience through the McDonnell International Scholars Academy at Washington University in St. Louis, where she taught International Leadership. She is a citizen of the Netherlands.

"Embrace yourself for a breathtaking journey in the multifaceted world of cultural beliefs and practices. A must for any student, professional, and world traveler wanting to increase their cultural IQ."

Dr. Nitish Singh
Professor of International Business, The Boeing Institute of International Business, Saint Louis University, USA

"This book offers a new approach to a better understanding of other cultures and would help prevent wrong ideas on how a businessperson or an international lawyer should behave when negotiating with partners from other cultures."

Joël L. Monéger
Emeritus Professor of Law, Jean Monnet Chair ad personam, Dr HC, France

SHAPING THE GLOBAL LEADER

Fundamentals in Culture and Behavior for Optimal Organizational Performance

Henry P. Biggs, Tom Bussen, and Lenny Ramsey

NEW YORK AND LONDON

First published 2020
by Routledge
52 Vanderbilt Avenue, New York, NY 10017

and by Routledge
2 Park Square, Milton Park, Abingdon, Oxon, OX14 4RN

Routledge is an imprint of the Taylor & Francis Group, an informa business

© 2020 Taylor & Francis

The right of Henry P. Biggs, Tom Bussen, and Lenny Ramsey to be identified as authors of this work has been asserted by them in accordance with sections 77 and 78 of the Copyright, Designs, and Patents Act 1988.

All rights reserved. No part of this book may be reprinted or reproduced or utilized in any form or by any electronic, mechanical, or other means, now known or hereafter invented, including photocopying and recording, or in any information storage or retrieval system, without permission in writing from the publishers.

Trademark notice: Product or corporate names may be trademarks or registered trademarks, and are used only for identification and explanation without intent to infringe.

Library of Congress Cataloging-in-Publication Data
Names: Biggs, Henry, author. | Bussen, Tom, author. | Ramsey, Lenny, author.
Title: Shaping the global leader : fundamentals in culture and behavior for optimal organizational performance / Henry Biggs, Tom Bussen, and Lenny Ramsey.
Description: New York : Routledge, 2019. | Includes index.
Identifiers: LCCN 2019016389| ISBN 9780367225186 (hardback) | ISBN 9780367225193 (pbk.) | ISBN 9780429275296 (ebook)
Subjects: LCSH: Organizational effectiveness. | Organizational behavior. | Corporate culture. | Leadership.
Classification: LCC HD58.9 .B4946 2019 | DDC 658.4/092--dc23
LC record available at https://lccn.loc.gov/2019016389

ISBN: 978-0-367-22518-6 (hbk)
ISBN: 978-0-367-22519-3 (pbk)
ISBN: 978-0-429-27529-6 (ebk)

Typeset in Bembo
by Lumina Datamatics Limited

Visit the eResources: www.routledge.com/textbooks/9780367225193

 Printed in the United Kingdom by Henry Ling Limited

CONTENTS

Introduction		vii
1	The What, How, and Why of Culture	1
2	Individualism – Collectivism	11
3	A Glass of Beer, a Shot of Sake, and Groupthink	31
4	Group Work and the Free-rider Effect	55
5	Achievement – Ascription	62
6	Power Distance: Hierarchical versus Egalitarian	76
7	Avoiding the Elixir of Power	100
8	Uncertainty Avoidance	109
9	The Loss Aversion Bias	126
10	Assertiveness	134
11	Pan-cultural Motivation	144
12	Attitudes in Time	161

13 Communication Is More – Much More – than
   Language   172
14 Ethnocentrism   186
Conclusion   210

Appendix   213
Index   220

INTRODUCTION

In the last 50 years, leadership scholars have tended to limit their research to Western subjects. However, Westerners' underlying values, beliefs, and way of getting things done often differ in profound ways from the rest of the world. So much so, in fact, that scholars Joseph Henrich and his colleagues coined an acronym to define this group: WEIRD (western, educated, industrialized, rich, and democratic). In fact, WEIRD are among the *least* representative people on Earth.[1]

This leads to questions about the generalizability of leadership research to other parts of the world. But several scholars in particular have conducted exhaustive work internationally to explain how culture varies and the ways in which this variance influences upon leadership models. Most notably, the work of Hofstede, Trompenaars, and the GLOBE (Global Leadership & Organizational Behavior Effectiveness) Study have stood out for its thoroughness; these works, therefore, serve as the fundamental core of our research here.

Management scholars are well versed in biases generally, but less often aware of the cross-cultural bias. The reason is that when we reference culture, we refer to the ways in which our minds are "cultivated" to act. Mental programming is the term used by Geert Hofstede, a scholar that many would fairly argue wrote the book on culture. Hofstede's choice of words implies that just as surely as a computer is programmed to behave in one way without variation—and without recognition that deviation is even a possibility—so, too, does culture operate this way on many people. For example, many westerners consider eye contact an essential character of the well-mannered, while in parts of Asia just the opposite is true. To "see" another way requires a reprogramming of our mindsets, and so what follows is something of a product listing for the different programs on offer in our world today.

We therefore introduce the reader to alternative approaches, doing our best to keep our own prejudices at bay as the "right way" of doing things. There are many ways, and students of international business do well to familiarize themselves with these core concepts which we introduce throughout this book.

Interplaying with culture, however, are phenomena of behavioral psychology. We see much that is innately human rather than culturally determined in behavioral contexts, such as obedience to authority, as revealed by Milgram; gender and racial stereotyping as revealed by Steele; and the effects of authority as unsettlingly disclosed by Zimbardo.[2] To be sure, culture does play a role in tempering or exacerbating these behaviors, and how certain behaviors play within cultures is fundamental to developing a truly insightful leadership policy.

It is said that President Theodore Roosevelt would discover the most passionate interests of important people he planned to meet—be it sailing, astronomy, philosophy, or anything else—and that he would spend the night before the meeting studying that topic and then would woo his counterpart during the meeting by engaging in a rich discourse on the subject.

This tactic worked to spectacular success. But imagine the reverse effect if, instead of learning about his counterpart's most passionate interests, he didn't bother to learn about even their most fundamental beliefs—their religion and language, whether tea or coffee or vodka or hookah should be served, whether they preferred formal greetings and direct and open exchanges, or gave greater credibility based on seniority. If Roosevelt built a sense of connection by highlighting similarities, neglecting culture is to perpetuate differences.

Appreciating this nuance is thus essential to good leadership but also good followership and to be a good citizen of the world. This is true for an American preparing to study abroad in Paris or a young Nigerian professional considering a transfer opportunity to Brazil. It is also true for a midcareer professional attending monthly or quarterly meetings at branch offices around the world, or considering whether and where to open a new office. This is even true for those with a personal rather than a professional interest in the cultures of the world—for those with a love of culture, a passion to travel in a way that goes beyond the guidebooks, or even to better understand a sometimes inscrutable significant other, in-law or friend from another culture.

So buckle up. We are about to embark on a global field trip, from the rugged mountains of central Asia to the savannas of Africa to the metropolises of eastern Asia and the small towns of middle America. In our travels, we'll explore classic behavioral experiments that help us better understand how biases and stereotypes often stalk cross-cultural organizations, and how personal and employee motivations can be both universally true (universal) or culturally specific (relativist). We'll explore what it means to be an ethical leader around the world, and see that ethics itself can prove rather protean. And we'll see the fundamental importance of communication and understanding in effective cross-cultural interactions.

But before beginning, let us pause to admire the following ode to culture and underscore first principles, that culture is something to be esteemed and admired, not minimized or avoided:

> Man is the only animal with a culture, and it is this culture that has enabled him to become preeminent in the animal kingdom. To appreciate the importance of culture, consider the possibilities of man's natural animal state. By nature, man is a tropical creature and cannot survive without culture in any cold climate. For defense, he has neither sharp teeth nor claws, nor does he have great speed. He has no natural tools for digging, climbing, or killing to obtain food. Human infants are unable to care for themselves for several years, during which time they prove an additional burden to the mother in seeking to survive.
>
> If man had to live without culture, he would be at a serious disadvantage in comparison to other animals and would certainly never exist in great numbers. Fortunately, he is not forced to live in this fashion, for by using his well-developed brain he has created culture, which helps him to overcome his physical disadvantages.
>
> Ernest Schusky and T. Patrick Culbert
> *Introducing Culture*[3]

References

1 Joseph Henrich, Steven J. Heine, and Ara Norenzayan, "The Weirdest People in the World?" 33 *Behav. Brain Sci.* 61, 79 (2010).
2 See Stanley Milgram, "Behavioral Study of Obedience," 67 *J. Abnorm. Soc. Psychol.* 371–378 (1963); see also Claude Steele and Joshua Aronson, "Stereotype Threat and the Intellectual Test Performance of African Americans," 69 J. Pers. Soc. Psychol. 797–811 (1995); see also C. Haney, C. Banks, and P. Zimbardo, *Interpersonal Dynamics in a Simulated Prison*, Stanford University (1972).
3 Ernest Schusky and T. Patrick Culbert, *Introducing Culture*, Prentice Hall Anthropology Series (Englewood Cliffs, NJ, 1967).

1
THE WHAT, HOW, AND WHY OF CULTURE

Vérité en deçà des Pyrénées, erreur au-delà.
(There are truths on this side of the Pyrenees which are falsehoods on the other.)
Michel de Montaigne
Sixteenth Century

Culture: A Brief Introduction

Leadership can be taught. Confucius knew this,[1] Machiavelli believed this, and most management educators subscribe to this idea as well.[2] But what if you are being taught the wrong thing? What if the information on leadership you've heard is coming from scholars of the same Western, educated, industrial, rich, and democratic – or WEIRD[3] – perspective. Furthermore, many of the behavioral tests themselves are being conducted on this limited cross-section, bringing the contended universality of the resulting behavioral findings into question. This is problematic but may help our readers understand why proposed leadership theories and behavioral research outcomes often fail to comport with the reality of cross-cultural environments and behaviors.

Leadership refers to the process by which an individual is able to "influence, motivate, and enable others to contribute toward the effectiveness and success of the organizations of which they are members."[4] But the ways in which people are influenced, motivated, and enabled is understood differently in different countries. Emerson, a Fortune 500 company with operations throughout the world and with more than 75,000 employees,[5] provides a good example of a multinational company that must pay close attention to such things. Jean Paul Montupet is eminently qualified to speak to these challenges. He has served as the business leader for Emerson Industrial Automation, the executive vice president for Emerson, the chairman of Emerson Asia-Pacific while in Hong Kong, and as president of Emerson Europe. Montupet worked closely first with longtime CEO Charles "Chuck" Knight and later with current CEO David Farr. He relates the following story, seemingly grounded in corporate governance but which ultimately has much broader implications:

> Corporations around the world have to deal with three main constituencies: customers, employees and shareholders. For American companies, the number-one priority is to achieve the financial results expected by the shareholders. In order to do that, you, of course, need to fully satisfy your customers and treat your employees well. But if it comes to the point where trade-offs have to be made, it is usually the financial objectives that prevail.
>
> In Europe and Asia, the priority is more often the protection of the employees, as illustrated by the Japanese practice of "employment for life," or the fact that during an economic downturn, German companies do not lay off as many people as a US company would. Instead, they put many redundant employees into training programs while waiting for better times to return.
>
> Another example of those trade-offs has to do with the offshoring of manufacturing jobs to low-cost countries: many American companies, Emerson being one, have taken advantage of NAFTA to move some manufacturing jobs to Mexico. While no American worker is happy to lose his or her job under such circumstances, the American workforce is usually abler to understand the economic motivation of such a move and can be receptive to the argument that, by improving its overall competitiveness, the company will ultimately be able to grow and create more jobs in the United States. In Europe, the employees and the unions that represent them are strictly focused on the protection of their jobs regardless of the consequences for the rest of the company.
>
> Emerson was confronted by that situation in the early 1990s when eastern Europe opened up and offered low-cost opportunities similar to those in Mexico. Emerson CEO Chuck Knight was keen to quickly take advantage of these opportunities. My view was that we could do it, but it would take more time as we would first need to get our European management to accept the idea, and then we would have to work with them to develop appropriate communication plans to which our European employees would be receptive. We would also have to be patient, as due to European laws the process takes longer and is also more expensive. Chuck Knight, who had worked in Europe in the early part of his career, was fully capable of understanding the differences with the United States, and in the end Emerson was successful in adding a best-cost eastern European manufacturing base to its already powerful western European setup.

Other American companies did not take the same prudent and disciplined approach and have run into serious problems, such as suffering from long and violent strikes with employees occupying the plants, who burned old tires out front. That never happened at Emerson because of the good communication programs and the proper adaptation to the local culture. The fact that CEOs Chuck Knight, and his successor, David Farr, had extensive international experience was also essential.[6]

The point is that what works "here" – wherever "here" is – may not, and often will not, work "there." Indeed, it is with a certain degree of arrogance that scholars assume the American standard for leadership, profoundly influenced by American culture, works well as a model for vastly different cultures.

Geert Hofstede is considered by most to be the first to make the case – through a dogged empiricism – that leadership principles touted in the United States were hopelessly blended with US-centric cultural beliefs that had more limited application for other cultures. Hofstede wrote: "If one thing has become clear, it is that the export of Western – mostly American – management practices *and* theories to poor countries has contributed little to nothing to their development."[7] Hofstede went on to note that some of the most famous management minds of all time, such as management theorists Frederick Taylor, Henri Fayol, and Peter Drucker, all sought universally applicable management styles. However, as Trompenaars, a leading scholar who followed Hofstede, later wrote: "the fallacy of the 'one best way' is a management fallacy which is dying a slow death."[8]

Between 1967 and 1971, Hofstede carried out cultural studies on tens of thousands of IBM employees across fifty countries,[9] and he updated this work in subsequent decades. The results of these studies provide a working foundation upon which to understand cultural dimensions across virtually the entire world. Although national cultures are in part perception, Hofstede writes: "National and regional differences are felt by people to be a reality – and therefore they are a reality."

Hofstede's work is a guide in our own investigation of cross-cultural leadership, and it is supplemented by the work of Fons Trompenaars and Charles Hamden-Turner, authors of the cross-cultural management classic, *Riding the Waves of Culture*, a work that includes survey responses from more than thirty thousand participants. Finally, our work is based on the *GLOBE Study of 62 Societies* by Robert House and colleagues. All these researchers categorize their findings through the use of their own cultural dimensions that overlap to varying degrees. Additionally, a fundamental grounding for our work here is to take a hard look at how to effectively lead internationally to apply many of the lessons from psychology and behavioral economics across territories.

When we discuss national culture, it is important to establish that a national culture simply represents the values held by a *majority* of members. This means we can say there is such a thing as an American culture or a Peruvian culture, but it is virtually assured that no single American perfectly encapsulates the American culture. This is partly because culture often varies between different categories of people – rich and poor, secular and sectarian, educated and uneducated, rural and urban, as well as by type of profession – within a country, thereby creating subcultures to the broader culture. Professionals, for instance, may be said to have their own subcultures that cross country lines: lawyers around the world may have a certain concept of justice, musicians may tend to be independent-minded nonconformists, and executives are more charismatic than your average person. Even sports teams may have cultures that elicit passionate advocacy, as the New York Yankees-Boston Red Sox or Leeds United-Manchester United rivalries illustrate.

If all this variation exists, why study national culture? The reason is that even if no single American perfectly encapsulates the American culture, we can say most Americans will encapsulate most of the American cultural values. We can add that the average American will more closely resemble the American culture type than that of Peru or any other country. Consequently, national cultures are not perfect representations of all national citizens, but as the Voltaire-inspired aphorism goes, we should not let perfect be the enemy of good.

With that in mind, it is best to begin by addressing the what, how, and why: that is, what culture is, how culture can be seen and understood, and why culture exists.

NOTE: For readers interested in the theoretical components of the cultural dimensions constructed throughout this book, and for greater detail on the workability of the system constructed, please refer to the appendix.

Culture Defined

Edward B. Tylor wrote in 1871: "Culture is that complex whole which includes knowledge, belief, art, morals, law, custom, and any other capabilities and habits acquired by [humankind] as a member of society." Or, as it has been put it more simply, "Culture is the way we do things here."[10] These definitions explain *what* culture is, but let's think about *how* culture appears to us, and *why* we have it.

Is Culture an Onion?

As articulated famously by the lovable ogre Shrek, ogres have layers and onions have layers, and we would argue so too does culture.[11] The outer layers might best be described as observable things, including the food, dress, and music of a society. A typical tourist in Paris or Rome probably goes no deeper than this outer layer. After all, when we say, "When in Rome, do as the Romans do," we typically mean nothing more than "try the wine" or "eat the gelato." But at the inner levels, we have a more immovable culture, and this is where doing as the Romans do becomes a greater challenge. It in this inner realm where our values are so closely held that we may not even be aware they are part of our culture – Collingwood has referred to this deeply layered culture as the "absolute presupposition about life."[12] Hofstede's "mental programming," a definitional companion to Collingwood's, makes clear how deep in the human psyche these cultural values lie.

The inner and outer levels are, however, linked rather than perfectly distinct. For instance, Russian men of the former Soviet Union began wearing Levi's jeans – thereby changing the visible outer layer – in order to reflect a solidarity with the liberal values of the Western world, which represented the inner layer.

Alternatively, the outer layer may change first, such as when more liberal attire for women is adopted, while gender equality still is not. This type of gap has been termed a "culture lag." "The concept of culture lag is useful for understanding why Americans may drive next year's cars by yesterday's traffic laws."[13] Consequently, there is a certain amount of hand wringing that perceived transgressions to the outer levels will feed into depredations at the inner levels. Governments and people from China to Iran, and even France, believe in the power of this connection and thus resist so-called "cultural imperialism" from the United States and other countries. As *The Economist* relates, China's government seeks to be become a "socialist culture superpower."[14] To this end, China is now explicitly using the outer layers of the onion to impact core values. It is, for instance, limiting the entry of foreign children's books to the country and is deemphasizing pop stars on television in lieu of classical poetry quiz shows and children's competitions in writing complex Chinese characters.[15]

The Composition of the Onion: Economic, Political, and Religious

The layers that collectively comprise the cultural "onion" include economic, political, and religious or ideological institutions, among others, that affect social interactions and beliefs. History also has profound effects on culture, but history may be better understood as underpinning the other factors rather than a standalone concept.

As just one example, consider economics. In the Central Asian nation of Kyrgyzstan, much of the population is poor, rural, and still today lives a seminomadic lifestyle in which a temporary home is set up in the pastures each summer. This is an inner level component of culture that has ramifications on the outer levels. One of these outer level reflections is a certain bewilderment at the idea of running for exercise.[16] Most of the population gets abundant exercise during their daily work, in a way that more sedentary folks – including many professionals – do not. Additionally, strenuous exercise is a privilege. These exercises consume additional calories and so require more sustenance. For many people in this nation, and indeed in many parts of the world, foods with high nutritional value give way to cheaper materials such as breads and broths.

In Kazakhstan, by contrast, physical activity is abundant. Almaty, the largest city, is dotted with fitness centers, tennis courts, soccer fields, swimming pools, and bike and ski rental shops. Kazakhstan is also much wealthier than Kyrgyzstan thanks to its oil and gas revenues, with the average person earning seven times more than in Kyrgyzstan.[17] Based on the ready participation of locals in physical activities, we might speculate that this wealth allows for more time to engage in "active-leisure" activities such as hiking or sports. And yet Kazakh and Kyrgyz culture are remarkably similar. They have a shared nomadic tradition, a similar history as Tsarist Russian and later Soviet subjects, nearly identical languages, and, up until independence in 1991, a similar economic history. The comparison of these historically and traditionally similar countries shows the powerful impact that economics can have on culture.

Secondly, we recognize that political systems are enormously varied throughout the world. There are democracies and dictatorships and systems in between. A vibrant democracy may gain vigor through freedom of speech, which may result in a cultural affinity for outspoken celebrities and politicians. There are societies with high transparency and low governmental corruption, such as the Scandinavian countries of Northern Europe, where trust flourishes, but societies such as Turkmenistan, Eritrea, and North Korea are virtually cut off from the world and social interactions are largely governed by state ideologies.

These political systems impact culture because of their profound effect on other factors. For instance, political systems can play a significant role in determining economic outcomes. Political systems may gain their legitimacy from religion, as is the case in Iran and to a certain degree Saudi Arabia, and one might mischievously argue England (where the titular head of government, now the queen, is the head of the Church of England), or they may foreclose religious freedoms (as in the former Soviet Union and as remains the law *de jure* in China, Cuba and elsewhere).

The innermost part of the onion may also relate to the dominant religion of a society. This, in turn, may result in societal values, norms or taboos regarding honesty, compassion, or respect for elders. Further out still, the values may be reflected in certain rules and systems of law, the violation of which result in punishment. If the laws do not reflect underlying values, we can note that disobedience is more probable. Finally, the outer part of the onion may include celebrities who exhibit great compassion in their lives, athletes with a reputation for honest play, or elder statesmen that personify the dignity and wisdom of a society.

Finally, religion plays a crucial rule in the culture of many societies. The world's major religions bring moral and ethical systems, many that overlap to a significant degree. However, in spite of this overlap, the resulting behaviors and societal norms vary enormously, not just among religions but even within sects. We'll discuss, for instance, how Catholics and Protestants vary in important cultural ways on the basis of religious norms, how Mormon outer layer cultural beliefs manifest culturally through abstention from caffeine, alcohol and tobacco, and how the conflict between Shias and Sunnis has proven unresolvable for more than a thousand years.

TABLE 1.1 Onion diagram

Inner	Middle	Outer
Ideology (e.g., Christian)	Honesty as a value	Fair play in sports
Ideology (e.g., liberalism)	Equality	Gender rights; Diverse fashion styles
Economics (e.g., wealthy)	Short working hours	Outdoor active; Coffee culture, and other social activities
Political (e.g., democratic)	Freedom of speech	Respect for outspoken leaders; Vibrant media

These institutions and belief systems are interdependent. Additionally, some of these may be more or less relevant to culture. For example, religion plays a minimal role on the culture of an officially atheistic country such as North Korea but a disproportionately important role in Saudi society. Regardless of the relative importance by county, looking at these broad categories allows us to see the ways in which culture manifests, as well as some of its underlying causes. In the following chapters, we'll look at specific cultural dimensions, and we'll see how some institutional and belief systems may drive those dimensions (see Table 1.1).

Culture: The Best Survival Mechanism Invented

We conclude this section by briefly discussing *why* we have culture in the first place. "Culture" comes from the same root as the verb "to cultivate," or "till the soil."[18] Culture is first and foremost about survival – giving a community the best chance to perpetuate its existence. A farmer in Equatorial Guinea and a farmer in Russia have a lot in common – both cultivating the land, manipulating the flow of water for their own benefit, and seeking markets for their products. But environmental factors result in different produce grown, different techniques of cultivation, and different seasonal schedules. Similarly, societies are cultivated in ways responsive to natural and humanmade realities. Furthermore, just as the farmers share commonalities and enjoy differences, societies too share some universal (or "pancultural") behaviors and ideas but also diverge.

Trompenaars demonstrates how these differences can beget more differences across a range of factors:

> People, like the Pueblo Indians, who own land in common and exploit it communally, are going to emphasize cooperation in their man-to-man relationships. Similarly, their gods are not likely to be seen as highly competitive figures; rather, the religion emphasizes the morality of working together.

We would note that the causation could go the other way – perhaps the Pueblo Indians owned land in common *because* they originally conceptualized their gods as collaborative figures. Regardless of direction, the fundamental point is that societies organize in such a way as to maximize the chances at survival and prosperity, and this form of organization impacts the economic, political, and religious institutions that give shape to cultures.

Human Nature versus Culture

> If you prick us, do we not bleed? if you tickle us, do we not laugh? if you poison us, do we not die? and if you wrong us, shall we not revenge?
> William Shakespeare
> *The Merchant of Venice*

Some cross-cultural scholars go far in suggesting that virtually everything has a culturally specific component. Hofstede, for example, argues that values are *"never* universal" (italics added).[19] We have already noted the Western bias of many authors of leadership programs. But to deny a degree of universalism – by which we mean values that are shared by the vast majority of people in geographically, socially, and economically dispersed environments – is to deny the bonds that hold us together. Without these shared traits, only our differences would define us. This is where behavioral psychology can inform us by identifying traits that are indeed common to us all, albeit sometimes expressed differently through the affecting prism of different cultures.

Even the authors of *The Weirdest People in the World?*, a book that addresses Western cultural biases, assert that "we expect humans from all societies share, and probably share substantially, basic aspects of cognition, motivation, and behavior."[20] Indeed, even the range of variability within human personalities – the so-called Five-Factor Model of Personality[21] – is considered universal. Or as Taiwanese singer Jolin Tsai put it in his song title, "We're All Different, Yet the Same."

A reason for this is our common ancestral origins. At a certain level, we all come from the same atavistic source, and research in certain areas oddly bears this out. For example, it has been discovered that cognition improves significantly when people are asked to walk in nature for one hour, while no change in performance occurs when people are instead asked to walk in an urban environment.[22] In the book *Natural Born Heroes*, Christopher McDougall summarizes: "That's all it takes, just a reminder of our ancestral past can be enough to flip a switch in the brain that focuses attention and shuts out distractions. You slip back into hunter-gatherer mode – and when you do, you're capable of remarkable things."[23]

So as we prepare to define those differences, let's recall the similarities. It is often these similarities that are so important in building trust and forming relationships with people across cultures (see Table 1.2).

TABLE 1.2 Common across cultures, or "pancultural"

Obedience	Feasting	Property rights
Dancing	Food taboos	Residence rules
Fire making	Housing	Status differentiation
Cooking	Community organization	Folklore
Kinship systems	Courtship (and sexual appetite)	Funeral rites
Body adornments	Division of labor	Mourning
Play	Education	Music
Trade	Family	Dream interpretation
Grammar[24]	Government	Personal names
Dress	Incest taboos	Surgery[25]
Religion	Inheritance rules	Age as a social variant[26]
Gender differences	Language	Facial displays of emotion[27]
Decorative art	Marriage	Displays of pride[28]
	Property rights	

References

1 Barbara Kellerman, *Leadership: Essential Selections on Power, Authority, and Influence* 9 (McGraw-Hill Education) (2010).
2 Jonathan P. Doh, "Can Leadership Be Taught? Perspectives from Management Educators," 2 *Acad. Learning Educ.*, 54 (2003).
3 See introduction for a definition and explanation of WEIRD (see page 7).
4 Robert J. House and Mansour Javidan, "Overview of GLOBE," in *Culture, Leadership, and Organizations: The Globe Study of 62 Societies* 15 (eds. Robert House, Paul J. Hanges, Mansour Javidan et al., SAGE Publications) (2004).
5 *#481 Emerson Electric*, Forbes (last accessed July 28, 2018), https://www.forbes.com/companies/emerson-electric/.
6 Jean Paul Montupet, Interview with Author.
7 Hofstede, *supra* note 4 at 86.
8 Fons Trompenaars and Charles Hampden-Turner, *Riding the Waves of Culture: Understanding Cultural Diversity in Business* 5 (Nicholas Brealey Publishing: London, 2nd ed.) (1997).
9 Geert Hofstede, "The Cultural Relativity of Organizational Practices and Theories," *J. Int'l Bus. Studies* 75, 76 (1983).
10 Brené Brown, *Daring Greatly: How the Courage to Be Vulnerable Transforms the Way We Live* 174 (Penguin Group: New York) (2012).
11 Trompenaars and Hampden-Turner, the first order cross-cultural scholars to whom we will defer throughout this book, created this analogy. See Trompenaars and Hampden-Turner, *supra* note 12 at 6.
12 *Id.* at 7.
13 Schusky and Culbert, *supra* note 3.
14 "The Chinese Party is Redefining What it Means to Be Chinese," *The Economist* (Aug. 17, 2017), https://www.economist.com/news/china/21726748-and-glossing-over-its-own-history-mauling-chinese-culture-communist-party-redefining.
15 *Id.*
16 Author Bussen lived in Kyrgyzstan for nearly three years, and his running was met with befuddled stares (and occasional outright laughter) by uncomprehending locals. This no doubt was exacerbated by the scarcity of foreigners in the country, which

itself can bear profoundly on the local culture as well. This is not confined to foreign cultures either. Odd glances are common in rural towns in the US and may even be greeted with a "Run, Forrest, run," with the movie *Forrest Gump* being their only exposure to long-distance running.

17 *GDP Per Capita,* World Development Indicators (last visited July 28, 2018), https://www.google.hu/publicdata/explore?ds=d5bncppjof8f9_&met_y=ny_gdp_pcap_cd&hl=en&dl=en#!ctype=l&strail=false&bcs=d&nselm=h&met_y=ny_gdp_pcap_cd&scale_y=lin&ind_y=false&rdim=country&idim=country:KAZ:KGZ&ifdim=country&hl=en_US&dl=en&ind=false.
18 Schusky and Culbert, *supra* note 3.
19 Geert Hofstede, "Problems Remain, but Theories Will Change: The Universal and the Specific in 21st-Century Global Management," 28 *Organ. Dyn.* 34, 43 (1999).
20 Henrich, et al., *supra* note 1 at 62.
21 These are extraversion/introversion, agreeableness, conscientiousness, neuroticism/emotional stability, and openness to experience. See Christopher J. Soto and Joshua J. Jackson, *Five-Factor Model of Personality*, Oxford Biographies (July 28, 2018), http://www.oxfordbibliographies.com/view/document/obo-9780199828340/obo-9780199828340-0120.xml.
22 Marc G. Berman, John Jonides, and Stephen Kaplan. The cognitive benefits of interacting with nature. in *Psychological Science* 19, no. 12 (2008): 1207–1212.
23 Christopher Mcdougall, *Natural Born Heroes: Mastering the Lost Secrets of Strength and Endurance* 222 (Vintage; Reprint Edition) (2016).
24 Henrich, et al., *supra* note 1 at 62.
25 Schusky and Culbert, supra note 3.
26 *Id.*
27 Henrich, et al., *supra* note 1 at 69.
28 *Id.*

2
INDIVIDUALISM – COLLECTIVISM

> Whosoever is delighted in solitude is either a wild beast or a god
> Aristotle[1]

Let's return to our discussion about the WEIRD nature of American culture as it applies to individualism. It may come as no surprise that the United States is considered one of the most individualistic countries on Earth.[2] And while the I in WEIRD actually stands for industrialized, it could just as well have stood for individualistic.

We can think of individualism as the degree to which one is responsible, first and foremost, for looking after oneself and one's immediate family. One's opinions, beliefs, and values need not be shared with the rest of one's family, and, if the typical American Thanksgiving table is any indication, opinion, beliefs, and values often are *not* shared with all members of the family. In collectivist societies, by contrast, ties are further reaching and may include immediate and extended family, and friends, and also in some cases one's community, ethnic group, or religious family (collectively referred to hereafter as one's "in-group").[3]

America is one of the most individualistic countries on Earth – *the* most individualistic, according to some studies – and a large share of leadership researchers are also Americans working at American institutions with American study participants. Leadership theory is therefore often based on the preconception that one's "followers" will be individualists who are driven in part by their own self-interests rather than those of a larger group.[4] But as we'll discuss more below, it is to the cross-cultural manager's benefit to recognize that collectivists are motivated differently than individualists in some important ways.

12 Individualism – Collectivism

Indeed, the vast majority of the world's people live in societies that lean toward this type of collectivism,[5] and high levels of in-group collectivism are seen in the regions of Southern Asia, the Middle East, Eastern Europe, Latin America, and East Asia.[6] Regions showing less in-group collectivism include the Anglo countries, Germanic Europe, and Nordic Europe.[7]

With all of these dimensions, we will see a clear spectrum. People overwhelmingly fall somewhere between the most assertive and the least assertive, a topic discussed in more detail in Chapter 10. One either acts to uphold gender egalitarianism (Chapter 14) or does not, or if one is more moderate on this dimension, then one's decisions and behaviors are less predictable. One may also be what is termed ascriptive and so ascribe status based on inherent characteristics, or be achievement-oriented, in which case status must be earned, or some combination of the two (Chapter 5). And depending on where one – or one's culture – falls on this spectrum, we have a pretty good idea of what this means and how to explain it.

This same spectrum exists when we speak of individualism and collectivism – even in the highly individualistic United States – as evidenced by US senator Cory Booker's quote: "I respect and value the ideals of rugged individualism and self-reliance. But rugged individualism didn't defeat the British, it didn't get us to the moon, build our nation's highways, or map the human genome. We did that together."

What we also find, however, is that collectivism is a complex idea closely interacting with many other dimensions. An individualist may seek status to stand above others. We tend to see this in countries that are individualistic and also assertive. Another individualist may have little interest in standing above, as long as he or she is able to stand apart from others by acting independently with a high degree of autonomy.[8] We see this often in individualistic countries that are egalitarian. Consequently, individualism will, throughout this book, be considered in light of its interdependence with other dimensions. But not to panic – as we move through each of the dimensions, we will work to connect these links of the chain until we have an interconnected whole in our mind's eye.

The next two sections will explore the causes of in-group individualism/collectivism (Table 2.1). Individual and societal wealth tend to be the predominant drivers, but societal histories and religions also are significant. After exploring the reasons for great variation between the societies of the world on this dimension, we will consider the ways in which the differences affect behavior in the workplace.

In-Group Collectivism and Economic Conditions

Indulge us for a moment and imagine two brothers – we'll call them Bob and Alan – from a faraway planet, arriving on Earth one day without preconception or understanding of culture. One goes to live in a society with high levels of income equality and a rather developed economy. The other lives in a community with little development and little wealth.

TABLE 2.1 In-group collectivism (from highest to lowest)[9]

1. Philippines	21. Zimbabwe	41. Italy
2. Georgia	22. Nigeria	42. Austria
3. Iran	23. South Korea	43. Qatar
4. India	24. Venezuela	44. Israel
5. Turkey	25. Poland	45. Japan
6. Morocco	26. Malaysia	46. Namibia
7. Zambia	27. Portugal	47. Germany (East)
8. Ecuador	28. Argentina	48. South Africa (white sample)
9. China	29. Bolivia	49. France
10. Kuwait	30. Spain	50. Canada
11. Albania	31. Slovenia	51. United States
12. Colombia	32. El Salvador	52. Australia
13. Mexico	33. Costa Rica	53. England
14. Thailand	34. Hong Kong	54. Finland
15. Indonesia	35. Greece	55. Germany (West)
16. Egypt	36. Kazakhstan	56. Switzerland
17. Singapore	37. Hungary	57. Switzerland (French speaking)
18. Guatemala	38. Brazil	58. Netherlands
19. Russia	39. Ireland	59. New Zealand
20. Taiwan	40. South Africa (black sample)	60. Sweden
		61. Denmark

Bob, in the underdeveloped society, quickly notices the struggles of his aging neighbors. Those with "good" children seem to be well-cared for; but those without children, either because they predeceased their parents, because they never had children, or because the children are estranged, struggle mightily.[i] The community sympathizes with the struggling elders, but they are not wealthy enough to care for them while meeting their own family's needs.

Bob now wonders what will happen as he and his spouse grow old. He asks a neighbor what to do, who tells him he must have children to ensure his support in old age. His neighbor smilingly refers to children as the "cane for the hand in old age."[10] Bob therefore decides to have children – in fact, he tells himself the more the better. Bob quickly sees there's another benefit to this plan: from the day of his arrival, his neighbors ask him why he didn't have children, and when he would have children. Clearly, child-bearing is a vital responsibility of community members, so Bob's esteem is certain to rise with each child. Although neither Bob nor his neighbors know it, they are just one of many collectivist cultures that have made child-bearing an almost sacred societal value as an evolved response, at least in part, to facing old age without wealth or institutional support.[11]

Bob knows from observation of his unfortunate elderly neighbors what happens when children lack loyalty to the family. Upon having children, therefore, Bob acts to enculturate them, as do collectivist parents throughout the world. He is quick to remind them that they are part of the family, that they must be obedient and loyal, and that they will one day care for their father and mother.[12] But not to worry, he tells them – one day their children will care for them, and the benevolent cycle will continue.[ii]

Many of these same values will be emphasized at the children's school, in their storybooks, and in the homes of their friends, furthering the enculturation. Additionally, Bob's limited resources mean the family lives in a small house, and consequently, the children and parents share a room and extended family regularly stay with Bob for sometimes lengthy periods of time. He inadvertently, but usefully, develops a sense of self in the children, which is inextricably linked with that of the other family members.

Bob seems to have figured out the solution to his fears about health and old age. But now he begins to wonder about the security of his family. He asks himself, what happens if outsiders owing no loyalty to the community try to take his land and his home or otherwise threaten him and his family? Without access to good education, how will he and his children obtain employment? He knows the government is unlikely to be willing or able to step in.

Bob learns about the social contract and determines that the best way to ensure protection is to make a pact with the community – if any one of them is threatened, the rest will come to the aid of the other. He proposes a binding contract. The response, however, is ambivalent, even a bit confused.

Bob does not give up. He reasons that if he builds a close bond with the members of his community, they will come to his aid out of a sense of loyalty and friendship, rather than obligation. He does this in numerous ways. For example, although he loves his wife dearly, the idea of marrying outside his community never occurs to him; to do so would be to weaken his bonds with the community. He is quick to invite his neighbors over for parties and important events. Although sometimes a neighbor may drink too much and say things that he disagrees with, he knows better than to argue with him – better to stay friendly than lose an ally over unimportant matters like differences of opinion. He even adopts their religion.

These relationships quickly pay dividends for Bob when he is in search of a new job. His neighbor has an uncle who runs a business. Although Bob lacks the experience desired for the job, the uncle agrees to hire him. When Bob asks why he would hire him, he tells him that his loyalty will be worth more than his skills. "You can teach skills," he says. "You can't teach loyalty."

Hiring employees based on connections just like these is common across numerous collectivist societies.[13] In the end, the community is not just loyal to Bob; Bob feels a strong sense of connection to his community. In many ways, these bonds are far stronger than any legal contract would be – especially since the country's judges are said to be bribable, so the law may not operate as bindingly as one might think.

Now contrast Bob with his brother, Alan, living in a more developed society. Alan and his wife met at university and later relocated to a community where neither had previously lived. It was an easy decision – it was close to work. Both now find great fulfillment in their professional careers.

Alan doesn't worry too much about his care in old age – he knows that as he and his spouse grow old, they will receive generous pensions; they know that as their bodies weaken, they will have medical care and support. He does worry, however, about leaving a mark on this world through unique professional accomplishments. Alan and his wife wait to have children. They pursue their professional careers instead while periodically taking advantage of their resources and children-free lifestyles to jet-set around the world.

One day Alan travels to meet his brother, Bob. Learning that Bob had children in order to care for him and his spouse in old age, Alan feels a bit sorry for Bob but especially sorry for Bob's children. He doesn't realize that Bob's children feel great pride to be part of his family.

Bob, for his part, confides to his wife that he finds his brother to be remarkably selfish – traveling the world and working long hours rather than starting a family! And that wife of his, working to pursue *her* professional career instead of nurturing her family? Scandalous.

Bob has adopted the family and values of his community. These values ensure the elderly are cared for and the community protected against outside dangers, but Bob fails to understand that in Alan's society, these protections are not upheld by the family and community through social bonds, but are instead guaranteed by the state as long as one pays taxes. The greater the societal earnings, the greater the taxes, and the stronger these benefits should become. Thus, Alan's society has less reason to value community bonding and more reason to value hard work and economic success.

Alan eventually has children. He doesn't do so to ensure his protection in older age: he does so because he thinks the idea of having little children of his own will bring him great happiness – and passing on his genes, he must admit, has appeal. Alan is now a consummate individualist. He encourages his children to be independent and pursue their dreams. Because Alan knows he is to be cared for in old age, there's no reason they can't move far away to reach those dreams. Perhaps one will even go to his home planet for work! As long as they call home and visit once in a while, it's okay with Alan. After all, he too once prioritized his professional and personal interests, though having children has made him more the family man.

Inadvertently, but usefully, this mind-set is enculturated in Alan's children. His relative wealth means he has a home large enough to give his children their own rooms from their first days of life. While Bob's children learn about the value of loyalty at home and in school, the teachers of Alan's children tell them that they are unique and special. Soon, the "mental programming" of Alan's children and Bob's children are profoundly different.

The story of Bob and Alan is admittedly simplistic, but it gets to the essence of individualism and collectivism. These cultural differences have less to do with our intrinsic selves and more to do with environmental realities. Individualism is correlated with higher-income societies than in-group collectivism, though politically open societies tend also to allow individualism to flourish. Though there are exceptions, individualists tend to have a strong and formal social contract with the government. They may expect a safety net – pensions, subsidized or free life insurance, nursing and more – and this makes individualism safer and collectivism less essential. With such governmental protections, the individual may be less reliant on the goodwill of the employer. We might think of the collectivist workplace consequently as a family, with the employer as parent and employee as child. Individualists might better be conceived of as mercenaries in which both employer and employee are constantly on the lookout for more plentiful booty.

In lower-income economies, the social contract with society may be weak or nonexistent[14]; instead, the social contract is made informally with one's in-group. You are expected and likely eager to help your in-group when they are in need, and they will likely come to your aid when you are in need.[15] Most of the world's countries are still developing, which helps explain why in-group collectivism is still the norm.

It is true that collectivism prevails in many wealthy East Asian societies, including Japan, Thailand, and South Korea. It is also true that collectivism in these countries was once even higher, although it has fallen as more robust governmental welfare programs have freed (or broken the link, depending on how your perspective) many people from their traditional economic reliance on family and community.[16] For example, in Japan's Edo period (1600–1868) most individuals had no legal rights; instead, the family entity held all rights of the individuals in his family.[17] It was only with rising incomes that individualism also rose in Japan and other parts of East Asia.[18] Other less-developed countries in the region remain highly collectivist. If and when North Korea opens to the outside world, for instance, it will be interesting to compare the collectivism of their economically depressed peoples with that of their wealthy, tech-savvy counterparts in the south.

Furthermore, it is not just higher-income societies that are more individualistic: higher-income individuals, perhaps unconcerned with these issues of welfare and security, tend to be more individualistic, even if they live within a lower-income, traditionally collectivist society.[19] In fact, one study involving Indonesia and New Zealand found that individual wealth better predicted individualism/collectivism than did country of origin.[20] It is therefore wise for students of culture to sometimes look beyond country statistics into the underlying drivers of collectivism, which may include economic wealth but also, as we will see in the next section, religion and historical factors.

Societal and Religious Drivers of In-Group Collectivism

Collectivism and individualism have not only economic but also societal, religious and historic causes. Hofstede, for instance, notes that countries such as Sweden and Scotland were individualistic even before they were wealthy.[21]

In the Middle East and parts of Southeast Asia, the words of the prophet Mohammed may foster collectivist values: for instance, the Quran stresses the "importance of working for the collective good, taking care of others and maintaining unity in the face of opposition or threat. The Quran also urges Muslims to see one another as well as non-Muslims as members of one human family striving toward common goals."[22]

In this area, Fons Trompenaars notes that within the Christian faith, "Calvinists had contracts or covenants with god for which they were *personally* responsible. Roman Catholics have always approached god as a *community* of the faithful" (emphasis added).[23] Consequently, Calvinists tend to be more individualistic and Catholics more collectivist. We would add that these factors moderate one another, such that a Catholic from a wealthy nation might exhibit some collectivist tendencies along with some individualistic behaviors.

Confucianism tends to promote unity and societal harmony, which are values of many collectivist societies. In the east, Confucius looms large in the minds of many, and it was a Confucian principle that, "A person is not primarily an individual; rather, he or she is a member of a family."[24] What is seen now in many economically developed East Asian countries, therefore, is something of a hybrid. On the one hand, collectivism and a sense of societal well-being prevail in a way that is unheard of in most Western societies. Still, in our haste to see collectivism, we may at times go too far. Trompenaars, for instance, relates that modern Japan has no word for adult individual, instead using a word that translates as "person among others."[25]

Finally, we can see distant historical roots in society's relative standing on this dimension. It has been argued that in times when hunter-gathering was the norm, individualism prevailed because "self-reliance and freedom are crucial for survival."[26] With the agricultural revolution, however, collectivism gained ground as cooperation between unrelated parties provided the most expedient way to get produce from the field to the table.[27] Indeed, the Stone Age is a period characterized by collective work and oftentimes communal ownership of property.[iii] For instance, in Japan it was found that planting and harvesting rice required the cooperation of twenty people.[28] Thus, Japan historically was existentially motivated to value collectivism.[29] By contrast, in highly arable America, the expected collectivism of agricultural societies did not follow because pioneer families were able to produce enough food on their own to survive.[30] This may therefore serve as one of many factors contributing to America's historically individualistic nature.[31]

Additionally, collectivism reigned unchallenged in medieval Europe, but the thinkers of the Renaissance, and subsequently the Enlightenment, slowly contributed to greater European individualism.[32] Given the undeniable effect of, in particular, Enlightenment Era thinkers on early American politicians and philosophers, this suggests another factor influencing America's individualistic predisposition. This trend was also visible in the new forms of housing that rose, first in Central Italy and later throughout much of the Western world: "Hitherto, the powerful families in Florence had existed largely as clans; and this was reflected in not only how they lived, but where they lived. Extended, almost tribal families would live together in the family palazzo, with one leader presiding over a largely communal existence; loyalty, and to a large extent individuality, would be subsumed into a clan identity... yet something different was beginning to emerge in the new palazzi which the leading families of Florence were now building for themselves. ...the family clans began to separate out into individual nuclear families – a development that was reflected in the interior design of these new palazzi, and in the way they were occupied."[33]

Finally, the world once was much poorer than it is today, and we have noted that poverty at a broad level mediates toward greater levels of collectivism. Yuval Noah Harari tells of this economic revolution in *Sapiens*: "In 1500, global production of goods and services was equal to about $250 billion; today it hovers around $60 trillion. More importantly, in 1500, annual per capita production averaged $550, while today every man, woman and child produces, on the average, $8,800 a year."[34]

This economic growth has been fostered through industrialization, the process by which machines gradually replace the labor of humans. Industrialization has brought greater wealth while at the same breaking the cooperative chain of the workplace, and consequently, the period of industrialization has been accompanied by greater individualism.[35]

We may be seeing this third shift in parts of East Asia. A look at economically prosperous but traditionally collectivist South Korea or Japan, for instance, suggests that these countries are relatively, but not extremely, collectivist. In this we might see the Confucian ideology mixing with – perhaps even battling with – the individualizing tendency of economic prosperity.

The individualism of the West is apparent in some respects in the funky dress styles of Tokyo youth, the artsy culture of Seoul, and the pursuit of material wealth in Singapore. This is perhaps best illustrated in Tokyo on a Friday evening. Pouring out of the subways are businessmen – and yes, most businesspeople in Japan still are men – almost all wearing a professional "uniform" consisting of black pants, a collared and well-starched white shirt, and a black tie. But some of those same men, perhaps unkindly reminding the uninitiated of a group of worker ants, will transform themselves by night into a mass of singularly important ants. Just as Clark Kent changes into Superman, many businessmen will return ready to belt out Japanese pop songs at karaoke, perhaps drinking highballs and wearing eclectic manga costumes.

As Bob and Alan's children in part illustrated, many societies begin this individualist/collectivist acculturation almost from birth: many Americans, for instance, have the comparatively unusual practice of providing newborns with their own bedrooms, which fosters a self-identification as distinct from the rest of the family.[36] As he or she grows older, the child may begin closing or even locking the door. The parents are not to enter without knocking first. The child will likely decorate the room as he or she sees fit. "Somebody growing up in such a space cannot help but imagine himself 'an individual,' his true worth emanating from within rather than from without."[37]

This enculturation can result in professional challenges. As Harvard's Barbara Kellerman writes: "Most young people in professional and executive ranks have had long training in individual performance [since elementary school, for most]. They learn that it is how they perform as individuals that counts, not how they relate to others. So it is not surprising that many young executives – even middle-aged executives – are still pirouetting for some scorekeeper, real or imagined, with little thought of their possible constituency. Their gaze is directed upward, at the executive staff meetings they want to worm their way into, at the executive vice-presidents they want to impress. They are not even paying attention to the people at their own level or below, whom they might hope to lead."[38]

Individualism is not, however, code for selfish or aloof (nor should collectivists be considered mindless automatons or "worker bees"). Americans, for example, are consistently ranked the most charitable on Earth, though admittedly that may have something to do with the perceived inefficacy of governmental spending and tax incentives.[39] Additionally, humans as a species are exceptionally social – we are built so.

As renowned social psychologist Jonathan Haidt notes, "Your brain secretes more oxytocin [a pleasure-inducing chemical] when you have intimate contact with another person, even if that contact is just a back rub from a stranger." We enjoy chocolate more if tasted with another rather than by ourselves and dislike particularly bitter chocolate more when in the company of another.[40] Finally, a study looking at brain activity used a simulated ballgame to study rejection. While having his or her brain activity recorded, the participant uses buttons to play a ballgame with two others (played by a computer). After a few tosses, the two "others" start throwing the ball at each other and ignoring the actual participant, making the participant feel left out and rejected. The brain areas that were then activated are the same regions that become active during physical pain.[41]

The degree to which these and other drivers of individualism and collectivism diverge help explain the relative strength of these traits on a particular society. It takes a deeper dig, however – and often personal experience supplemented with an open mind – to reveal the ways in which these elements manifest, and thus serves as a reminder that the system presented here is the beginning, not the end, of the cross-cultural inquiry.

In-Group Collectivists in the Workplace

Individualists view themselves as distinct from the organization.[42] They believe they are hired for their abilities; they expect to be paid a salary reflective of those abilities and contributions; and they are prepared to leave the organization when better opportunities arise.[43] In-group collectivists, by contrast, tend to come from societies with fewer structured rules and are more likely to be hired due to their relationships and social backgrounds.[44] Consequently, we would expect their foremost loyalty to be to the manager hiring them. Because this hiring manager is an extension of their in-group, they would be prepared (and these managers would expect them) to make sacrifices on behalf of the organization.[45] They would expect to hold their positions even in hard times and would anticipate compensation packages representative of collective contributions to the organization, the needs of individuals (such as number of children, marital status or health concerns), and ascriptive characteristics such as seniority or even gender.[46]

Praise for good work, so sought after by many individualists, may in fact embarrass the collectivist. Collectivists often prefer group praise and rewards, including the equal distribution of raises or bonuses throughout a working group.[47] As a result, researchers have found that "pay-for-performance" incentives often fall flat in Africa, as well as in large parts of Asia.[48]

As an example, consider these two stories by cross-cultural negotiation specialist Jeannie M. Brett, the first involving an individualistic manager:

> A US manager... said that his team was using his ideas but he was not getting any recognition. He was tired of "doing all the work and not getting any of the credit." He described a team that typically generated multiple alternatives, considered their pros and cons, and then selected the alternative that had the most team support. "By the time the team members reach a decision, they all own my alternative," he complained. That the group appeared to be using a pretty good process was not what this man wanted to hear.

Contrast this with a collectivist's perspective:

> I [Brett] sent materials for a four-day course in decision-making to China two months in advance so that they could be translated. The young woman who was assigned to assist me had done a great job by any standard in organizing all the materials. Yet when I praised her in front of other staff members, I could tell that she felt very uncomfortable. "I'm just doing my job, Professor," she said.
>
> The public recognition that was so embarrassing to my Chinese assistant was exactly what the male manager required to maintain his meaningful participation in his team.[49]

Why the difference?

A Japanese proverb, heard in various forms in other cultures as well, may prove illustrative: "the nail that stands out gets hammered down."[50] It is important, in short, to stay within the confines of the group. As work in collectivist cultures is more likely to be a group effort, the connection to that group may be particularly strong. This is because collectivists often work long-term with a team, whereas individualist teams are often fluid and restructured with each task based on areas of expertise.[51] Furthermore, collectivists tend to set goals that are consistent with those of the in-group, while individualists are more focused on setting personal goals.[52] In these cultures, singular praise may indeed be misplaced and may result in disharmony. Japanese employees were indeed found to perform better when setting group goals rather than individual goals.[53]

Finally, Park and Usugami found that "employees who are outpaced by a coworker in promotion often lose their motivation, and some quit their job."[54] The employee receiving the promotion, therefore, faces the emotional burden of causing a loss of face. Indeed, social anxiety in the West is caused by excessive worry about embarrassing oneself. In Japan, it is caused by excessive worry about embarrassing *others*.[55]

Trompenaars presents an alternative that may appeal to the collectivist mindset: "A group bonus scheme used by Shell Nigeria... was a water well and irrigation scheme for the town the employees lived in, which materially benefited their homes and neighborhoods besides raising their status in the community."[56] In this way, Shell responded in a way that provided rewards for high-level performance, but in a way that elevated, rather than diminished, individual esteem. Organizations should pay attention to emotions and behaviors, including how employees respond when they are singled out, as well as work-group dynamics. If a collectivist culture prevails, it acts to reward group participants in a way that does not unduly single anyone out and ensures that benefits accrue equally or proportionally to all members of the team.

This tendency to wish to be appreciated as part of a group rather than apart from it has one other important implication: collectivists may be more likely to attend meetings in delegations, rather than in the small working groups that, for individualists with an eye on efficiency, often prove favorable. One reason is that because collectivists are often expected to personally hold the opinions and beliefs of their in-groups, they are less focused on the merits of the decision than on the preferences of the in-group. Consequently, changing the mind of a collectivist counterpart may be impossible without changing the mind of the group as a whole.[57]

Emerson Electric's former executive vice president Montupet provides a compelling example: "I was negotiating a JV [joint venture] with a Japanese company and we were progressing to the point where we said basically, we are ready for a deal and then on my side I knew I was speaking on behalf of the company [and it] would be approved. The Japanese guy came back a few weeks later and said, "Well, I could not get my people to come to a consensus to do what we were planning to do; therefore, we are not going to do it." And it was not the voice from above, because his CEO very much approved of the deal, but it came from the people below, and that killed the whole project."[58]

In this case we see that collectivism and the need for consensus was stronger than the views of any one person, including the boss. Asked if, in retrospect, Emerson could have helped the company to reach consensus, Montupet explained: "I don't think so, because consensus building is internal to the Japanese companies, and they don't allow outsiders to be part of that process."

The collectivist need to gain consensus may result in decision-making that moves at a speed that feels positively glacial to the individualist. Taking the time, however, to establish relationships may be a worthy investment. As Trompenaars aptly notes about individualists, "saving time in decision-making is often followed by significant delays due to implementation problems."[59]

In collectivist cultures, the time taken to fully vet important decisions with all interested parties may help identify potential problems at an earlier stage when they are still avoidable. Or, as Montupet puts it, "if you don't allow your Japanese managers to take the time to build consensus in the organization... nothing is going to work."[60] So, individualists, prepare your workforce, warn your boss, and check your own expectations: a bigger time commitment may be required at the front end of budding relationships and before important decisions.

Employee Loyalty and Social Relationships

As we've seen, collectivist societies often have a sense of reciprocal obligations premised on loyalty and trust. This sense of reciprocity is heightened in hierarchical as opposed to egalitarian societies (Chapter 6), where those in power are expected to care for those lower in the hierarchy. It is also heightened in particularist as opposed to universalist societies (Chapter 8), where exceptions to the rules – such as access to desirable jobs and other favors – are expected to be made for one's family, friends, or other connections. Taking care of one's employees is considered not just a professional but a moral responsibility. For example, employees might wonder, *If you don't take care of us, who will?* The manager is therefore often expected to provide "a broad array of satisfaction to employees: security, money, goodwill and socio-emotional support."[61] We refer to this as paternalism.

This has an upside: in particularist, collectivist, and hierarchical societies, the relationship-oriented approach to business means that relationships are often deeper than in universalist, individualistic, and egalitarian cultures. Indeed, the personal relationship may even predate the working relationship in organizations operating in these cultures. Employer-employee relationships in these societies are often less transactional than in the world of many universalists, individualists, and egalitarians.

For example, GLOBE contributing authors Hayat Kabasakal and Muzaffer Bodur relate the following story: "a Turkish company owner escorted the son of his employee to England for medical care because the family did not speak English. As a consequence, this employee would not leave the organization in the future even for better salary or promotion opportunities."[62] Thus, particularism, collectivism, and hierarchy are all expected to contribute to employee loyalty.

By contrast, universalists' worldviews, premised on equal treatment, leave them with little debt or any real loyalty to organizations or even people – after all, anything received was fair, not preferential. You are paid to perform a task, and that individualists' first loyalty is to themselves – often, the organization is merely serving as a means to that end. Turnover is consequently high and organizational loyalty rather low.

In the United States, for example, the average millennial is expected to change jobs four times by age thirty-two.[63] This turnover is often lucrative for the individual, but it is costly for organizations that must constantly battle to keep their best employees and spend heavily on training programs.

Creating Loyalty through Transformational Leadership

Many organizations would benefit from stronger employer-employee relationships of the sort we see in these collectivist cultures. So how can individualist, universalist, and egalitarian organizations learn from their opposites? First, loyalty is a two-way street. For organizations to get it, they have to be willing to give something. This mutuality results in a social bond, and researcher Dan Ariely argues that companies building these social bonds gain exceptional loyalty from their employees.[64] This is true for organizations from all types of cultures, though as we saw with the Turkish case, this may be understood at a deeper level in paternalistic cultures.

One way to create these social relationships is through the use of transformational leadership, in contrast to transactional leadership. Transactional leadership is the traditional leadership style in which organizations motivate employees through compensation and other benefits, or through the possibility of punishment for bad behavior or inferior results. It is therefore "transactional" in the sense that employees give something (usually their time and effort) in return for something else (such as compensation). Transactional leadership is thus an emotionally bankrupt form of leadership. It is well encapsulated in the phrase "it's not personal – it's just business." Indeed, former Emerson CEO Chuck Knight once told a senior manager: "always remember that I get mad at facts but not people."[65]

But it *is* personal, and that's exactly why Knight felt the need to emphasize that his anger was *not* directed at the individual but instead at the situation. We are all humans, and even people from the most independent-minded of societies have a genetically inherited preference for group relationships and acceptance. As researcher Jonathan Haidt explains, we are "hivish," and this deep-seated need for inclusion allows organizations to "activate pride, loyalty, and enthusiasm among [their] employees..."[66]

In sharp contrast to transactional leadership, transformational leadership can help bring out our "hivish nature" and thereby create those social relationships

24 Individualism – Collectivism

that make even universalists and individualists loyal to an organization or its leader. Here's how Haidt distinguishes transactional leadership from transformational leadership through the lens of the "hive":

> Transactional leadership appeals to followers' self-interest, but transformational leadership changes the way followers see themselves – from isolated individuals to members of a larger group. Transformational leaders do this by modeling collective commitment (e.g., through self-sacrifice and the use of "we" rather than "I"), emphasizing the similarity of group members, and reinforcing collective goals, shared values, and common interests.[67]

Such leadership is more personal than transactional leadership. It helps leaders forge personal relationships with employees, feeding a sense of connection to the organization rather than building a team of mercenaries.

For example, in the construction industry in the United States, personal relationships forge stronger bonds than is typically seen in most industries. This is not accidental. Managers of construction companies, typically known as project managers, oversee crews carrying out potentially dangerous work, using multimillion-dollar machinery and subject to a vast array of environmental, financial, and governmental contingencies. Tom Kalishman spoke directly to this issue. Kalishman, a Kellogg School of Business MBA and a Wharton alum, began his career with Bain & Company and rose through the ranks of the multinational company Insituform. Kalishman is now CEO and chairman of SAK Industries, a company that is one of the most respected specialty contractors in the world and which has grown from two people in 2008 to more than five hundred full-time employees as of 2017. Kalishman also serves as the finance chair of the Young Presidents Organization international chapter and travels throughout the world in an advisory role.

Kalishman says, "I can think of no industry where the ability to affect profitability lies further away than the CEO's office than this industry. It's the individual decisions that are made, minute to minute, in the field, that determine success or failure, because every situation is different. We can't control these things, so we have to have people who are thinking and making good decisions. As a result, we have to have people who we trust, and we have to turn them loose and empower them. Top managers must have full trust in lower-level workers."[68]

This trust is built, Kalishman says, by making the professional life of the workforce an extension of their personal lives. He says, "We spend a tremendous amount of time, and I believe we've done a very good job of building the team culture at SAK, where people feel a part of a team, and the team has accomplished something pretty unique. The relationships [of the workforce] are deep inside and outside of the work environment. It cannot be *transactional* when the relationships permeate your social life and your family life as well" (emphasis added).[69]

Indeed, Kalishman sounds a bit like our Turkish business owner in saying that part of building this connected culture is to recognize that not everyone is the same, and that different people merit different treatment. He says, "We can't expect two people to have the same strengths and weaknesses, or the same backgrounds or the same needs, or the same family backgrounds. We have to be very open to the individual, and flexible to the individual, while achieving our group goals."

This is a far cry from "it's not personal, it's just business," and this social relationship can lead to increased loyalty and interconnectedness. Remember, however, that loyalty is a two-way street. Now that you've created a relationship, you've made it personal. Many businesses struggle because they fail to recognize that they can't have it both ways.[70] They tell employees or even customers that they are "part of the family," but then they make business decisions – raising prices or cutting a workforce – and reassert that, "It's not personal. It's just business."[71] But we hold our friends and family – those with whom we have social relationships – to much higher standards than we do businesses with whom we have only a transactional relationship. When they disappoint, we are much more aggrieved than when the television company lets us down by raising the monthly bill, and the moment the employee or customer buys into the social arrangement, they hold the companies to these higher standards. For better or worse.[72]

Consequently, leaders benefit enormously from creating social relationships with their employees. Using transformational rather than transactional leadership is one way to create this relationship. However, only those leaders able to uphold their end of the bargain – to consistently view the relationship as a personal rather than merely business relationship – should adopt this style.

Institutional Collectivism

Finally, we will note the rise of a second type of collectivism – institutional collectivism. In-group collectivists show great loyalty in their social lives, and often these social relationships bleed into their professional lives. Thus, loyalty is shown to the organization through the person with which the social relationship exists. In countries with high institutional collectivism, there is a greater separation between the social and organizational relationships, but the end result is, similarly, loyalty to employers, coworkers and the organization itself.[73]

Institutional collectivism is correlated with greater economic prosperity and a strong performance orientation, global competitiveness, and, unlike in-group collectivism, it is correlated with strong public institutions that support that economic prosperity.[74] We're most likely to see institutional collectivism in Nordic Europe and East Asia,[75] with the most institutionally collective countries being (from highest to lowest) Sweden, South Korea, Japan, Singapore, New Zealand, Denmark, and China.[76] The least institutional collectivism is seen in Latin America, Latin Europe, and Germanic Europe.[77] The United States lands around the middle of the pack.[78] While Confucianism helps explain the high levels of

26 Individualism – Collectivism

institutional collectivism in East Asia, we might speculate that high degrees of trust that prevail in Nordic Europe contribute to the institutional collectivism of those countries (Table 2.2).

Many inhabitants of countries that score high on institutional collectivism show very little collectivism in their personal lives.[79] For instance, the United States tends to be highly individualistic when it comes to in-group collectivism but exhibits moderate levels of institutional collectivism.[80] In societies that both practice and value in-group collectivism, institutional collectivism is rarely practiced due to the weak state of business. Instead, the loyalty or connection is to an individual, such as a supervisor or manager, rather than to the organization. However, these same people would show institutional collectivism were their workplaces sufficiently strong and stable to warrant this behavior.[81] Indeed, with the exception of the United States and other Anglo and East Asian countries, the people of most countries would prefer to have greater institutional collectivism than they actually do.[82]

What this shows – and what the transformative businessmen of Tokyo exemplify – is that personal individualism is likely to continue thriving, but it can mingle comfortably with institutional collectivism. This provides the opportunity for managers to benefit from the loyalty seen in collectivist relationships. The key is to draw out this hivish nature using transformational leadership to forge mutually beneficial social relationships (Table 2.3).

TABLE 2.2 Institutional collectivism (most to least collectivism)[83]

1. El Salvador	21. Nigeria	41. Hong Kong
2. Brazil	22. Morocco	42. Australia
3. Iran	23. Mexico	43. South Africa (white sample)
4. Ecuador	24. Zimbabwe	44. Namibia
5. Greece	25. Malaysia	45. Slovenia
6. Venezuela	26. France	46. Switzerland (French speaking)
7. Colombia	27. Egypt	47. England
8. Argentina	28. Germany (West)	48. South Africa (black sample)
9. Portugal	29. Philippines	49. Israel
10. Turkey	30. Zambia	50. Poland
11. Guatemala	31. Austria	51. New Zealand
12. Spain	32. India	52. Denmark
13. Indonesia	33. Switzerland	53. Canada (English speaking)
14. Costa Rica	34. Germany (East)	54. United States
15. Taiwan	35. Ireland	55. Finland
16. Kuwait	36. China	56. Kazakhstan
17. Qatar	37. Singapore	57. Japan
18. Italy	38. Netherlands	58. Sweden
19. Thailand	39. Hungary	59. South Korea
20. Bolivia	40. Albania	60. Russia
		61. Georgia

TABLE 2.3 Collectivism onion

Inner	Middle	Outer
Economics (poor)	In-group collectivism	Seek harmony with friends and extended family; obtain employment through family network; expect support from the workplace, rather than the state; take care of your elderly parents, and expect your kids to do the same for you
Economics (wealthy)	Individualism	Rely on governmental support programs in old age and during times of illness; obtain employment most likely via online searches, with wide-ranging geographic scope; have little loyalty to, or expectation of loyalty from, employer; pursue individual interests and expect the same of your children
Ideology (Catholics)	In-group collectivism	Act as a "community of the faithful"
Ideology (Protestants)	Individualism	Be personally responsible for salvation
Ideology (Confucianism)	Institutional collectivism	Value organizational consensus; show loyalty to organization; show embarrassment by singular praise; work hard willingly for benefit of in-group and toward group goals
Politics (democratic)	Individualism	Vibrant press; show respect for outspoken leaders; maintain equality of representation (one person, one vote)

In the next chapter, we explore how the cohesion and loyalty of collectivist organizations can both contribute to – and help solve – the dreaded groupthink.

Notes

i It's said that in Cambodia, for example, parents without familial care may join the monastery in old age to ensure their care.
ii For example, in Kyrgyzstan the youngest son – and ultimately that son's wife and family – lives with his parents. The wife, known as a "kailin," is expected to take care of the aging parents. Only after the parent's deaths may this family move into an independent living situation, at which point the situation repeats itself.
iii Exhibit visited by author, Bussen, at The National Museum of Kazakhstan.

References

1. BrainyQuote, https://www.brainyquote.com/quotes/aristotle_399587.
2. *Individualism*, Clearly Cultural (last accessed July 28, 2018), http://www.clearlycultural.com/geert-hofstede-cultural-dimensions/individualism/; see also Michele J. Gelfand, Dharm P.S. Bhawak, Lisa Hisae Nishii and David J. Bechtold, "Individualism and Collectivism," in *Culture, Leadership, and Organizations: The GLOBE Study of 62 Societies* 469 (eds. Robert House, Paul J. Hanges, Mansour Javidan et al., SAGE Publications) (2004) (showing US in bottom ten of in-group collectivism).
3. Hofstede, *supra* note 13 at 79.
4. *Id.* at 85.
5. Hofstede, *supra* note 4 at 92 (showing that about 80 percent of societies are collectivist).
6. Gelfand, et al., *supra* note 32 at 479–480.
7. *Id.* at 480.
8. *Id.* at 444.
9. *Id.* at 469.
10. This is an Iranian expression. See Mansour Javidan, "Part IV: Empirical Findings," in *Culture, Leadership and Organizations: The GLOBE Study of 62 Societies* 240 (eds. Robert House, Paul J. Hanges, Mansour Javidan et al., SAGE Publications) (2004).
11. Many collectivist societies have children to ensure care in old age. See *Id.*
12. Children of collectivist societies are "expected to be obedient and to take care of their parents when they are in need." See *Id.*
13. See Hayat Kabasakal and Muzaffer Bodur, "Humane Orientation in Societies, Organizations, and Leader Attributes," in *Culture, Leadership, and Organizations: The GLOBE Study of 62 Societies* 566 (eds. Robert House, Paul J. Hanges, Mansour Javidan, Peter W. Dorfman, and Vipin Gupta, SAGE Publications) (2004) (writing: "Organizations in these societies [with weak social contracts] tend to choose employees on the basis of the individual's relationship to the employer or patron, rather than the organization's needs or the skills of the individual (Kiray, 1997; Ong, 1987)."
14. See, for instance, Robert J. House, Preface, in *Culture, Leadership, and Organizations: The GLOBE Study of 62 Societies* XVII (eds. Robert House, Paul J. Hanges, Mansour Javidan, Peter W. Dorfman and Vipin Gupta, SAGE Publications) (2004), referring to the "poor due process" of in-group collectivist societies.
15. Hofstede, *supra* note 13 at 79.
16. Hofstede, *supra* note 23 at 40.
17. Edo Japan, Wikipedia, (last accessed July 28, 2018) https://en.wikipedia.org/wiki/Edo_period (James B. Lewis, *Frontier Contact between Choson Korea and Tokugawa Japan*. Routledge, 2005).
18. Hofstede, *supra* note 23 at 40.
19. Gelfand, et al., *supra* note 32 at 449.
20. *Id.*
21. Hofstede, *supra* note 23 at 40.
22. http://peopleof.oureverydaylife.com/collectivism-islamic-society-9230.html.
23. Trompenaars and Hampden-Turner, *supra* note 12 at 52–53.
24. Martin J. Gannon, *Cultural Metaphors: Readings, Research Translations and Commentary* 34 (SAGE Publication) (2001).
25. Trompenaars and Hampden-Turner, *supra* note 12 at 64.
26. Gelfand, et al., *supra* note 32 at 450.
27. *Id.*
28. Neal Ashkanasy, Vipin Gupta, Melinda S. Mayfield, Edwin Trevor-Roberts, "Future Orientation," in *Culture, Leadership and Organizations: The GLOBE Study of 62 Societies* 288 (eds. Robert House, Paul J. Hanges, Mansour Javidan, Peter W. Dorfman and Vipin Gupta, SAGE Publications) (2004).
29. *Id.*
30. *Id.*

31 Id.
32 Paul Strathern, *The Medici: Power, Money and Ambition in the Italian Renaissance*, 24 (Pegasus Books) (2016).
33 Id. at 146.
34 Yuval Noah Harari, *Sapiens: A Brief History of Humankind* 341, (Penguin Random House: London) (2011).
35 Gelfand, et al., *supra* note 32 at 450.
36 Although this may be beginning to change, Americans were the only nationality to do this in a survey involving 100 nationalities. See Henrich, et al., *supra* note 1 at 4.
37 Harari *supra* note 66 at 128.
38 Kellerman *supra* note 5 at 167.
39 Henrich et al., *supra* note 1 at 75.
40 Adam Grant, *Originals: How Non-Conformists Move the World* 120 (Viking: An Imprint of Random House LLC) (2016).
41 N.I. Eisenberger, M.D. Lieberman, and K.D. Williams, "Does Rejection Hurt? An FMRI Study of Social Exclusion," 302 *Science* 290–292 (2003).
42 Gelfand et al., *supra* note 32 at 446.
43 Id.
44 Id. at 446, 473.
45 Id. at 447.
46 Id. at 447. See also Id. at 455.
47 Trompenaars and Hampden-Turner, *supra* note 12 at 52.
48 Id. at 2.
49 Jeanne M. Brett, *Negotiating Globally: How to Negotiate Deals, Resolve Disputes, and Make Decisions Across Boundaries* 164 (Josey-Bass) (2001).
50 As Tim Nowak, executive director of the World Trade Center, St. Louis, noted, a Chinese leader phrased it similarly: "It is always the tallest blade of grass that is mowed down first." Nowak, Interview with Author.
51 See Trompenaars and Hampden-Turner, *supra* note 12 at 191 (stating fast-changing work groups "offend family feeling with their on-again/off-again relationships and their 'two fathers'").
52 Gelfand et al., *supra* note 32 at 443.
53 Gelfand et al., *supra* note 32 at 456.
54 Jiro Usugami and Kyung-Yeol Park, "Similarities and Differences in Employee Motivation Viewed by Korean and Japanese Executives: Empirical Study on Employee Motivation Management of Japanese-Affiliated Companies in Korea," 2 *Int'l J. Hum Resource Manag* (2007).
55 Susan Cain, *Quiet: The Power of Introverts in a World That Can't Stop Talking* 91–92 (Penguin Random House: New York) (2012).
56 Trompenaars and Hampden-Turner, *supra* note 12 at 194.
57 Id. at 60.
58 Montupet, *supra* note 10.
59 Trompenaars and Hampden-Turner, *supra* note 12 at 61.
60 Montupet, *supra* note 10.
61 Trompenaars and Hampden-Turner, *supra* note 12 at 41.
62 Kabasakal and Bodur, *supra* note 44 at 589.
63 Heather Long, "The New Normal: 4 Job Changes by the Time You're 32," *CNN Money* (April 12, 2016), http://money.cnn.com/2016/04/12/news/economy/millennials-change-jobs-frequently/index.html.
64 Dan Ariely, *The Upside of Irrationality: The Unexpected Benefits of Defying Logic* 81–82 (Harper Perennial; Reprint Edition) (2011).
65 Montupet, *supra* note 10.
66 Jonathan Haidt, *The Righteous Mind: Why Good People Are Divided by Politics and Religion* 44 (Vintage, Reprint Edition) (2013).
67 Id.

68 Tom Kalishman, Interview with the Author.
69 *Id.*
70 Dan Ariely, *Predictably Irrational: The Hidden Forces That Shape Our Decisions* 79, 82 (Harper Perennial) (2010).
71 *Id.* at 79.
72 *Id.*
73 As distinguished by Gelfand, et al., *supra* note 32 at 438–502.
74 *Id.* at 482.
75 *Id.* at 476.
76 *Id.* at 470.
77 *Id.* at 476.
78 *Id.* at 468.
79 See *Id.* at 473 (showing very low in-group collectivism where institutional collectivism is high).
80 See *Id.* at 468, 469.
81 *Id.* at 467.
82 *Id.* at 476.
83 Id. at 470.

3

A GLASS OF BEER, A SHOT OF SAKE, AND GROUPTHINK

> Think not those faithful who praise thy words and actions, but those who kindly reprove thy faults.
>
> Socrates

The Surprising Importance of Choosing a Glass of Beer: Individualist and Collectivist Biases

You made it: it's Friday afternoon. You're sitting down for happy hour with your friends from work. You look over the beer menu and order last. How likely is it that you allow your friends' orders to determine your eventual order? For most of us, there's a pretty good chance just that would happen. But exactly how your friends affect your beer choice depends on whether you're more of an individualist or a collectivist. And this, in turn, has important implications for optimal decision-making in the workplace.

Dan Ariely, in *Predictably Irrational*, relates a study in which he and a colleague went to a popular brewery at the University of North Carolina at Chapel Hill, approached a table of customers, and offered each of them the choice of one of four types of beer for free. The names and full descriptions of each beer were provided.[1] In return, the lucky customers simply had to fill out a short survey documenting how much they'd enjoyed the beer or whether they regretted their decision.[2] Naturally, he had little trouble finding takers, and by the end of the day he'd visited one hundred tables and run up a bill of $1,400.[3]

Ariely was surprised to notice a trend, which the data confirmed: once one type of beer was chosen by a member of a table, it was *less likely* to be chosen by another member of the table. This seemed illogical, to say the least. After all, a beer is no less tasty just because your table mate is drinking it. The survey results showed that the first person to order was typically the most satisfied with her choice, suggesting that subsequent people were making choices based on the choices of their tablemates, which left them less satisfied.[4]

What was going on? Ariely changed the conditions to find out. He asked the next set of customers not to verbally voice their preferred beer as in the first sample but instead to write their preferences on a small menu and keep their decisions private until the rest of the table had ordered.[5] Again they received their beers and filled out the satisfaction surveys.[6] This changed everything. Now, uninfluenced by the choices of their tablemates, more people ordered the same one or two kinds of beer and *satisfaction was higher*.[7]

What Ariely discovered through this experiment was that when people ordered aloud, they made decisions not based on their actual preferences. Instead, the order was used to signal to the rest of the group that they were unique, autonomous beings.[8] The more someone had this "need for uniqueness," the more likely he or she was to order something different from the rest of the group.[9] And they did this regardless of their actual preferences, and in fact, this diminished their satisfaction.

It was, in short, about ego, about avoiding the horror of (gasp) conformity. It is not a reach to extend this behavior to business environments, suggesting that at times colleagues may simply disagree in order to distinguish themselves.

There's more to this story, however. American undergraduate students are consistently rated more individualistic than the average American adult – this, in a society that is already one of the most individualistic on Earth. Did this explain the ego-enhancing decisions of the beer-drinking students? Ariely provided the answer to this question through a study with Hong Kong undergraduate students.

These students came from a relatively collectivist culture, though slightly less so than those from less prosperous, less politically open, mainland China. Here, he found the opposite occurred: when ordering verbally, students didn't order differently from their tablemates in order to stand apart; rather, they ordered more similarly in order to stand together![10] They behaviorally showed their collectivist rather than individualist colors.

Once Ariely asked students to write their preferences in private, there was *more* variance in the types of beer ordered than in the condition when they ordered verbally. Recall that in America, exactly the opposite occurred.

But there was one similarity between American and Hong Kong students: in both cases, the students made decisions that left them less satisfied when they were aware of the decisions of their tablemates,[11] and they did it on the basis of their relative preferences to be seen as independent or part of the group, respectively.

We can surmise from this study that Americans' willingness to celebrate their uniqueness may make group work difficult and may create decisional conflicts that are, ultimately, more about ego than actual differences. In collectivist societies, however, where being the nail sticking up is to be avoided, a conformity bias may pose its own problems.[12]

Ultimately, the results suggest that for opposite reasons, group decisions are better made – at least initially – in a more anonymous format, such as anonymous polling or through individual interactions, avoiding the relevant bias of either culture.

The Bay of Pigs and Humility

This "need for uniqueness" has obvious downsides. An eagerness to dissent, however, can perhaps be exploited to avoid the dreaded, but often misunderstood, groupthink phenomenon. Groupthink is the process by which a group makes an irrational or suboptimal decision by failing to consider the strengths and weaknesses of a decision or relevant alternatives.

Overcoming groupthink is key, however, because if conducted appropriately, a group decision is generally superior to that of an individual one. This was a recurring theme among business and administrative leaders interviewed for this book. For instance, we spoke to Nicholas Keuper, who most recently was CEO of lifestyle brand India Hicks. Though India Hicks has now closed its doors, Keuper spent twenty-three years with Boston Consulting Group, moving between offices in Munich, Bangkok and Los Angeles. Keuper noted that a leader "can make good decisions for a short term but not in the long run. The diverse group always makes the best decisions."

Former CEO of McDonnell-Douglas, John McDonnell, also related a story with a similar turn: "one training exercise we participated in [showed] us that multiple minds can usually result in better decisions ... It was an exercise where your small airplane crash-landed in a desert. You had twenty items on board, and you were supposed to prioritize them as to importance for survival. First, we each did the exercise individually; then we formed groups of five or six and redid the exercise. Sure enough, the group decisions were better than any of the individuals (unless the group had a dominate participant who overruled the others). That was billed as an exercise in group dynamics."[13] This serves to emphasize the importance of overcoming groupthink in order to leverage the benefits of group decision-making.

To take the idea one step further, consider the oft-cited parable of the ox, as perhaps most recently related by James Suriewicki in his book *The Wisdom of Crowds*. At a town fair, the locals were asked to guess the weight of an ox – while individually they had quite varied and generally limited success, their guesses collectively averaged within a pound of the correct weight (1197 average versus 1198 actual weight)![14] Collective thinking in short can be extraordinarily powerful.

Irving Janis is something of a godfather to the idea of groupthink.[15] Writing in 1973, Janis used as his focal point the US Bay of Pigs invasion. This was a CIA-backed operation in which US military-trained Cuban exiles invaded Cuba and attempted to overthrow the government. Instead, the invasion was thwarted within three days under Castro's direct leadership, further cementing his power in Cuba and his animosity toward the states. In meetings leading up to the operation, many of Kennedy's advisors felt the idea significantly problematic but held their tongues. Groupthink won.

Groupthink is, of course, not only found in the Oval Office but is a scourge seen throughout all facets of organizations, in our classrooms and across cultures. Washington University in St. Louis Chancellor Mark Wrighton in his interview with the authors: "We are recruiting some of the finest students in the country. It's a great student body, but one of the things that amazes me is that when they get together, the combined decision-making process leads them to do some really dangerous things. It never ceases to amaze me that some of these talented students do the dumbest things when they get together. So you can't just depend on a group of smart people to do the right thing, or the best thing or the most productive thing."[16]

Indeed, it is often the smartest people who are most prone to inflated egos, and groupthink may be driven by a lack of humility that kills critical thinking. Relatedly, groupthink flourishes when dissent is smothered out of fear that challenging the idea of a powerful superior will result in retaliation. Groupthink is also often based on the desire for harmony and unity within a group, and to achieve this goal, bad decisions go unchallenged.

To avoid groupthink, Janis posited that we must openly voice our dissent when we think a decision is bad.[17] Before we are even able to consider raising such concerns, however, we need to first be sufficiently critical of our decisions to poke holes, find problems, and consider alternatives. There are consequently two steps to avoiding groupthink: first, an internalized belief that a decision is bad; and second, a willingness to communicate that belief (to dissent) with coworkers or bosses.

To reach the belief that a decision is bad requires critical thinking. And to think critically about decisions, we need the humility to admit that our ideas are not always perfect. This is true not only for us but for our teams and bosses: you are unlikely to question your own decisions if you are firmly convinced of your brilliance. You are unlikely to question your team's decisions if you think the team is brilliant. And you are unlikely to question your boss if you believe she is brilliant.

Carol Dweck, a Stanford University professor of psychology, provides the following explanation for America's ill-fated Bay of Pigs invasion:

> Groupthink can occur when people put unlimited faith in a talented leader, a genius. This is what led to the disastrous Bay of Pigs invasion. ... President Kennedy's normally astute advisers suspended their judgment. Why? Because they thought he was golden and everything he did was bound to succeed.[18]

Similarly, Dweck argues that Enron's failures can also be attributed to Groupthink that was caused by a sense of overconfidence. Enron is now synonymous with corporate scandal, a cautionary tale for business ethics courses and accounting lecture halls. At its most scandalous, Enron artificially inflated its stock by using elaborate accounting tricks to hide billions of dollars in debts, and managers ultimately sold off their personal stock to amass fortunes while simultaneously assuring lower-level employees that all was well.[19] Eventually, the house of cards collapsed; within months of the first signs of scandal, the value of the company's once-vaunted stock cratered. Complete immolation followed – a loss of more than twenty thousand jobs, wide-scale financial losses to stockholders (including many former employees who had been paid bonuses in Enron stock), with many of the perpetrators behind bars (though some deemed too leniently punished) and paying millions in fines.[20]

How did a company that *Fortune* magazine named the most innovative company in America six years in a row get to this point? Dweck again:

> Groupthink can happen when the group gets carried away with its brilliance and superiority. At Enron, the executives believed that because they were brilliant, all of their ideas were brilliant. Nothing would ever go wrong. An outside consultant kept asking Enron people, "Where do you think you're vulnerable?" Nobody answered him. Nobody even understood the question. "We got to the point," said a top executive, "where we thought we were bulletproof."[21]

In this case, it wasn't just the belief that the CEO and chairman Kenneth Lay was brilliant but in fact a corporate culture in which intelligence was prized above all. Reportedly, among the worst labels within Enron was not lazy or obstructive but "just not smart enough."[22]

Ego is most closely related to the assertiveness cultural dimension. As we will see, the highly competitive and confident culture of American energy darling Enron pointedly aligns with this dimension.

Grant, for his part, raises a similar argument. Polaroid, which launched the famed Polaroid camera, was at the height of its success in the eighties and nineties. But the company's conviction of its own genius spelled its doom. Illustrative of this overconfidence was long-time Polaroid CEO and founder Edwin Land's devastating refusal to adopt digital camera technology, a technology that revolutionized the camera industry.[23] Despite an offer for collaboration from Sony founder Akio Morita in 1980, Land was sure he knew the future and that it involved print photos.[24] A later CEO, Mac Booth, reportedly said: "Polaroid doesn't sell what it didn't invent."[25] This, in Grant's view, represented "overconfidence in the company's ability to predict the future and create the best products."[26]

Edwin Land *was* brilliant, but even he couldn't do it all himself. Billionaire entrepreneur and PayPal founder Peter Thiel puts it this way: "Great leaders...know better than to assume that they are the only ones with value to add. Great leaders bring out the best in those around them. In this way, Ayn Rand was only half right. Her villains were real, but her heroes were not. There is no Galt's Gulch. To believe yourself invested with ... self-sufficiency is not the mark of a strong individual but of a person who has mistaken the crowd's worship – or jeering – for the truth."[27] Polaroid would be forced to declare bankruptcy in 2001 and again in 2008.

The damage from egotistical leadership goes beyond groupthink. In Jim Collins's *Good to Great*, Collins found among other things that modest leaders tend to outperform their immodest counterparts. Indeed, Collins found that 2/3 of failing or mediocre companies were under the leadership of men with a "gargantuan personal ego."[28] Unfortunately for our WEIRD readers out there, the research shows that it is people from the West who tend to have a particular weakness for such outsized egos.

> The most widely endorsed assumption regarding the self is that people are motivated to view themselves … more positively than objective benchmarks would justify. For example, in one study, 94 percent of American professors rated themselves as better than the average American professor (Cross 1977). However … self-serving biases tend to be more pronounced in Western populations than in non-Western ones (Heine and Hamamura 2007; Mezulis et al. 2004) – for example, Mexicans (Tropp and Wright 2003), Native Americans (Fryberg and Markus 2003), Chileans (Heine and Raineri 2009), and Fijians (Rennie and Dunne 1994) score much lower on various measures of positive self-views than do Westerners. Indeed, in some cultural contexts, most notably East Asian ones, evidence for self-serving biases tends to be null, or in some cases, shows significant reversals, with East Asians demonstrating self-effacing biases (Heine and Hamamura 2007).[29]

This is known as the "self-serving bias" and leads to overestimating the quality of one's work, with some research indicating that we believe our work to be nearly five times better than others'.[30] This perception of excellence is a danger, but Westerners in particular are susceptible to this bias.

At McDonnell-Douglass, former CEO John McDonnell related one strategy for ensuring full input on larger decisions. Decisions that affect many people, we should note, are the most likely to deter lower-level or less-outspoken employees from speaking up. Consequently, a subtler approach was taken. "We had what was called the 'green sheet' process," McDonnell said, where a "green sheet" was sent around to each function and/or department that could be affected by a decision. They would each in turn sign their approval or state their issues with a decision.[31] This helped to avoid a groupthink bias as the green created a structure where one actually felt compelled to speak out, because by not speaking out and problems arising from your division would negatively implicate – and impact – that employee.

Obedience to Authority: Respectful or Dangerous?

Humility is not enough, however; it is also important to critically assess decisions, and those of employees and employers. If, however, an employee sees problems in the group decision, this is no guarantee that dissent will be registered.

To avoid groupthink, critical thinking is necessary but not sufficient; employees must also be prepared to openly question their coworkers, and at times their superiors, and to do so in a way that does not create disharmony or distrust.

Many collectivist cultures are hierarchical, an environment in which the boss therefore holds substantial power, and in hierarchical cultures, people may hesitate to challenge the ideas of the boss, or anyone higher in the power structure. Dissent can be hard to come by, however, in both individualistic and collectivist societies. After all, it is one thing to stand apart from the beer preferences of one's peers; it is quite another to stand up to the wishes of one's powerful superiors.

Stanley Milgram showed just how compliant people can be in the face of authoritative figures. In his "obedience experiments," Milgram told participants they were part of a memory test. Their role was to push a button shocking a test-taker should the test-taker answer incorrectly, and to increase the severity of the shock with each missed answer. The test was purportedly to see if such punishment improved the performance of the test-taker, although in reality the test-taker was an actor and no shock was being administered. There was also an experimenter in a lab coat uniform in the room. Even hearing the test-taker screaming in apparent agony, a remarkable two-thirds of participants continued to shock the test-taker up to the maximum level, often upon a prompt by the authority figure in the lab coat. At the maximum level, the test-taker had gone entirely quiet, and the participants could reasonably believe the shocks had left the test-taker unconscious or worse.

The experimenter would verbally prod the volunteer or "teacher" to continue if he or she hesitated to administer a shock, but participation was completely voluntary. The lab coat uniform, Milgram held, created an authority figure that must be obeyed, and all independent decision-making went out the window. Milgram hypothesized that these psychological behaviors showed why people with no history of violence or hatred committed the heinous crimes they did during the Holocaust.[32]

Suggestions have been made that the idea of obedience has changed over the years (as the initial experiments were done in the sixties and seventies), but multiple replications over time have shown that obedience to authority has remained distressingly stable. There are, however, a few factors that make a difference. The authority of the experimenter plays a huge role. Having an experimenter tell the participants to *not* deliver a shock, having an ordinary member of the public in everyday clothes (not a lab coat) take over the role of experimenter, or not having an experimenter in the same room (distancing that authority) increases disobedience of the participant.[33] Moreover, if the experimenter does not urge someone to continue or lets the participant pick the voltage used, the number of participants continuing to the highest voltages is significantly decreased.[34] Defiance decreases, however, when the participant chooses whether the shock should be administered but another person actually pushes the button to give the shock.[35]

Milgram called this effect of authority the agentic state, in which participants give the responsibility to the experimenter. In a replication done in Puerto Rico, when participants were explicitly told the experimenter assumed all responsibility, all participants were fully obedient. When they were however told that they, as a teacher, were responsible for what happened to the learner, only 33 percent of the participants were fully obedient.[36]

The initial studies were all done with male participants, but replications have shown similar results for women as well (around 65 percent obedience), though in general women show more tension and anxiety.[37]

Replications of the study have taken place outside the United States, as well (Jordan, Italy, South Africa, Spain, India, Austria, Germany, and Australia).[38] Participants in these studies showed very similar rates of obedience across this wide variety of cultures and regions.[39]

Discouraging Blind Obedience to Authority

In the business context, the notoriety of the "yes-man" is evidence of this willingness to obey without question. Jim Collins, documenting this in his leadership review, found employees in companies without great leadership hesitated to speak until they'd first heard from the one considered the decision-maker for the company. A yes-man culture had developed, and this is an environment that is often initiated from, or is nurtured by, the leader. As Collins put it: "The moment a leader allows himself to become the primary reality people worry about, rather than reality being the primary reality, you have a recipe for mediocrity, or worse."[40]

But a yes-man or yes-woman might also be a collectivist and a member of a hierarchical society where dissent is not considered appropriate. Consider this story involving an egalitarian manager and a hierarchical employee, as told by international dispute resolution specialist Jeannie Brett of the Kellogg School of Management:

> A Canadian manager described his experience with an outstanding Chinese woman who worked at his company as a computer programmer as part of a two-year government program. As the end of the two years approached, she became more and more angry as aspects of the program that she believed had been promised were not delivered. He knew she was unhappy, but she would not tell him why. He ultimately decided that if she could not talk about it, he could not do anything about it. Both parties were trapped within the norms of their respective cultures. Coming from a hierarchical culture, she could not make claims against the boss and head of the international program without making him lose face. Coming from an egalitarian culture, he relied on her to tell him what the problems were.[41]

The Japanese seem to have found a solution to all of this. Japanese professionals are infamous for their long work hours, followed by after-hour, hard drinking of saké with their work colleagues (often at karaoke parlors). This drinking experience is often mandatory to employees, as it is seen as a bonding exercise for the workforce.

The drinking and thus bonding in the Japanese culture. It is also an antidote to groupthink.

Typically, it is impossible to disagree with a manager in the Japanese workplace – but while drinking saké? Go for it. This is the only time that disagreements may be voiced to the boss. Perhaps the alcohol is seen as a plausible excuse in the event a new idea is rejected, or perhaps the mutual embarrassment of voicing disagreement is minimized by said alcohol. Or perhaps it is simply a recognition that employees need an outlet to express their concerns, and the confines of a karaoke parlor provide just such a medium. Regardless, the Japanese are responding – and perhaps finding a solution – to the groupthink "virus" that can affect organizations anywhere in the world. Indeed, this isn't the first time in history alcohol has been used to ward off groupthink: "Herodotus, writing in the fifth century BC, reported that the ancient Persians used a version of [this technique] to prevent groupthink. Whenever a group reached a decision while sober, they later reconsidered it while intoxicated."[42]

Without your authors explicitly endorsing the vast consumption of alcohol, the Japanese do stand for the proposition that even in strongly cohesive, harmony-seeking organizations, outlets for dissent can be creatively found.

It is, consequently, incumbent on leaders to do that which may be unnatural: to demand that employees question their decisions, and those of colleagues. Great leaders, or "level 5" leaders in the parlance of Collins, were able to nurture an environment in which all voices were heard. We'll see in Chapter 6 that nurturing relationships of trust – a trust that dissent will be heard and not punished – is an effective tactic. This does however require a substantial investment of time.

Indirect methods can also accomplish the goal. For instance, encouraging dissent by email can help overcome fears arising in hierarchical cultures where dissent is more difficult. The indirect nature of emails helps reduce inhibitions and thereby facilitates communication between those lower in the hierarchy and those at higher levels.[43] Involving a third-party intermediary to mediate between a lower-level and higher-level employee can also help bridge the gap in power. As Brett writes: "Behavior that might be labeled tattling in an egalitarian culture is the way information gets conveyed in a hierarchical culture."[44]

An additional cross-cultural tactic is that of empowering employees to identify bad news or prevent the implementation of bad ideas. Renowned corporate consultant W. Edwards Deming traveled from the United States to Japan, a collectivist culture, and consulted for Sony Corporation. There, he recommended, and Sony implemented, a policy in which any and every employee could call out a problem without fear of punishment. In essence, they could "stop the assembly line." Later, Toyota also adopted this approach, saying, "You don't have to ask permission to take responsibility." It is evident that collectivist cultures too are able to empower employees to act as dissenters.

A leader can also resist providing his own opinion until everyone else in the group has weighed in, or, as Janis suggests, the leader may physically remove himself from the room until the other members have freely debated the issue.[45]

Relatedly, leaders can ask questions rather than seeking to uphold a sense of omnipotence by always providing answers.[46] An aggressive version of this interrogatory method was the tactic favored by former Emerson CEO Chuck Knight. Knight was known to use a confrontational approach at large meetings with question and answer sessions. Knight used these meetings to squeeze out every bit of relevant information.

As Jean Paul Montupet, the former executive vice president of Emerson Electric, explains: "Whatever you present, he is going to initially take the opposite view and challenge you very hard on everything you are presenting. He will make you feel like what you are presenting is wrong and he does not agree with it. So what I have to explain to people unfamiliar with Chuck's style is that the biggest mistake you can make is to cave in and quit defending your plan, because in fact it is likely he actually agrees. But he pushes to make sure you know what you are doing."[47]

Why does Knight pretend to disagree when he actually is in agreement? Perhaps he intuits what researchers confirm, and what we all might have suspected on the basis of those undergraduate beer drinkers: that, "knowing others' preferences [in this case, the preferences of the CEO] degrades the quality of group decisions."[48]

Montupet notes that most European and American employees were willing to speak up at these meetings. "In those meetings, we had complete exchanges of views. In Asia, we had the same meetings and it was initially a lot more difficult to get the Asians in general to open up."

How did Knight respond in this case? He adjusted to the culture rather than allowing his ego to demand conformity to his managerial style. Knight, in his book, *Performance without Compromise*, writes, "We realized early that the management process works because it deals with strategic business issues, which don't change with geography. Tactics, however, may differ by geography, particularly in employment practices."[49]

Montupet explains how his former boss did this: "In the US he was known for being very outspoken. An understatement; he was yelling at people, using bad words. But move him to an Asian environment and he would behave differently. So he was not out of control, he was perfectly in control, but it was his sense of US culture – perhaps pushed to an extreme – but he was careful in Asia, and he even changed his tactics in some ways in Europe."

Reiterating the philosophy espoused by Knight, Montupet says, "You can achieve the same thing in a different culture, but you have to do it in a different way."[50] At Emerson, employees are expected to conform to the big-picture management practices that Knight mentions above, but beyond those large-scale practices, Montupet says, "you run your business based on your local needs and habits."[51] This represents an attempt to respect local culture while also acknowledging that as an American company, certain goals and strategies will necessarily remain consistent across cultures.

TABLE 3.1 Discouraging obedience to authority, or, encouraging dissent

1. Sake and karaoke: find creative outlets to dissent
2. Use indirect methods to hear dissent – such as email or third-party intermediaries
3. Play dumb: managers wait to provide their own opinion until everyone has spoken; or even physically absent themselves until the rest of the team has debated the issue
4. Stop the assembly line: empower employees to identify bad news
5. The military machine: empower a cadre of trusted lieutenants, not "yes-men."

And that's okay. "Companies are becoming more and more transparent, and there are many studies published telling you what companies are the best companies to work at," Montupet says. "So people have a pretty good view of what working in a place will be like."[52]

If all else fails, follow the lead of Winston Churchill and carve out a core of trusted, brutally honest lieutenants. "[Churchill] feared that his towering, charismatic personality might deter bad news from reaching him in its starkest form. So, early in the war, he created an entirely separate department outside the normal chain of command, called the Statistical Office, with the principal function of feeding him – continuously updated and completely unfiltered – the most brutal facts of reality."[53] Churchill found a way to ensure dissent reached him, despite the hierarchical nature of his rule. This relied on empowering, indeed demanding, open communication from select members of his staff (Table 3.1).

Conformity in the Workplace

Disagreeing with a group can be difficult. It marks one as an outsider, a nonconformist. Most just want to fit in, to be embraced by others.

While Milgram shows us how obedient to authority we may be, Solomon Asch shows us in his now classic conformity experiments from the 1950s how people – even individualists – can be willing to conform to avoid the decidedly uncomfortable position of dissenting with the group. Asch did this by asking college students to participate in a vision test and had actors (who the test subject believed were fellow participants) seated in a row. Then the real participant would come in and take the last spot. The participants are then shown a paper with a line on the left side and three lines of different lengths on the right, and they are to choose which of the three lines matches the length of the line on the left (Figure 3.1). The actors state their answers one by one, with the actual participant answering last.

While the answer was obvious – a "clear and simple fact" as Asch writes – in some cases the actors were instructed to unanimously answer incorrectly. How does the actual participant respond in this case? Faced with the prospect of opposing the group, 37 percent of the time participants conformed by giving the wrong answer (and 75 percent of the participants conformed at least once).[54]

42   Glass of Beer, Shot of Sake, and Groupthink

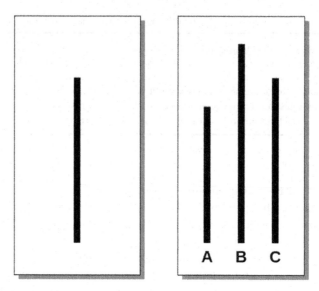

FIGURE 3.1 In the famous Asch experiment, students had to choose which of the three lines on the right matched the length of the line on the right.

Asch explains: "Whereas in ordinary circumstances individuals matching the lines will make mistakes less than 1 percent of the time, under group pressure the minority subjects swung to acceptance of the misleading majority's wrong judgments in 36.8 percent of the selections. Of course, individuals differed in response. At one extreme, about one quarter of the subjects were completely independent and never agreed with the erroneous judgments of the majority. At the other extreme, some individuals went with the majority nearly all the time. The performances of individuals in this experiment tend to be highly consistent. Those who strike out on the path of independence do not, as a rule, succumb to the majority even over an extended series of trials, while those who choose the path of compliance are unable to free themselves as the ordeal is prolonged."[55]

There are two main reasons for conforming to a group: one is that we doubt our own judgment when others give a different answer; the other is that we do not want to stand out. As the difficulty of the task increases, we become less sure of our answers and are therefore more likely to look at others for confirmation. In the Asch experiments, however, the vision test was straightforward and the correct answers obvious. Therefore, the participants had no reason to doubt their own judgment, and disagreement by others could not be seen as reasonable answers; they were unambiguously incorrect answers. The second reason for conforming then is explanatory: the participants wanted to conform to the group.

Asch modified the experiment – changing the size of the group from one person next to the participants up to fifteen people – to confirm that this explained the conformity. Here's what Asch found:

> [With] only a single individual who contradicted his answers, [the subject] was swayed little: he continued to answer independently and correctly in nearly all trials. When the opposition was increased to two, the pressure became substantial: minority subjects now accepted the wrong answer 13.6 percent of the time. Under the pressure of a majority of three, the subjects' errors jumped to 31.8 percent. But further increases in the size of the majority apparently did not increase the weight of the pressure substantially. Clearly the size of the opposition is important only up to a point.[56]

Consequently, when the dissent involves just one person, there is no group to stand out from and thus conformance is minimal. Even two people dissenting, however, caused a minority of subjects to go against the "clear and simple facts." Once the dissent reached three people, the full effects of groupthink set in.

We'll return to the Asch experiments in a moment. First, however, let's consider what separates the conformity seen in the Bay of Pigs disaster and the Asch case from that of the individualist beer drinkers who actually wanted to stand apart from the crowd. In both the Bay of Pigs case and the above Asch case, there was a *cost* to disagreeing that was not present for our nonconforming beer drinkers. There was a possible professional cost in disagreeing with the newly minted and highly popular US president in the Bay of Pigs disaster. While the beer drinkers for their part could order differently without signaling their rejection of their tablemates' choices, there was a social cost in the Asch experiment because answering differently signaled indirectly that the participants believed other respondents were wrong.

What is perhaps most striking is that this study was done using American participants that, as we know, tend to have a "need for uniqueness," which is less apparent in collectivist cultures. Additionally, collectivists may have the additional burden in these situations of being enculturated to maintain harmony by limiting dissent with their in-groups. Cross-cultural studies indeed indicate that non-Western societies are *more* susceptible to this conformance bias than Western societies.[57] For instance, there are studies showing an increased conformity in China, Brazil, and Ghana (countries scoring low on the individualism dimension) in comparison to Americans, and a decreased conformity in Germans (a country scoring more similarly to the United States).[58]

After the Asch study, researchers wondered whether the participants *knew* they were giving the wrong answer and simply feared openly disagreeing with the group, or whether they'd actually been convinced by the group. Author Susan

Cain, noted for her acclaimed TED Talk and bestselling book, *Quiet*, relates a study that relies on brain-scanning technology to understand mental processing:

> Gregory Berns decided to conduct an updated version of Asch's experiments. Berns and his team recruited thirty-two volunteers, men and women between the ages of nineteen and forty-one. The volunteers played a game in which each group member was shown two different three-dimensional objects on a computer screen and asked to decide whether the first object could be rotated to match the second. The experimenters used an fMRI scanner to take snapshots of the volunteers' brains as they conformed to or broke with group opinion.
>
> The results were both disturbing and illuminating. First, they corroborated Asch's findings. When the volunteers played the game on their own, they gave the wrong answer only 13.8 percent of the time. But when they played with a group whose members gave unanimously wrong answers, they agreed with the group 41 percent of the time.
>
> But Bern's study also shed light on exactly *why* we're such conformists because the scan showed the conformists exhibited less brain activity in the frontal, decision-making regions and more in the areas of the brain associated with perception.[59]

In other words, the volunteers did not just consciously change their answers to agree with the group. Instead, the brain scans revealed that the volunteers' very perception of the correct answer was changed.

The reason for this behavior is known as "cognitive dissonance."[60] In essence, this means that there is a disconnect in our brains – why, after all, would I be agreeing with the group on X, Y and Z if I didn't really believe X, Y and Z? The brain is happy to "fill in" the answer – "Oh, I'm saying it because I believe it. No more cognitive dissonance."

What to do about all this? We discussed the utility of probing questions aimed to root out the logic behind decisions, and to create environments where dissent is permissible, to help avoid blind obedience. These tactics will be equally useful in avoiding group conformity.

Additionally, just as we saw Emerson's CEO Knight adjusting his tactics to correspond to the target culture, so too must leaders react differently in cultures where obedience is particularly valued. Where conformity prevails, Wharton's Grant offers this advice: "disguise your ideas as acts of conformity. Find admired companies that are doing something similar and share those examples – people are surprisingly eager to jump on the bandwagon. It's not that hard to go from "You want to ignore pedigree and GPA in hiring decisions? You're insane," to "Google is ignoring pedigree and GPA in hiring decisions? Why aren't we doing that yet?!"[61]

Juan Ferreira, currently president for Latin America at Sumitomo Chemical, provides meaningful real-world experiences that echo these findings. Ferreira might be considered "Mr. International" in the business world. He is a Colombian national who earned his MBA in the United States from Florida International University and formerly worked for Monsanto on four continents, serving as company president for Europe, then the Middle East and then Africa. He has served as the former president of Monsanto for Europe, the Middle East, and Africa. Ferreira's strategy is to repackage dissent as a positive and to thus create an opportunity to move to more productive discussion.

Ferreira tells the story of an encounter with an Indian American employee prior to the beginning of an all-hands meeting in China: "A guy in our IT department gave me some feedback on a program we are investing a lot of money in, and it is not going as great as we would like it to. I thank him for his feedback and continue to our meeting. I am in the town hall meeting, and I say I got really good feedback. Now, he did not give the information that way – he said, 'This is a problem that we have.' But instead of positioning it as a bad thing, as criticizing people, I said, 'We have an opportunity to better serve our customers, and I am appreciative that that is the way that everyone is thinking here.'"[62]

Through these techniques, organizations can begin to overcome the double threats of obedience to authority and group conformity. In the next section, we provide additional techniques with a twist on the well-known devil's advocate technique and provide clear steps to cultivate what we refer to as an "authentic devil's advocate."

Discouraging Conformity: An Authentic Devil's Advocate Is an Authentic Dissenter

> Politeness is the poison of collaboration.
>
> Edwin Land[63]
> *Scientist, Inventor, and Polaroid Co-founder*

Imagine this scenario: your company is trying to decide whether to open a new office in Peru or Kenya.[64] Before you come to your own decision, the boss suggests that Peru may be the best option. He encourages other suggestions, but the rest of the team quickly agrees with the plan. Do you dissent? To do so would require going against both your boss and your team. We know from Asch's conformity experiments that we're unlikely to disagree with the team; we know from Milgram's shock experiment that we're unlikely to dissent with the boss; and consequently, for most of us, the answer is no – we'll hold our tongues. In fact, Bern's research tells us that we're likely to quickly convince ourselves that Peru is indeed the best option, regardless of whether we would have come to that conclusion independently.

As if this weren't enough, we also know that once we've come to this conclusion, we'll now seek all evidence possible to confirm this decision. We'll give less weight to information that presents Kenya favorably, taking more notice of that which portrays Kenya in a more negative light and Peru in a positive light. In fact, in a study with more than two hundred business and governmental leaders in Germany involving just this question, participants were given access to equal numbers of articles on both Peru and Kenya. But for those who favored Peru, they read 26 percent more articles on Peru than on Kenya. This contributes to the "confirmation bias," as these participants are more likely to find information in those extra articles that supports their favorable view of Peru.[65]

We now have all the pieces of the puzzle needed to see the many pressures that lead us to groupthink: the willingness to obey those in authority, the fear of non-conformity, the ability to rationalize our conformance through cognitive dissonance, and the ability to double down on our rationalizations through confirmation bias.

We return to the famous Asch experiments for a first possibility of a solution. After revealing extensive conformity on the vision test, Asch decided to close out his experiments with a twist, and this is where things get interesting. Asch brought in just one "supporting partner." While the rest of the group continued to provide obviously incorrect answers, this partner was prepped to provide the correct answer before the test subject was asked to provide his own answer. The question was whether this supporting partner would give the test subject the courage to answer honestly, or whether the subject would still go along with the majority in answering incorrectly.

Here's what happened:

> The presence of a supporting partner depleted the majority of much of its power. ... subjects answered incorrectly only one-fourth as often as under the pressure of a unanimous majority. The weakest persons did not yield as readily. Most interesting were the reactions to the partner. Generally, the feeling toward him was one of warmth and closeness; he was credited with inspiring confidence.[66]

Asch thus hits upon a possible solution to the problem. While one person may be too meek or uncertain to speak up, having just one other person dissenting with the group's consensus provides vast reserves of strength. This led to the idea of a devil's advocate, a person ready and willing – and often appointed – to disagree with the others in the group. Not only might this lead to uncovering previously missed concerns and problems, but Asch's study shows us how it might empower those in the group that already had reservations.

Many researchers, including Janis, have argued that appointing a devil's advocates is a solution to groupthink.[67] By explicitly tasking an individual to raise concerns about the otherwise accepted decisions of the organization, so the thinking goes, the others in the room may be willing to raise concerns themselves. Stepping a bit out of our customary intellectual spaces, even Hollywood trotted out this tried-and-true management technique in the zombie flick *World War Z*. In that movie, a character explains to star Brad Pitt that the Israeli government anticipated the pending apocalypse after appointing a devil's advocate in top-level government meetings.

Given the propensity of students to rather eagerly follow the ideas of their instructors, this is a tried-and-true classroom technique. Many instructors will argue one side of a point and immediately switch to the opposite perspective. The best instructors do so in a way that leaves students unsure which side the instructor actually believes, which forces those students to objectively evaluate the merits of the argument.

It turns out, however, that in the business context, this simple solution to groupthink is not quite as effective as we once thought. The reason is that devil's advocates are relatively unpersuasive, in part because it is often known that they are just playing the role of the dissenter, or because most people argue more persuasively for things they believe in than those they don't. Put differently, it is usually quite clear which answer they agree more with. To argue truly persuasively, we need "authentic" devil's advocates.

Grant cites the following study as proof of this idea, taking us back to the German business and governmental leaders studying an expansion plan into Peru or Kenya. After members of the group had chosen their preferred country – and after the participants had exhibited confirmation bias as discussed just above, a devil's advocate was appointed. Grant writes:

> His role was to challenge the majority preference for Peru, identifying its disadvantages and questioning the group's assumptions. With a devil's advocate present, the managers became more balanced: they read only 2 percent more pro-Peru articles than pro-Kenya articles. Yet the advocate's input ultimately wasn't sufficient to change their minds. The managers paid lip service to the advocate by selecting an evenhanded mix of articles, but their confidence in their original preference dropped by only 4 percent. Because of confirmation bias, they were persuaded by the arguments that affirmed their preference and discounted those that didn't.[68]

A devil's advocate had little impact. But Grant wondered about an *authentic* devil's advocate and not just someone pretending to disagree, but someone who sincerely held a differing opinion. You might call it diversity, and here we see its real power to change the way we think about devil's advocates and how to arrive at the best group decision:

> The researchers formed another set of groups with two managers who favored Peru. For the third member, instead of assigning a devil's advocate to argue for Kenya, they picked someone who *actually* preferred Kenya. Those groups selected 14 percent more articles against the majority preference than for it. And now, they were 15 percent less confident in their original preference. While it can be appealing to assign a devil's advocate, it's much more powerful to unearth one. [emphasis added][69]

In a related experiment, Charlan Nemeth found that authentic devil's advocates led to 48 percent more solutions to problems than assigned devil's advocates.[70] The solutions, moreover, were of a higher quality.[71]

We know from Asch's experiment that when just one other person stands up for an idea that we too hold, we are more likely to join them in dissenting. We know from Grant's and Nemeth's study that even if no one else has a dissenting opinion, an authentic devil's advocate can go far in encouraging critical thinking. The question then is how we get people to serve as authentic devil's advocates and ardently stand up for these beliefs?

Coherence and Diversity

> If we can capture diversity we [w]ould have much better decision making. But ... the execution is more important than the strategy. If people of diverse backgrounds – different educational and professional levels, nationalities, and so forth – are bringing us the best idea but screwing up our execution – what do we gain?
>
> Tom Kalishman
> CEO and Chairman, SAK Industries

Cohesion and diversity are required to facilitate authentic devil's advocates. Having a diverse workforce makes it more likely that natural disagreements will arise. Many leaders hire employees based on one's likelihood of fitting in – that is, their similarity to the existing corporate culture. And the more established a company gets, the more likely they are to trend toward homogeneous thinking by hiring based on cultural fit and weeding out nonconformists.[72] But Grant warns that when you hire for cultural fit, you end up facilitating groupthink.[73] Instead, you need to look to people who are different, have different life experiences and worldviews, and yes, come from different national cultures, to be able to stand up to the conventional wisdom.

Apple CEO Tim Cook agrees: "if you're a CEO, the most important thing is ... pick people around you that aren't like you, that complement you. Because you want to build a puzzle; you don't want to stack Chiclets up and have everyone be the same. And so I believe in diversity with a capital D."[74]

Secondly, creating a workforce that is cohesive and trusting of one another facilitates open communication. In this situation, communication increases as employees are more secure and thus more likely to challenge ideas.[75] Consequently, when cohesion is high, groupthink should actually *decline*. This goes against our perceived wisdom. When articulating the groupthink concept, Janis argued that when a group's desire for unanimity trumps a desire for maximal decision making, groupthink can occur.[76] Consequently, highly cohesive teams were most susceptible to groupthink in Janis's view. As a result, organizations concerned with groupthink have for decades sought ways to reduce cohesiveness.

But intuitively, Grant's affirmation of cohesion makes perfect sense. In the Asch study, one can imagine a heightened discomfort in disagreeing with total strangers' clearly illogical decisions. It would have been much easier to make light of the situation, to jest, "You need to get your eyes checked if you think those lines are the same length," if the participants were one's family or close friends. Indeed, we can recall that in all the cases referenced in this chapter, the test subject and the experimenters were strangers, so cohesion of the sort Grant advocates was absent.

Diversity and cohesion may at first glance appear to be mutually exclusive ideas but, as we will see, thoughtful managers can foster just this environment in several ways. Racial, religious and other differences are inevitable and increasing in the twenty-first century workplace, and many cultures recoil from diversity. But Jonathan Haidt advises that these differences are not as important as we tend to think; he argues that we can drown race and other differences "in a sea of similarities, shared goals, and mutual interdependencies."[77]

Applying this approach to the organization, businesses can unite through a shared corporate culture, the use of stories and myths, insider language and metaphors, a unified sense of purpose, and a sense of shared pride in past accomplishments. This argument has empirical support: researchers have found that workers in so-called "dirty" industries – such as gravediggers, prostitutes, or pawnbrokers – tend to subconsciously use precisely these techniques to build unusually strong organizational cultures as a bulwark against low public status.[78]

Additionally, Japanese corporations such as Toyota build this connectedness through companywide exercises before the workday begins; sports teams and warring armies do this with "group chants and ritualized movements."[79] More mundane activities, such as office-wide parties or outings to the bowling alley, can also help build this connectedness.[80]

SAK's Tom Kalishman notes further that increasing diversity improves decision making but can inhibit cohesiveness. There is a "push-pull tension," he says, but "the key is to build an organization of candor, and that's a very challenging thing. Candor and communications are the keys to building an organization that can handle diversity."[81] Put differently, cohesive teams communicate well, and teams that communicate well build cohesion. In the latter case, specific strategies can be used to encourage communication.

This candor is best facilitated in small working groups where relationships can be formed and misunderstandings overcome. Indeed, the larger the group, the less cohesive.[82] Instead, in-group competition tends to rise with the size of the group.[83] More problematically with regards to groupthink is that as group size increases, "the amount of communication initiated by individual members decrease[s]."[84] Individuals feel more inhibited and more threatened by teammates.[85] Consequently, both cohesion and dissent decline as group size increases.

For this reason, Kalishman says, "Communication that takes place formally in large groups is just as important as communication which takes place informally in small groups. If a new person is understandably uncomfortable voicing their opinions or challenging conventional wisdom, there's nothing we can do about that, that's human nature. That's why it's important to have camaraderie and informal conversations where the risks of speaking are far less."[86]

Relatedly, face-to-face interactions, and relationships built over the long-term, help to increase rapport between individuals and thus cohesiveness within an organization. These points are discussed further in Chapter 13.

Sumitomo Chemical's executive Juan Ferreira builds on this idea. He notes that Monsanto's global footprint means there are corollary global biases to address:

> "You know, the Italian doesn't want a German, the German doesn't want a Spanish person, and the Spanish person dreads a German. Some people had rough times with the Americans. We have these entirely unconscious biases sitting in everyone's minds, including yours and mine. So, you need to acknowledge it" [build an organization of candor], "but then encourage them to leave it to the side as much as they can to really listen to the person or culture that they are working with. Ultimately, we are able to do this because we live in a results-oriented world and we are in a results-oriented organization, and you just need to accomplish something."[87]

Finally, Emerson's Montupet raises the issue of leveraging competition. He notes that "Americans like to win. Period. [But] in every culture people like to win in various degrees. With any management group, you can motivate by saying 'here is the competition, and we are going to beat them.' That is a big motivator."

For example, St. Louis beer company Anheuser-Busch leveraged its competition with Milwaukee brewer Miller to bring together management and labor during a time of strife. Among other things, the company took to printing shirts for its employees that read "I am a Miller Killer."[88] These sorts of activities build up the in-group, thereby strengthening harmony.

This competition can also be internal, by increasing competition within the organization. However, that competition should take place between *teams*, not *individuals*. Haidt finds that "pitting individuals against each other in a competition for scarce resources (such as bonuses)" destroys trust and connectedness. By contrast, creating "friendly rivalries between corporate divisions, or intramural sports competitions" effectively builds trust.[89] And, as long as the competitions are kept friendly, trust within the group is built far more than relationships are harmed between the groups.[90] In this way, bonds may be formed amongst the members of an organization.

However, let's briefly consider in closing this chapter what to do once the dissent is registered. Committed team members should be willing to put their egos aside and to hear alternative opinions; to dive back into the research if merited, or to reconsider their own preconceptions. The fact is, however, that even the most well-intentioned of people will not always find a common ground for resolution. In this case, dissent threatens to ripen into conflict.

Amazon's Jeff Bezos proposes the following when all else fails: "Recognize true *misalignment* issues early and escalate them *immediately*. Sometimes teams have different objectives and fundamentally different views. They are not aligned. No amount of discussion, no number of meetings will resolve that deep misalignment. Without escalation, the default dispute resolution mechanism for this scenario is exhaustion. Whoever has more stamina carries the decision...".[91]

In other words, dissent is necessary, and those arguments should be heard, but not all dissension will be resolved. It is up to the manager to determine when a debate is in a death spiral. After everything else, there must come a time when the team – or if not the team, the boss – makes an authoritative decision.

Groupthink is a complex phenomenon with oft-cited negative implications. The good news is that coherence, diversity and humility not only reduce groupthink, they can benefit the organization as a whole. Cohesion weakens the pull of cross-cultural conflict; diversity is widely considered to bring about superior performance; and, as we'll see in the next chapter, cohesion can help collectivists overcome the problem of free riding (Figure 3.2).

Steps to overcoming groupthink

→ Remain humble
→ Encourage dissent and avoid conformity

How to remain humble:

→ Pay attention to history and the many failures of brilliant minds and exceptional companies
→ Recognize that we tend to see ourselves more favorably than do others – the "self-serving bias"
→ When mistaken, admit it – especially if you are a leader!

How to encourage dissent and avoid conformity:

→ Drink sake – or at least, find a viable outlet for dissent
→ Disguise ideas as acts of conformity, or give dissenting ideas a positive spin
→ Leaders reward dissent
→ Leaders resist giving opinion until others weigh in, instead asking probing questions
→ Empower employees throughout the organization to dispute the prevailing opinion and to "stop the assembly lines" (whether metaphorical or real)
→ Identify an authentic devil's advocate, and make sure she speaks up
  + Find authentic devil's advocates by hiring for diversity, not cultural fit
→ Increase trust to facilitate open communication
  + Facilitate shared corporate values and cultures
  + Keep work groups small
  + Increase competition between groups, not individuals, or with other companies
  + Increase face-to-face interactions
  + Foster repeated, long-term relationships

FIGURE 3.2 A summary of groupthink prevention.

References

1. Ariely, *supra* note 102 at 233–234.
2. *Id*. at 234.
3. *Id*. at 233.
4. *Id*. at 236.
5. *Id*. at 235.
6. *Id*. at 235.
7. *Id*. at 235–236.
8. *Id*. at 237.
9. *Id*. at 237.
10. *Id*. at 238.
11. *Id*. at 235, 238.
12. Henrich, et al., *supra* note 1 at 71.
13. John McDonnell, Interview with Author.
14. James Surowiecki, *The Wisdom of Crowds: Why the Many Are Smarter than the Few* 2 (Anchor) (2005).
15. Irving L. Janis, *Groupthink: Psychological Studies of Policy Decisions and Fiascoes* (Houghton Mifflin: Boston) (1973).
16. Mark Wrighton, Interview with the Author.
17. Grant, *supra* note 72 at 164.
18. Carol S. Dweck, *Mindset: The New Psychology of Success* 110 (Random House: New York) (2007).
19. For an overview on the accounting methodology used by Enron, see Troy Segal, *Enron Scandal: The Fall of a Wall Street Darling*, Investopedia (updated Jan. 3, 2018), https://www.investopedia.com/updates/enron-scandal-summary/. For executive stock sales, see "Enron Execs Sold $1.3B in Stock," *CNNMONEY* (Jan. 22, 2002), http://money.cnn.com/2002/01/22/companies/enron_stocks/index.htm.
20. Richard A. Oppel, Jr., "Employees Retirement Plan Is a Victim as Enron Tumbles," *The New York Times* (Nov. 22, 2001), http://www.nytimes.com/2001/11/22/business/employees-retirement-plan-is-a-victim-as-enron-tumbles.html.
21. Dweck, *supra* note 132 at 111.
22. Thomas Clarke, *International Corporate Governance* 321 (Routledge: London and New York) (2007).
23. Grant, *supra* note 72 at 169.
24. *Id*.
25. *Id*. at 170.
26. *Id*.
27. Peter A. Thiel and Blake Masters, *Zero to One: Notes on Startups, or How to Build the Future* 136 (Crown Business) (2014).
28. Jim Collins, *Good to Great: Why Some Companies Make the Leap … and Others Don't* (HarperBusiness) (2011).
29. Henrich et al., *supra* note 1 at 503/5723 (e-book).
30. Ariely, *supra* note 96 at 64, 65.
31. McDonnell, *supra* note 127.
32. Milgram, *supra* note 2.
33. Nick Haslam, Steve Loughnan, and Gina Perry, "Meta-Milgram: An Empirical Synthesis of the Obedience Experiments," 9 *PLOS One* 1, 8 (2014).
34. *Id*. at 8.
35. *Id*.
36. Thomas Blass, "A Cross-Cultural Comparison of Studies of Obedience Using the Milgram Paradigm: A Review," 6 *Social and Personality Psychology Compass* 196–205 (2012).
37. Thomas Blass, "The Milgram Paradigm after 35 Years: Some Things We Now Know about Obedience to Authority," 29 *J. of Applied Social Psychology*, 955, 969 (1999).

38 *Id.* at 966.
39 Blass, *supra* note 150.
40 Collins, *supra* note 142 at 72.
41 Brett, *supra* note 81 at 100.
42 Dweck, *supra* note 132 at 111.
43 Brett, *supra* note 81 at 148.
44 *Id.* at 100.
45 Ed Griffin, *A First Look at Communication Theory* 240 (McGraw-Hill) (1991).
46 Collins, *supra* note 142 at 75 (writing: "Leading from good to great does not mean coming up with the answers and then motivating everyone to follow your messianic vision. It means having the humility to grasp the fact that you do not yet understand enough to have the answers and then to ask the questions that will lead to the best possible insights").
47 Montupet, *supra* note 10.
48 Grant, *supra* note 72 at 329 (citing to Andreas Mojzisch, and Stefan Schulz-Hardt, "Knowing Others' Preferences Degrades the Quality of Group Decisions," *Journal of Personality and Social Psychology* 98 (2010): 794–808).
49 Chuck Knight and Davis Dyer, *Performance without Compromise: How Emerson Consistently Achieves Winning Results*, Harvard Business Review Press 178–179 (2005).
50 Montupet, *supra* note 10.
51 *Id.*
52 Montupet, *supra* note 10.
53 Collins, *supra* note 142 at 73.
54 Solomon E. Asch, "Studies of Independence and Conformity: A Minority of One against a Unanimous Majority," 70 *Psychological Monographs: General and Applied* 1, 9–10 (1956).
55 Solomon E. Asch, "Opinions and Social Pressure," 193 *Scientific American* 1, 3–4 (1955).
56 *Id.* at 5.
57 Henrich et al., *supra* note 1 at 71.
58 "Culture and Conformity: A meta-Analysis of Studies Using Asch's (1952b, 1956) Line Judgment Task." R Bond and PB Smith, *Psychological Bulletin* (1996).
59 Cain, *supra* note 87 at 91–92.
60 Janis and King, 1954, 1956.
61 https://www.forbes.com/sites/danschawbel/2016/02/02/adam-grant-why-you-shouldnt-hire-for-cultural-fit/2/#7eef027dbcb5.
62 Juan Ferreira, Interview with the Author.
63 BrainyQuote, https://www.brainyquote.com/quotes/edwin_land_193299.
64 This scenario is derived from the experiment cited below by Grant, *supra* note 72 at 175–176.
65 *Id.* at 175.
66 Asch, *supra* note 168 at 5.
67 Grant, *supra* note 72 at 175.
68 Grant, *supra* note 72 at 175–176.
69 *Id.* at 176.
70 *Id.* (citing to Charlan Nemeth, Keith Brown, and John Rogers, "Devil's Advocate versus Authentic Dissent: Stimulating Quantity and Quality," *European Journal of Social Psychology* 31 (2001): 707–720.
71 *Id.*
72 *Id.* 168.
73 "Dan Schawbel and Adam Grant, "Why You Shouldn't Hire for Cultural Fit," *Forbes* (Feb. 2, 2016), https://www.forbes.com/forbes/welcome/?toURL=https://www.forbes.com/sites/danschawbel/2016/02/02/adam-grant-why-you-shouldnt-hire-for-cultural-fit/&refURL=https://www.google.com/&referrer=https://www.google.com/.

74 Tim Cook Quotes, Brainy Quotes (last accessed July 29, 2018), https://www.brainyquote.com/authors/tim_cook.
75 Grant, *supra* note 72 at 165 (citing to Sally Riggs Fuller and Ramon J. Aldag, "Organizational Tonypandy: Lessons from a Quarter Century of the Groupthink Phenomenon," *Organizational Behavior and Human Decision Processes* 73 (1998): 163–184.
76 Irving Janis, *Victims of Groupthink: A Psychological Study of Foreign Policy Decisions and Fiascoes* 9 (Houghton Mifflin: Boston) (1972).
77 Haidt, *supra* note 98 at 186.
78 Blake E. Ashforth and Glen E. Kreiner, "'How Can You Do It?': Dirty Work and the Challenge of Constructing a Positive Identity," 24 *Acad. Manag. Rev.* 413, 431 (1999).
79 Haidt, *supra* note 98 at 186.
80 *Id.*
81 Kalishman, *supra* note 100.
82 Susan A. Wheelan, "Group Size, Group Development, and Group Productivity," 40 *Small Group Research* 247, 247 (2009).
83 *Id.*
84 *Id.* at 248.
85 *Id.*
86 Kalishman, *supra* note 100.
87 Ferreira, *supra* note 175.
88 William Knoedelseder, *Bitter Brew: The Rise and Fall of Anheuser-Busch and America's Kings of Beer* 164, (Harper Business) (2012).
89 Haidt, *supra* note 98 at 186.
90 *Id.*
91 Jessica Stillman, "Here's How Amazon's Jeff Bezos Makes Great Decisions, Super Fast," *Inc.* (Apr. 14, 2017), https://www.inc.com/jessica-stillman/heres-how-amazons-jeff-bezos-makes-great-decisions-super-fast.html.

4
GROUP WORK AND THE FREE-RIDER EFFECT

Andrew Carnegie once said that "Teamwork is the ability to work together toward a common vision. The ability to direct individual accomplishments toward organizational objectives. It is the fuel that allows common people to attain uncommon results."[1]

Carnegie was right, but he may not have known just how surprising the effects of teamwork can be on productivity. Moving from the heights of Carnegie, let's now take a moment to consider roaches:

> In 1969, Robert Zajonc, Alexander Heingartner, and Edward Herman wanted to compare the speed at which roaches would accomplish different tasks under two conditions. In one, they were alone and without any company. In the other, they had an audience in the form of a fellow roach. In the "social" case, the other roach watched the runner through a Plexiglas window that allowed the two creatures to see and smell each other but that did not allow any direct contact.
>
> One task that the cockroaches performed was relatively easy: the roach had to run down a straight corridor. The other, more difficult task required the roach to navigate a somewhat complex maze. As you might expect (assuming you have expectations about roaches), the insects performed the simpler runway task much more quickly when another roach was observing them. The presence of another roach increased their motivation, and, as a consequence, they did better. However, in the more complex maze task, they struggled to navigate their way in the presence of an audience and did much worse than when they performed the same complex task alone.[2]

The study shows that cockroaches do better at simple, well-practiced activities when in the presence of other cockroaches. However, when the task is more complex, working alone seems to result in superior outcomes.

Of course, we wouldn't be talking about a couple of cockroaches if this only applied to the bug world: the same simple-complex phenomenon has been observed in a variety of animals and in humans. For example, one study found that people solved twice as many anagrams when working in private as when working in public.[3] And who among us cannot recall a time we performed better on the golf course when playing alone, scored higher on a practice test than on the real thing in a public setting, or watched an athlete wilt under the pressure of a big game? Conversely, the true masters are so well-practiced that certain activities become almost routine, and thus they perform better in public spectacles. Marathon runners, for instance, can attest to a race day performance elevated over that on the basement treadmill.

Social pressure can thus motivate or undermine effective work. But in the above cases, people – and cockroaches – are responsible for their own performance even if the setting involves others. When individuals begin to work in groups, the interplay becomes even more complex. At this point, there is the nagging fear familiar to many the diligent student assigned to a group project: the fear that teammates will free-ride on their efforts. Free-riding, also known as social loafing, occurs when certain members of a group do not work as hard or contribute as much as they might if working alone.[4] As the diligent professional could attest, the student's fear of free-riding does not dissipate in the professional workplace, and as the data will show, the anxiety of student and professional alike is well placed.

Let It Burn

Consider what would happen if firefighting services were privatized. In theory, each individual or family unit would need to hire a firefighter. Imagine, however, that one day a fire breaks out at your neighbor's home. This neighbor ran into some money trouble and recently laid off his firefighter. Do you ask your firefighter to put out the next-door blaze? Absolutely! Although it rewards the behavior of your neighbor, you know the fire may well spread to your home if not snuffed out.

The next day, you learn that numerous members of your community have dismissed their own firefighters. After all, they reason, if your firefighter will put out the neighborhood fires, why should they bother keeping their own on staff? They can, in essence, free-ride on your efforts. Perhaps you grudgingly continue paying your firefighter, or perhaps, embittered, you too lay off your firefighter rather than support your neighbors' selfish behavior. Either way, the result is undesirable.

The same problem arises when organizational groups free-ride: some put in the effort, but all members benefit. The question, then, is how to get everyone to participate in schemes where free-riding is possible. Often, the cause of free-riding is a lack of accountability – free-riders will neither face individualized punishment for poor performance nor additional rewards for high performance, and so the self-serving incentive to perform well is undermined.[5] At the societal level, accountability is ensured by making the service a public good, thereby making the government assume responsibility for the provision of services and in turn requiring everyone to contribute to the cost through taxes. This is seen as a more viable response than letting the houses of free-riders burn, which would increase accountability but would also be dangerous to the community as a whole.

But such an outsourcing of responsibility is not available at the organizational level. So how can we increase accountability? Maybe let the house burn. Or at least let the members affected by the free-riding decide whether to let the house burn.

Let's explain how this can work. Researchers found that when members of a team are given the opportunity, they are indeed willing, in essence, to "let the neighbor's house burn," even at some cost to themselves. And as the fear of negative consequences rises for free-riding group members, participation increases.[6] While useful, as we will see, the applications of the study are limited to Western societies. First, however, let's explore the conditions in which we can give participants the tools to let the metaphorical house burn.

The study, referred to as the "Ultimatum Game," gave participants the chance to go home with some money. The game proceeded as follows:

In one such game, a first player was given a sum of money and told he could divide it as he wished with the second player and then the second player was given the option to decide whether the arrangement was agreeable. If the second player rejected the offer, then neither player would receive any money.[7] The rational actor model would of course predict that the second player would accept any offer greater than zero, as he would be financially enriched in doing so. This, however, did not prove the case.

As it happened, the more skewed the first player's offer moved from an equitable 50/50 division between players, the less likely the second player was to accept the offer, choosing instead to receive nothing rather than participate in an unfair distribution of money.[8]

This situation is analogous to free-riding because when participants offered unfair amounts, they functioned essentially as free-riders, trying to gain more benefit than is equitable. In this case furthermore, the participants were willing to experience personal harm – to "let the house burn" – in order to punish the free-rider.

Interestingly, the interactions between the players was a "one-off" exercise – they dealt with each other only once. There was therefore no expectation that by punishing the player the first time they would get more cooperation later. Or to continue the analogy, there was no expectation that by letting the house burn this time, the neighborhood would be safer in the future. What this suggests is that it was a sense of fairness that motivated the behavior, even when that sense of fairness would result in harm to the player doing the punishment.[9] Consequently, this behavior is termed "altruistic punishment."

Ernst Fehr and Simon Gächter's classic article, "Altruistic Punishment in Humans," extended the Ultimatum Game study by increasing the number of interactions among the players, which allowed the researchers to measure whether the altruistic punishment would improve fairness. They found that where such punishments were made possible, overall team performance dramatically increased as would-be free-riders realized that it was to their benefit to cooperate.[10] Consequently, these studies showed that altruistic punishments could be used to reduce free riding. Put differently, many people will self-police their teams if given the resources to do so, which will ultimately improve team performance.

For a period of time, it was believed that Fehr and Gächter had revealed a universal truth about humans.[11] As is so often the case, however, it seems that this lesson does not apply equally to all cultures. Researchers extended the Ultimatum Game study to "small-scale human societies, including foragers, horticulturalists, pastoralists and subsistence farmers, drawn from Africa, Amazonia, Oceania, Siberia and New Guinea.[12] They found that "these populations made low offers and did not reject."[13] In other words, no self-policing took place, and thus, free-riding would be expected to continue unabated in these societies.

Additionally, researchers extended the study from "Altruistic Punishment in Humans," which had been tested only on Zurich undergraduate students, to a globally dispersed group of students. They found that in many of the participant groups, there was punishment for uncooperative behavior, but there was also what they termed "antisocial punishment," wherein subjects were punished for being *too* cooperative – that is, contributing more than fairness would seem to compel. In fact, the antisocial behavior was so significant amongst many participants that it entirely offset the benefits from punishing free-riders.[14]

Henrich, Heine and Norenzayan, the researchers who coined the term WEIRD, concluded as follows: "Possibilities for altruistic punishment do not generate high levels of cooperation in these populations. Meanwhile, participants from a number of Western countries, such as the United States, the United Kingdom, and Australia, behaved like the original Zurich students. Thus, it appears that the Zurich sample works well for generalizing to the patterns of other Western samples (as well as the Chinese sample), but such findings cannot be readily extended beyond this."[15]

The result is that in most Western societies, the ability to use "altruistic punishment" may help keep free-riders honest. "Cooperation flourishes [in these societies] if altruistic punishment is possible and breaks down if it is ruled out."[16]

For example, group members may be permitted at least partial discretion in distributing rewards such as bonuses for the completion of tasks. Similarly, groups may be responsible for choosing which members present the results, thus excluding free-riders from certain social benefits. In some cases, groups may also be asked to rank the efficacy of their group members in a way that indicates to managers whether all members performed. All these steps would help increase the accountability of group members that would in turn increase participation.

However, be it due to antisocial punishments meted out in some societies to overeager group participants or a refusal to punish free-riders in others, the evidence suggests this will not be particularly effective in many non-Western societies. The WEIRD societies strike again. Of course, many non-Western professionals behave in some WEIRD ways, so it may be worth experimenting with altruistic punishment to see whether it can be usefully adapted.

Free-riding in Collectivist Cultures

While altruistic punishment is expected to be less effective outside of the Western world in combating free-riding, research also suggests that non-Westerners are less prone to free-riding than traditionally individualistic Westerners. In fact, collectivist individuals often perform significantly better when working in groups than when working alone.

P. Christopher Earley, for example, carried out an experiment involving individualistic Americans, collectivist Chinese and collectivist Israeli subjects.[17] She asked the subjects to work in private on a task but told them in one condition that they were working alone and in another condition that they were working as part of a group of ten people.[18] When the Americans worked alone, their individual performance was superior to that of the other country nationals under both conditions.[19] But when told they were working as part of a group, their performance was on average worse than any other country national's.[20] This study therefore confirmed what we already know: individualists are subject to free-riding.

But for the collectivists, the results were more surprising. When told they were working as part of a group, some of the subjects were told they were working with people of very different backgrounds: coming from different parts of the country, adhering to different religions, with different interests, lifestyles and family backgrounds.[21] They were told, in short, that they shared virtually nothing in common. The other subjects were told the opposite about their supposed teammates: that although they didn't know the other members of their group, they shared much in common and would likely be friends if they met.[22]

The researchers in this way constructed "in-groups" and "out-groups." What they found was that both Israelis and Chinese participants did their best work when they thought they were working as part of an in-group.[23] When they thought they were working individually, they performed significantly worse.[24] And when they thought they were working as part of an out-group,

60 Group Work and the Free-rider Effect

they performed at their worst (though still better than the Americans when they thought they were working in either of the groups).[25]

It seems, therefore, that individualists are highly susceptible to free-riding, but they are also responsive to self-policing by other members in the group and thereafter to change their behavior for the better. Achievement oriented as many individualists are, they are also likely to perform better when they know they will be rewarded for their individual contributions within a group and held accountable for their individual shortcomings, rather than seeing their contributions or shortcomings lost in the mix.[26]

Collectivists are also susceptible to free-riding but primarily only when working in out-groups. Other studies have shown that out-group dynamics affect performance in other ways as well. For instance, out-groups often communicate poorly with one another, even if they work for the same organization.[27] Additionally, collectivists are more competitive than individualists when competing against out-groups. This is not inherently problematic, but studies suggest this competition can be taken to such a degree as to harm the in-group.[28] In Japan, for example, executives are known for their competitiveness against other companies (an out-group) and do indeed often take this competitiveness to such an extreme as to harm their own organizations.[29] For instance, Peter Drucker wrote that the Japanese "see intense, if not cutthroat, competition both among the major banks and among the major industrial groups." There is "bitter factional infighting," "unremitting guerilla warfare," and "competition tends to be ruthless between companies in the same field and between groups of companies – for example, between Sony and Panasonic or between Mitsui Bank and Fuji Bank."[30]

We saw that individualists can reduce groupthink with greater cohesiveness. Here, we see that collectivists can similarly benefit by increasing in-group identification (Table 4.1).

TABLE 4.1 Reducing free-riding for individualists and collectivists

1. Individualists	Free-riding common both when working with in-groups and out-groups.
	Performance at its highest level when working alone.
	The solution: If given opportunity for altruistic punishment, free-riding is reduced or eliminated.
	Not the solution: Transforming perception of team members as part of an out-group to that of an in group will have some benefits in general (including the reduction of groupthink), but not with respect to free-riding.
2. Collectivists	Free-riding common when working with out-groups.
	The solution: Free-riding not a problem when working with in-groups – performance at its highest level in this case. Therefore, transform perception of team members as part of an out-group to that of an in-group.
	Not the solution: Altruistic punishment likely ineffective to reduce free-riding.

References

1 Dave Kerpen, "15 Quotes to Inspire Great Teamwork," *Inc.* (Feb. 12, 2014), https://www.inc.com/dave-kerpen/15-quotes-to-inspire-great-team-work.html.
2 Ariely, *supra* note 96 at 45–46 (citing to Robert Zajonc, Alexander Heingartner, and Edward Herman, "Social Enhancement and Impairment of Performance in the Cockroach," *Journal of Personality and Social Psychology* 13 (2) (1969): 83–92).
3 Ariely, *supra* note 96 at 44.
4 P. Christopher Earley, "Social Loafing and Collectivism: A Comparison of the United States and the People's Republic of China," 34 *Administrative Science Quarterly* 565 (1989).
5 Kipling Williams, Stephen Harkins, and Latané, "Identifiability as a Deterrent to Social Loafing: Two Cheering Experiments," 40 *Journal of Personality and Social Psychology* 303–311 (1981).
6 Fehr and Gächter, "Altruistic Punishment in Humans," 415 *Nature* 138 (2002).
7 Henry Biggs, "Toward a More Comprehensive Approach to the Promotion of Creativity," 38 *University of Dayton Law Review,* 402, 408 (citing to Werner Güth, Rolf Shmittberger, and Bernd Schwartz, "An Experimental Analysis of Ultimatum Bargaining," *Journal of Economic Behavior and Organization* 3 (1982): 367, 371).
8 Id. (citing to Werner Güth, Rolf Shmittberger, and Bernd Schwartz, "An Experimental Analysis of Ultimatum Bargaining," *Journal of Economic Behavior and Organization* 3 (1982): 367, 374).
9 Id.
10 Fehr and Gächter, *supra* note at 214 at 138.
11 Henrich et al., *supra* note 1 at 65.
12 Id.
13 Id.
14 Id. at 70.
15 Id.
16 Fehr and Gächter, *supra* note at 214 at 137.
17 Christopher P. Earley, "East Meets West Meets Mideast: Further Explorations of Collectivistic and Individualistic Work Groups," 36 *The Academy of Management Journal* 319–348 (1993).
18 Id. at 327.
19 Id. at 338.
20 Id.
21 Id. at 331.
22 Id. at 332.
23 Id. at 338.
24 Id.
25 Id.
26 Id. at 341.
27 Id. at 322.
28 Id.
29 Javidan, *supra* note 42 at 244.
30 Peter Drucker, "Behind Japan's Success," *Harvard Business Review* (1981), https://hbr.org/1981/01/behind-japans-success.

5
ACHIEVEMENT – ASCRIPTION

> At home, a young man must respect his parents; abroad, he must respect his elders.
> Confucius

The unusual nature of Western culture – what Heinrich referred to as WEIRD (see Chapter 1) – returns in this section. Most English speakers are achievement-oriented, as are most members of Nordic Europe.[1] This means "you are judged on what you have recently accomplished and on your record."[2] Common accomplishments from which status is earned in achievement societies include how well one performs professional duties and the outcomes of that work, including professional and economic success. Some achievement-oriented businesspeople take this to the extreme, with a sort of "yes, but what have you done lately?" pressure.

An achievement-orientation is premised on a certain notion of equality and is underpinned by a universalist perspective in which rules and standards in principle apply equally. Achievement is indeed an objective indicator and in theory open to all. Achievement-oriented societies are therefore based in large part on meritocratic principles.

This mentality, however, would be out of place in ascription societies that comprise the majority of the world's people. Here, status is not achieved but attributed or "ascribed." Common attributions include age, birth, kinship, gender, connections, educational record and alma mater, and type of profession.[3] The preference to ascribe status is often driven by religion or ideology, as in East Asia by Buddhism and Confucianism, which tend to emphasize status relationships.[4] Many small Western businesses, for example, promote employees on the ascriptive basis of family links. The larger the organization becomes, however, the more likely that achievement will take precedence and a non-family member will get the job. Not so in many Eastern societies. In South Korea, for example, the leadership of conglomerates, termed "chaebols," are traditionally inherited by members of the family. We see this in such blue-chip companies as Samsung,[5] as well as throughout the many subsidiaries of Hyundai.[6]

The ascription-orientation may also have historic roots that impact society, such as the ancient French class system, the Indian caste system (which stubbornly refuses to fully disappear), or the decidedly un-meritocratic social order of Edo era Japan in which emperors sat atop a pyramid composed of distinct social classes (Table 5.1).[7]

As with so many of these dimensions, the failure to recognize and adapt to these relational differences can be consequential. In the following extreme example, an ascription-based society attempted to implement trainings better fit for achievement-oriented societies:

> Korean Air... is one of South Korea's, and the world's, largest commercial aircraft companies. Throughout the 1970s and 1980s, Korean Air had one of the world's worst safety records, with collisions and crash landings tarring their reputation and costing lives. Its equipment was not deficient, and its people were top notch. But despite all the hours Korean Air pilots spent in simulations, their training was inherently defective. The problem? Korean Air was training its pilots and copilots in the way the Western world had told it to, and in the way that had proven effective in so many parts of the world. But it turned out that when you asked a twenty-something South Korean copilot to warn his older and more experienced pilot that something was amiss, the Korean culture of respect meant that too many times those copilots remained silent, with tragic consequences.[8]

TABLE 5.1 Respondents who believe that respect is determined by family background (from most agree to least agree)[9]

1. Kuwait	16. Belgium	31. Spain
2. Saudi Arabia	17. Switzerland	32. Hungary
3. Austria	18. South Korea	33. France
4. Oman	19. Russia	34. Portugal
5. Thailand	20. Germany	35. Australia
6. India	21. Ethiopia	36. Czech Republic
7. Hong Kong	22. Pakistan	37. Sweden
8. Serbia	23. Bulgaria	38. Canada
9. Philippines	24. Japan	39. United States
10. Kenya	25. Singapore	40. UK
11. Burkina Faso	26. Greece	41. New Zealand
12. Bahrain	27. Italy	42. Finland
13. Cuba	28. Poland	43. Denmark
14. Argentina	29. China	44. Ireland
15. Brazil	30. Mexico	45. Norway

Status: A Self-Fulfilling Prophecy

Meritocracy, in which ability determines success, has obvious advantages in ensuring the best and brightest reach positions of influence and power. But Trompenaars, in exploring societies where seniority is an ascribed status, explains how it is that so many ascription societies – particularly Confucian-inspired East Asian societies – are able to flourish economically. Along with gender, one of the most visible parts of the ascription onion is the emphasis on seniority as an indicator of merit.[10]

Trompenaars argues that promoting based on seniority may be a self-fulfilling prophecy. That is, the more senior a person, the more he (and we'll talk about "she" in a moment) is respected within these societies. This respect results in increased loyalty and support from the organization itself and other members, which may result in greater access to information and greater access to training.[11] Consequently, the senior person will become more able *because of* his seniority.[12] Researchers have found a similar self-fulfilling prophecy among Italian and French managers, arguing that in an attempt to live up to an ascribed status, people work hard to ensure that their performance matches expectations.[13]

Unfortunately, the prophecy cuts both ways.

Margaret Shin, Shatinsky, and Ambody tested whether Asian women were influenced by stereotypes. The researchers wanted to test whether the stereotype that women were bad at math actually caused women to be worse at math, and conversely, they wanted to test whether the stereotype that Asians were good at math caused Asians to perform better. In both cases, these stereotypes are ascribed (based on gender and ethnicity, respectively).

Shin and her colleagues set out to "prime" participants in their study.[14] Simply put, this means they sought to remind the participants of their ascribed status as women or Asians by drawing attention to the fact. Working with a group of Asian American women, they asked one group questions relating to gender – for example, about their preferences regarding co-ed dorms.[15] They asked the other group of women questions to make them think about race, such as the languages they spoke at home and the family's history in the United States.[16] After this priming was complete, the participants were asked to complete a math examination. What they found, amazingly, was that the participants performed worse when they were reminded of their gender, and better when they were reminded of their race.[17] Remember, the researchers did not remind the participants of the stereotypes about them but indirectly reminded them of their status as women or Asians. The participants' subconscious then drew upon – and conformed to – the stereotypes.

Similar results have been found when dealing with black and white golfers. Researchers have shown that African American athletes are often stereotyped to have athletic ability superior to white athletes but inferior intelligence.[18] Jeff Stone and his colleagues sought to build on this finding and asked eighty-two Princeton University students with no background in golf to compete on a ten-hole miniature golf course.[19] For half of the participants, the task was described as one testing "sports intelligence."[20] For the other half, the task was said to describe "natural athletic ability."[21] In reality, the tasks were identical. But when described as testing "sports intelligence," the white athletes performed better.[22] When the task was said to test "natural athletic ability," the African American athletes performed better.[23]

The results of these studies show that high-status people may live up to their status, just as Trompenaars hypothesized with respect to seniors in certain ascription societies. But it also suggests that people can live down to their status too, which gives us a taste of the dangers of stereotyping. As we'll see in Chapter 14, all societies are subject to stereotyping and discrimination.

When Meritocracy Meets Ascription Societies: A Moral Conundrum

The reader will note that the self-fulfilling prophecies discussed above took place in America, which is typically considered an achievement-oriented society. What we're seeing is that most societies are not entirely achievement or ascription oriented; as with most of these dimensions, societies instead lean one way or the other. Indeed, Americans often ascribe status based on one's alma mater (think Ivy League grads) or profession (think doctors, lawyers, and CEOs), rather than achievement status (based on the effectiveness of that Ivy League doctor, lawyer or CEO).

And these dimensions regularly blend together. In certain parts of America, for example, one of the most common questions upon introduction to a new acquaintance is not "what do you do," as is the case in much of America, but "where did you go to high school?" The real question being asked is "how wealthy are your parents?" What else can I presume about you – perhaps your politics, religion, other stereotypes – based on the school you attended and the place in which you came of age? Achievement still matters – and "what do you do?" may eventually come up in conversation – but it is clear that ascription is simultaneously at work.

The question then is not simply whether a society is ascription- or achievement-oriented but often more the combination of ascription and achievement. For instance, graduating from an Ivy League university brings status; but graduating from an Ivy League university *and* being a successful tech entrepreneur brings even more in the United States. Similarly, we see successful actors with achieved status such as Ronald Reagan and Arnold Schwarzenegger transforming into politicians, as with boxer Vitali Klitschko (mayor of Kiev, Ukraine), and champion Manny Pacquiao (Philippines senator). Even the infamous drug kingpin Pablo Escobar made a run for the Columbian House of Representatives, a move that would have helped protect his illicitly earned wealth but also would result in an ascribed-status to bolster his questionably achieved status.

When one society's expectations about that proper combination of achievement and ascription run up against the expectations of another, however, both may be left feeling discouraged. For example, what happens when young, high-achievement people are sent to deal with senior partners in ascription-oriented societies? Just as a person from an achievement-oriented society might be offended if an inexperienced intern is sent to meet with the CEO, sending a young person to meet with a senior may be viewed as disrespectful to the status of that senior.[24] Where an employee has the knowledge to succeed in an achievement-oriented society but not the age to transmit that knowledge to an ascription-oriented audience, Trompenaars advises a sort of ascription-achievement hybrid, in which someone high in ascription status works in coordination with the high-achieving person.[25]

When dealing with questions of age, this may be acceptable – albeit frustrating – to younger people from achievement societies. The issue is considerably thornier, however, when status is ascribed on the basis of gender, religion or ethnicity. Indeed, for all the disunity that exemplifies the American populace as we write these words, Americans are nonetheless among the least class-conscious people in the world.[26] Certain human rights are seen as universally inalienable in the United States and many other parts of the world. Many Americans and others of achievement-orientation would feel considerable discomfort when Trompenaars extends his proposed ascription-achievement hybrid to include a situation where a woman is the achiever but is working in an ascription society where women are viewed as lower in status than men.[27]

Trompenaars acknowledges the moral questions raised by his proposal and rightly notes that "you cannot replace [local culture] with American cultural norms if you are to be effective in [the local society]."[28] We agree, and this is why we take pains in this book to demonstrate the origins and legitimacy of a variety of cultural values. We can also reiterate that neither ascription societies nor achievement-oriented societies are a guarantee of equal treatment across society. But when morality conflicts with the cultural values of another society, how is a business to react? The question is not merely philosophical: we live in a world where businesses that fail to think through these questions pay very real consequences, both with respect to public relations and legal repercussions.

Google, for instance, shut down its Chinese search engine in 2010 after refusing to meet the Chinese government's demands to filter search requests and after coming under a cyberattack that targeted Chinese human rights activists.[29] Google effectively packed up and left, maintaining just a small and indirect presence in the country and losing out on billions that have instead accrued to the market leader, Baidu.[30] In so doing, Google tacitly asserted that the right to privacy and freedom of information is, or should be, a universal human right.

This question of whether morals are universally true in all places and at all times, or more relativist and dependent on the situation, is an age-old question without an objectively right answer. Suffice it to say that many values are pan-cultural – honesty, non-violence, and fairness among them – but the ways in which those values manifest can vary enormously. It is up to organizations and individuals to clarify their own values; to determine those values that are flexible, and those that are held to be true in all places and at all times; and to determine, ultimately, when one might be willing to sacrifice money and material success for values (Table 5.2).

TABLE 5.2 Ascription/achievement onion diagram

Inner	Middle	Outer
Ideology (Buddhism/ Confucianism)	Ascription-oriented	Respect for elderly, males, family names, or a university degree
Ideology (Hindi)	Ascription-oriented	Status based on caste
Political history (French)	Ascription-oriented	Status based on family name or social place; organizations likely to promote access to information for those ascribed status, and those with status likely to make efforts to live up to their reputations
Political history (American)	Achievement-oriented	Class blind (relative to many other societies); meritocratic promotions; high need for achievement (see below); assertive (competitive, ambitious)

Status: Achieved or Ascribed, We All Want It

Regardless of whether status is ascribed or achieved, status itself still carries real value and is everywhere sought. Grant, writing in *Originals*, notes that status "cannot be claimed," and that without status, one lacks power.

Researcher Carmen Medina devised a study to measure how people react when they view themselves as lacking status. She asked all the participants to come up with a task, any task, which another participant could carry out in return for $50, but before doing so, half were told to imagine that they were high-status people admired and respected by their peers, and the other half that they were low status and not admired or respected. Here's what Medina found:

> When the power holders were randomly assigned to learn that their peers admired and respected them, they chose mostly reasonable assignments: for the $50 bonus, their peers would have to tell a funny joke or write about their experiences the previous day. But when power holders learned that their peers looked down on them, they retaliated by setting up some humiliating tasks, such as telling their partners to bark like a dog three times, say "I am filthy" five times, or count backward from five hundred in increments of seven. Just being told that they weren't respected nearly doubled their chances of using their power in ways that degraded others.[31]

Lack of status, therefore, causes a feeling of inferiority, and this in turn has negative consequences. We can imagine coworkers and employees similarly lashing out, as we saw in the Medina study, when they believe they lack (or have lost) power and status. This represents an attempt to regain or assert our own authority,[32] and this has important implications on employee satisfaction and honesty.

The reason we care about status so much, especially when we don't have it, is precisely because we know that others care about status so very much. Researchers Susan Fiske and Amy Cuddy discovered what is known as the "status endowment effect." This shows that people assume, "to an extraordinary degree," that people with "high status have traits reflecting intelligence, competence, capability and skill." Conversely, low-status people are presumed "incompetent, incapable, and unskilled."[33]

Unsurprisingly given our review of the Milgram shock experiments, we are more prepared to listen to the new ideas, or the dissenting opinions, of high-status people; when low-status people give those same opinions, we are likely to view them as "difficult, coercive, and self-serving."[34]

What is perhaps most remarkable about the status endowment effect is that "it approaches a potential human universal"; that is, the Fisk and Cuddy study was completed and the results replicated across nine European nations, three East Asian nations, Costa Rica and Israel (using both a Muslim and a Jewish sample).[35]

If we view low-status people in such a disparaging way, is it such a surprise that people would lash out against others – as they did in Grant's study – when their status is low? And if the results were so extreme in Grant's study above, when the low-status revelation was temporary and artificial, how much antipathy must be felt by those whose everyday reality is that of low status?

We get some idea by looking at an often-underappreciated segment of society: workers in the service industry. An old truism says that you can tell a lot about a person by how they treat the waiter or waitress at the restaurant, but we rarely stop to ask how that same waiter or waitress might respond to disrespectful behavior. Researchers from Bayley University and the University of Houston looked into this and found that among American servers, 65 percent admitted to providing slow service to troublesome customers, 11 percent forged a higher tip, 19 percent confronted the customer, while 14 percent insulted the customer, and 6 percent admitted to – yes, you guessed it – spitting on or otherwise contaminating an offensive customer's meal.[36] These service workers may consequently give us some idea of how workplace behavior can be affected when disrespectful behavior lowers our perceived status and authority.

Need for Achievement

> A person with too much ambition cannot sleep in peace.
>
> Chaldian Proverb[37]

When status is associated with prestige factors such as intelligence and competence, it is natural that people will seek to obtain status. Recall, however, that status can only be given, not taken. People still behave in ways that they believe will cause others to foist upon them a status of high repute. Those from ascription societies may seek to highlight those characteristics that are most valued, be it their age, family histories, or ethnic origins. They may even have reason to exaggerate or fabricate some of these attributes, much as some may recall from Alexandre Dumas's *Count of Monte Cristo* when the lead character, Edmond Dantès, falsely claims nobility as part of his disguise and all the more effectively achieves his just revenge. It is perhaps even more compelling as Dumas, the son of a French aristocrat and an African slave, would have a unique perspective to provide on the nature of ascribed status.

By contrast, people in achievement-oriented societies tend to exhibit a high "need for achievement."[38] An achievement-orientation does not, however, result in identical behaviors: if the society most values material wealth, then that is the focus of many in that society; likewise, if the accumulation of power is highly valued, so too will it become the center of focus. Need for achievement is generally correlated with one's relative willingness to do unpleasant or time-consuming work, as long as it allows one to claim those achievements that add status.[39]

People with a high need for achievement tend to behave assertively (something we will address further in Chapter 10).[40] They may also be willing to gamble or take shortcuts rationalizing a "no risk, no reward" perspective. Finally, people with a need for achievement tend to see time as nonrenewable and of high value and therefore act with a sense of urgency. This sense of urgency does indeed result in a higher preponderance of "achievements" than for individuals with less of a sense of urgency.[41] One such man of achievement, Charles Darwin, famously wrote: "A man who dares to waste one hour of time has not discovered the value of life."[42]

Collectivist societies, among others, tend to expend substantial time building relationships and establishing trust, which can collide painfully with high achievers who tend to focus less on relationships and more on transactions.[43] They also tend to take a low-context – that is, highly direct and straightforward – approach to communication, part and parcel of this more impatient profile.[44] There is no shortcut to relationship building, however, and so high achievers expecting to succeed in these situations must slow down, show the expected deference and respect and maintain a long-term perspective.

Max Weber famously argued that in contrast to Catholics, Protestants tend to have a high need for achievement.[45] He called this the "Protestant work ethic" and attributed it to the religion's early focus on achievement in the temporal world as a direct pathway to salvation.[46] Confucianism has been said to also excite a strong work ethic.[47] However, more recent studies suggest today there is little or no correlation between religion and a particular society's need for achievement (Table 5.3).[48] Put differently, Protestantism and Confucianism likely implanted a high need for achievement upon historically Protestant and Confucius societies, but converting to these religions is unlikely to alter one's need for achievement.

Americans are predominantly achievement-oriented, short-term-oriented, assertive, with weak uncertainty avoidance – a perfect storm, if you will, for a high achievement orientation. This need for achievement is therefore built into our society such that not only is status determined by achievement, but so too is self-worth.

TABLE 5.3 Need for achievement (from highest to lowest)[49]

1. Switzerland	21. Switzerland (French speaking)	41. Thailand
2. Singapore	22. Germany (West)	42. Nigeria
3. Hong Kong	23. India	43. Poland
4. Albania	24. Zimbabwe	44. Georgia
5. New Zealand	25. Denmark	45. Turkey
6. South Africa (black sample)	26. Japan	46. Finland
7. Iran	27. Ecuador	47. Guatemala
8. Taiwan	28. Zambia	48. Sweden
9. South Korea	29. Costa Rica	49. El Salvador
10. Canada (English speaking)	30. South Africa (white sample)	50. Namibia
11. United States	31. France	51. Slovenia
12. Philippines	32. Mexico	52. Argentina
13. China	33. Germany (East)	53. Bolivia
14. Austria	34. England	54. Portugal
15. Indonesia	35. Israel	55. Italy
16. Australia	36. Brazil	56. Kazakhstan
17. Ireland	37. Spain	57. Qatar
18. Malaysia	38. Morocco	58. Hungary
19. Netherlands	39. Kuwait	59. Russia
20. Egypt	40. Colombia	60. Venezuela
		61. Greece

Implications of the Need for Achievement

Although there are countries with low need for achievement but high economic development (Nordic Europe, for instance), a high need for achievement tends to foster economic prosperity.[50] One reason is that cultures with a high need for achievement value and reward, even more than other cultures, "hard work, ambition, high standards, and performance improvement. They lead to the formation of corporations that are ambitious, hardworking, competitive, and successful. The success of the private sector, in turn, drives the overall prosperity of the economy and the population."[51]

Despite the macro benefits of societies with a high need for achievement, however, this can be taken too far at the individual level. To work long hours is often a badge of honor in American society, but it is a badge that comes with a high cost. While societies with a high need for achievement are in fact slightly happier, on average, than their opposites,[52] they also have lower "psychological health."[53] High achievers are, in short, stressed out, and this can take its toll.[54] For instance, high-achievement societies do not necessarily have the longer life expectancies one would expect given the strong economies and strong institutions that tend to accompany a societal need for achievement.[55]

Indeed, in Japan, death from overwork is so common that there is a word, *karoshi*, to specifically describe this phenomenon. These instances of *karoshi* often make international headlines, inevitably accompanied by headlines condemning the

Japanese culture of overwork. But people in glass houses shouldn't throw stones: the United States actually exhibits a higher need for achievement than does Japan,[56] and according to the OECD, Americans work more hours on an annual basis than the Japanese.[57]

Interestingly, people from almost everywhere in the world tend to wish for a greater achievement-orientation within their society.[58] In fact, the need for achievement is desired more in societies that are not already doing the things associated with the need for achievement indicator than in countries that are actively manifesting a high need for achievement.[59] The implication is that the behavior that arises from the need for achievement is almost everywhere valued,[60] but for those practicing it, the reality proves to be somewhat less rewarding than anticipated. Japan, for instance, practices a high need for achievement but would rank sixty-first out of sixty-two countries on need for achievement if the people of the society behaved in the way individuals there would prefer.[61] While societal norms make it difficult for any one person to break this pattern, behavior is beginning to change in the aggregate as the average Japanese worked one hundred hours less in 2016 than in 2000,[62] and even stricter labor laws are under consideration to bolster this process.[63]

The evidence indicates, however, that even while many other countries seek to rein in their work addictions, many Americans continue to value work for the sake of work.[64] The drawbacks to a high need for achievement should serve as a warning against a blind or single-minded pursuit of achievement.

> For instance, embattled Facebook COO Sheryl Sandberg approvingly cites former US Secretary of State Colin Powell for the proposition that work for the sake of work is inefficient, and, moreover, that a balanced lifestyle is a worthy pursuit, Sandberg writes: "In his latest book, General Colin Powell explains that his vision of leadership rejects 'busy bastards' who put in long hours at the office without realizing the impact they have on their staff. He explains that 'in every senior job I've had, I've tried to create an environment of professionalism and the very highest standards. When it was necessary to get a job done, I expected my subordinates to work around the clock. When that was not necessary, I wanted them to work normal hours, go home at a decent time, play with the kids, enjoy family and friends, read a novel, clear their heads, daydream, and refresh themselves. I wanted them to have a life outside the office. I am paying them for the quality of their work, not for the hours they work. That kind of environment has always produced the best results for me.'"[65]

Sandberg concludes: "It is still far too rare to work for someone as wise as General Powell."[66]

Additionally, an interesting study by researchers John Darley and Daniel Batson illustrates some of the negatives that can result in an overworked, time-stressed environment.

The subjects were theology students who were assigned the task of giving a short sermon about the Bible story of the good Samaritan. In this story a Jewish man on his way from Jerusalem to Jericho is attacked by robbers and abandoned. Various role models who stood for piety at the time, such as a priest and a Levite, saw the man lying there but passed him without helping. Then a Samaritan came along. Although Jews were the enemies of the Samaritans, the Samaritan cared for the Jewish man and brought him to a hostel, where he paid for his stay. The theme of the sermon was "helpfulness."

After the students were finished with their preparations, they were told that the sermon would be filmed in another building on the university campus. The theology instructor gave them directions. On the way to the other building they passed a man who needed help. This man, who was part of the researchers' plan, appeared to have collapsed in the doorway. His head was bowed and his eyes were closed. At the moment that the student passed him, he gave a well-practiced groan and coughed twice. Would the theology students help the man?[67]

When the theology students received plenty of time to walk to the other building, they almost all helped the man, but when the researchers ensured that the students set off late, the proportion prepared to help fell to 63 percent. More than a third of the students did not stop for the man. But here's the real shock. When the instructor encouraged the students to get to the other building as fast as possible, because there was no time to lose, the percentage plummeted, only 10 percent still stopping to help. Of the theology students on their way to preach about helpfulness, 90 percent ignored a man in need of help. Some students even stepped over him.[68]

It's not that the students actually became willfully unethical or inconsiderate. Rather, their brain power was singularly focused on resolving the crisis at hand. It is this drive to solve problems that makes the human species such a high achiever, so creative and innovative, but it's also the reason countless millions are kept up every night obsessing about one unsolvable dilemma or another. We become more unethical and narrow-minded, failing to see the forest for the trees, and this makes us less effective teammates, bosses, and employees, and also less considerate friends, spouses, mothers and fathers.

We have all been there and we get it. You have a job, a boss (or teacher) to please and maybe some employees relying on you; you have bills, you may have a spouse and children, and if you're lucky, you might even have a social life to maintain. As Powell asserts, however, it is precisely this variety – this breakaway from a singular focus on work – that makes your work more productive. So reserve a day of the week for hobbies, or family time, or socializing. Take a note from Google's old playbook (and still many others) and adopt the "20 percent rule" by allowing employees to spend one day each weekday working on a pet project.[69] Follow the lead of KPMG, Microsoft and Google (again), and provide greater flex time for professional workers, such as the ability to show up earlier or later in the day, to work four-day weeks, or to work a few hours on the weekends in return for meeting the kids at the bus during the week.[70] Although the 20 percent rule was abandoned by Google as it grew into an established and more stable organization,[71] Google News, AdSense and Gmail are all products derived in thanks to the 20 percent rule, while those "flexible work practices lead to increased productivity, higher job satisfaction, and decreased turnover intentions."[72]

It is therefore clear that a busy schedule should no longer serve as a claim to fame or source of pride – something so often trumpeted on Facebook or LinkedIn – and instead focus on efficient and effective work of the sort Colin Powell and Sheryl Sandberg, among many others, now advocate. This does not mean to stop achieving; ultimately, quite the contrary.

Take your high-achieving self wherever you go and use that ambition to set challenging goals and motivate your workforce. Your workforce is likely to respond: just as we saw that the desire for achievement is pan-cultural, respondents from all countries surveyed by GLOBE expressed the belief that managers with a high need for achievement make for good leaders.[73] Remember, however, that the need for achievement may be deeply enculturated in you or your workforce, and thus not always based on purely rational calculations. You can avoid the moral and psychological pitfalls by moderating your ambitions to that which are truly important, balancing your work-life schedule, and, perhaps most essentially, giving your employees the courage to do the same.

References

1 Trompenaars and Hampden-Turner, *supra* note 12 at 104.
2 Concepts of achievement versus ascription first introduced by Parsons and Shils (1951), see Javidan, *supra* note 42 at 242.
3 Id.
4 Trompenaars and Hampden-Turner, *supra* note 12 at 107.
5 Lucinda Shen, "Meet the Samsung's Billionaire Lee Family, South Korea's Most Powerful Dynasty," *Business Insider* (June 19, 2015), https://www.businessinsider.com.au/lee-family-power-war-for-samsung-scandals-and-bribes-2015-6.
6 Don Kirk, "As Korean Heirs Feud, an Empire Is Withering: Change and Frail Finances Doom the Old Hyundai," *The New York Times* (Apr. 26, 2001), http://www.nytimes.com/2001/04/26/business/korean-heirs-feud-empire-withering-change-frail-finances-doom-old-hyundai.html?src=pm.
7 Conrad D. Totman, *Japan before Perry: A Short History* 135–136 (University of California Press: Berkeley) (1981).
8 Dr. Nitish Singh and Thomas J. Bussen, *Why Compliance Professionals Need to Think About National Cultures*, Ethikos (2014) (*citing to* Malcolm Gladwell, *Outliers: The Story of Success* (Little, Brown: New York) (2008).
9 Trompenaars and Hampden-Turner, *supra* note 12 at 106.
10 Trompenaars and Hampden-Turner, *supra* note 12 at 107.
11 Id. at 109.
12 Id. at 107.
13 Id.
14 Ariely, *supra* note 102 at 169.

15 Id.
16 Id.
17 Id.
18 Jeff Stone, Mike Sjomeling, Christian Lynch, and John Darley, "Stereotype Threat Effects on Black and White Athletic Performance," 77 *Journal of Personality and Social Psychology* 1213, 1215 (1999).
19 Id. at 1216.
20 Id.
21 Id.
22 Id. at 1217.
23 Id.
24 Trompenaars and Hampden-Turner, *supra* note 12 at 113–114.
25 Id. at 114.
26 Henrich et al., *supra* note 1 at 75.
27 Trompenaars and Hampden-Turner, *supra* note 12 at 114.
28 Id.
29 Kaveh Waddell, "Why Google Quit China – and Why It's Heading Back," *The Atlantic* (Jan. 19, 2016), https://www.theatlantic.com/technology/archive/2016/01/why-google-quit-china-and-why-its-heading-back/424482/.
30 Id.
31 Grant, *supra* note 72 at 67–68 (citing to Nathanael J. Fast, Nir Halevy and Adam Galinsky, "The Destructive Nature of Power without Status," *Journal of Experimental Social Psychology* 48 (2012): 391–394).
32 Id. at 67.
33 Susan T. Fiske and Amy Cuddy, "Stereotype Content across Cultures as a Function of Group Status," 252 in *Social Comparison and Social Psychology* (ed. Serge Guimond, Cambridge University Press) (2005).
34 Grant, *supra* note 72 at 67 (citing to Alison R. Fragale, Jennifer R. Overbeck, and Margaret A. Neale, "Resources versus Respect: Social Judgments Based on Targets' Power and Status Positions," *Journal of Experimental Psychology* 47 (2011): 767–775).
35 Fiske and Cuddy, *supra* note 271 at 252.
36 Samantha Zabell, "Do Servers Actually Spit in Your Food?" *REALSIMPLE* (Sept. 5, 2014), https://www.realsimple.com/work-life/do-waiters-spit-food.
37 https://safarijunkie.com/culture/african-proverbs/.
38 Need for achievement as a theoretical concept was first introduced by McClelland. See Javidan, *supra* note 42 at 240.
39 Trompenaars and Hampden-Turner, *supra* note 12 at 104.
40 Javidan, *supra* note 42 at 243.
41 Id. at 244.
42 Francis Darwin, ed., *The Life and Letters of Charles Darwin, Including An Autobiographical Chapter* (London: John Murray) (1887).
43 Javidan, *supra* note 42 at 245.
44 Id. at 245.
45 Id. at 239, (writing: "Arguably, the most influential and renowned treatment of performance orientation was Max Weber's classic analysis in *The Protestant Ethic and the Spirit of Capitalism* (1904/1930, 1904/1998).")
46 Id. at 240.
47 See Id. at 241 (writing: "Hofstede and Bond (1988) supported Kahn's (1979) hypothesis that one of the main reasons for the impressive economic growth and prosperity of Southeast Asian countries during the period 1965–1985 was the Confucian or neo-Confucian cultural roots of the region").
48 Id. at 258.
49 Id. at 250.
50 Id. at 254.
51 Id.

52 Id. at 257.
53 Id.
54 Id.
55 Id.
56 Id. at 250.
57 "Average Annual Hours Actually Worked Per Worker," OECD.STAT (last accessed July 29, 2018), https://stats.oecd.org/Index.aspx?DataSetCode=ANHRS.
58 Javidan, *supra* note 42 at 248.
59 Id. at 254.
60 Id. at 241.
61 Id. at 251.
62 OECD.STAT, *supra* note 293.
63 Leo Lewis, "'Death by Overwork' in Japan Exposes Dangers of Overtime Culture," *Financial Times* (Jan. 12, 2017), https://www.ft.com/content/982b1c46-d75b-11e6-944b-e7eb37a6aa8e.
64 Javidan, *supra* note 42 at 251.
65 Sheryl Sandberg, *Lean In: Women, Work, and the Will to Lead* 120–121 (New York: Alfred A. Knopf) (2013).
66 Id. at 121.
67 Muel Kaptein, *Workplace Morality: Behavioral Ethics in Organizations* 67 (Emerald Group, 2013) (citing to J.M. Darley and C.D. Batson, "'From Jerusalem to Jericho'": A Study of Situational and Dispositional Variables in Helping Behavior," *Journal of Personality and Social Psychology* 27 (1973): 1, 100–108).
68 Id.
69 Id.
70 Christopher M. Barnes, Kai Chi Yam, and Ryan Fehr, "With Flextime, Bosses Prefer Early Birds to Night Owls," *Harvard Business Review* (May 13, 2014), https://hbr.org/2014/05/with-flextime-bosses-prefer-early-birds-to-night-owls.
71 Alastair Ross, "Why Did Google Abandon 20% Time for Innovation?" *HRZONE* (June 3, 2015), https://www.hrzone.com/lead/culture/why-did-google-abandon-20-time-for-innovation.
72 Jillian D'Onfro, "The Truth about Google's Famous '20% Time' Policy," *Business Insider* (Apr. 17, 2015), http://www.businessinsider.com/google-20-percent-time-policy-2015-4 (citing to Boris Baltes, Thomas Briggs, Joseph Huff, Julie Wright, and George Neuman, "Flexible and Compressed Workweek Schedules: A Meta-Analysis of Their Effects on Work-Related Criteria," *Journal of Applied Psychology* 84 (4) (1999), 496–513).
73 Javidan, *supra* note 42 at 267.

6

POWER DISTANCE: HIERARCHICAL VERSUS EGALITARIAN

> Every man having been born free and master of himself, no one else may under any pretext whatever subject him without his consent.
>
> Jean-Jacques Rousseau
> *The Social Contract*

Regardless of whether status is achieved or ascribed, status differentials are pan-cultural. This section discusses the degree to which status brings about high levels of power. Power, defined as the "control over resources needed or valued by others,"[1] is most effectively wielded in combination with status. But not all holders of status exhibit large amounts of power, and equally, not all low status people are willing to accept power plays by those at the top. The greater the distance in power between the upper echelons of society and the bottom, the more hierarchical is the society. The less so, the more egalitarian.

Washington University in St. Louis' Chancellor Mark Wrighton gives an example of arguably one of the more egalitarian work places: academia. "I remember when I went to MIT when I was very young, and I asked my department chair, 'Is there anything you would like me to do?' He probably had never been asked that question before. He finally said, 'well, you're here to do whatever you think is interesting and important.' It wasn't a hierarchy," Wrighton continues, "or a group of people telling you what to do. The mentality was 'you're just getting started. We hope you're successful; we hope you do something significant. But *you* choose, not us.'"[2] This level of professional freedom, or autonomy, is unheard of in many parts of the world, and indeed in most professions of the world. But as we'll see in the section below, this autonomy also provides enormous opportunities to act quickly and effectively in the rapidly evolving Information Age.

A more visible manifestation of egalitarian cultures – the outer part of the onion – is the physical arrangement of the office. At egalitarian workplaces, group work spaces are the norm. There are no offices, even for top executives.[3] By contrast, more hierarchical workplaces are characterized by the prized corner-office dynamic.

In terms of power-distance, or degree of egalitarianism, the geographically dispersed countries of Morocco, Nigeria, El Salvador, Zimbabwe, Argentina, Thailand, and South Korea exhibit the highest levels around the world.[4] The United States on the other hand was ranked as the thirteenth most egalitarian country of the 62 countries studied, while Denmark, the Netherlands, Bolivia, Albania, Israel, Qatar and black respondents of South Africa, were ranked most egalitarian.[5]

However, the results for the United States are somewhat misleading from an organizational perspective. The GLOBE authors studied power distance within a country's society generally – for instance, the power distance between a father and his children – and also the power distance within organizations. And while typically societal and organizational behavior overlap to a significant degree, in the case of power distance we saw several regions with significantly *higher* organizational power distance than in society generally. This was true for Anglo societies including the United States, as well as East Asia, Southern Asia, and Eastern Europe.[6]

This result is particularly consequential when we consider that even societal power distances were, on average, at the high end of the spectrum.[7] However, GLOBE also asked respondents how much power distance they would *prefer* to have in their societies and organizations. More than any other dimension studied by GLOBE, respondents indicated that they would in fact prefer much less power distance in their social and organizational lives.[8] The one exception to this was Middle Eastern countries, where respondents indicated relative satisfaction with their high levels of power distance.[9]

On the whole, this variation means that, even more than usual, generalizations are dangerous: managers must look beyond societal practices and explore the actual practices within an organization. This also means, however, that unless that organization is located in the Middle East, its employers are likely to prefer less power distance than is actually practiced. This is true regardless of whether the actual power distance practiced is low or high.

This in turn suggests that managers attempting to incorporate more egalitarian organizational norms are likely to face a receptive audience even in hierarchical cultures. However, the very long power distance within so many of the world's societies and many organizations also cautions against too rapid a pace of change. For instance, we will see that people from high power distance cultures may exhibit less productivity when given greater autonomy than those that already come from egalitarian cultures, perhaps in part because people from egalitarian societies are enculturated to act with autonomy in their educational and professional lives.

Paternalism and the Gini Coefficient

Hierarchical countries, counter-intuitively, are often collectivist and particularist. These three dimensions all imply strong relational obligations. The reader will recall, for instance, that many collectivist societies are paternalistic. This means that the individual may be expected to conform with the ideals of her in-group, but in return she often expects to be cared for in times of need. Particularists, similarly, reserve special, at times preferential, treatment for those in their in-group.

In hierarchical societies, it is the person holding power that is expected to provide for the safety and security of the group. In return, those in a subordinate position are expected to remain loyal, not just to the in-group as in collectivist societies, but specifically to those at the upper levels of the hierarchy. And if that hierarchical society is also collectivist, then it is up to those atop the hierarchy to decide, first and foremost, the ideals that the group as a whole should uphold.

Nicholas Keuper relates one such example from his time working with the Boston Consulting Group, relating specifically to his time in Thailand. Keuper recalled that "In Thailand my first project was for a state bank, and Thailand has a very paternalistic management culture. The boss takes care of the employee, and the employee never questions their boss. And it's very difficult to work as a consultant on a more transformational project in a place like this. So, you just have to adapt to what you're used to doing in the United States, which is 'here is the analysis, here are the numbers; let's do it.' That just does not work in these more paternalistic cultures. It's a much more dialogue-based process with that boss."[10]

This paternalism, however, occurs as a rule with many exceptions. One predictor of the paternalistic environment is the strength of the middle class within the society. Middle class people tend to be well educated and to hold managerial or administrative positions, and they often demand equal opportunity within their respective societies. Many societies with strong middle classes are therefore relatively egalitarian,[11] including many western European and North American countries. However, we also see a strong middle class in high-power countries like South Korea, Singapore, and Japan, and it is in these countries that we tend to see the mutually beneficial, but hierarchical, relationships.

One way to identify the relative impact on a country's middle class is through the combined analysis of the Gini coefficient, and the gross domestic product per capita (GDP/capita). Although economic analysis is not the point of this book, an understanding of how these concepts interact provides the tools to predict paternalistic behaviors in a diversity of societies and is worth some analysis.

GDP measures the total economic production of a country. GDP/capita divides that number by the total population. For the sake of simplicity, if we assumed that the GDP of a country were $1,000 and the population included ten people, then the GDP/capita would be $100. GDP/capita allows us to compare the wealth of countries and gives some indication of how much wealth is available for each person rather than a large, population-based aggregate figure. China, for instance, has a relatively large GDP of nearly $11.2 trillion (second largest in the world).[12] When this GDP is divided by its population of more than one billion people, however, this results in a figure of just over $8,000 for every man, woman, and child, giving it a GDP/capita ranking of 68th in the world.[13] By contrast, tiny Luxembourg has a GDP of just more than $60 billion (ninety-fourth largest in the world), but per capita income is among the highest in the world at more than $100,000.[14]

Next, we can look to the Gini coefficient (or Gini index) to see how well that money is dispersed across society. Gini coefficients measure the relative economic equality within a country and are read on a scale of 1–100. If all the economic activity within a country were split entirely equally, the Gini coefficient would be 1. If all economic activity were held in the hands of just one person, the coefficient would be 100. This is true regardless of the size of the GDP but allows us to put that GDP/capita into context.

In looking back at China, we can see that the Gini coefficient was 42.2 when last measured in 2012.[15] That coefficient indicates that the resources of China will fall within the hands of a relatively small percent of the population and further indicates that the majority of the population actually has an annual wealth totaling something less than that $8,000 GDP/capita. Luxembourg, by contrast, had a Gini coefficient of 31.2 as of 2014, which made it the nineteenth most-equitable country on earth.[16] Consequently, we expect Luxembourg's GDP to be more equally spread throughout its population, so the high GDP/capita more closely reflects the actual wealth of an average Luxembourg citizen.

Returning to the Far East, we see that South Korea's 2012 Gini coefficient of 31.6 puts it, along with Luxembourg, as one of the more equitable countries.[17] It also has the twenty-seventh highest GDP/capita in the world, so a strong middle class is predictable.[18] Yet South Korea has a very high power distance.[19] Together, these statistics suggest that South Koreans with power are paternally using their positions to support those with less power (at the very least, they have not used their power corruptly to aggrandize the country's wealth). Unsurprisingly, South Koreans and other respondents from East Asia were more accepting of continuing differences in power than seen in the global averages.[20]

By contrast, Equatorial Guinea has, in recent years, had one of the highest GDP/capita rankings in Africa and one of the worst Gini coefficients in the world.[21] This high Gini coefficient suggests that power is used to entrench the financial interests of those holding it.

Identifying this high inequality is important not just as one predictor of the relative paternalism within society – though that does have important implications on the leadership styles expected within these societies. It also signals that the people of Equatorial Guinea and other unequal countries are unlikely to have an extensive appetite for middle-class consumer goods such as iPhones, Apple computers, or Volkswagen sedans. It also indicates that educational levels are probably insufficient to maintain a highly skilled workforce, points to a higher risk of political stability, and, in fact, predicts a less-developed legal system. All of these may be essential considerations in determining whether that branch office should be opened in Peru, Kenya, or somewhere else entirely.

Though Equatorial Guinea is the most extreme, many (collectivist-leaning) African and Latin American countries exhibit a similar dynamic. In these countries, economic growth tends to flow mostly to those at the top, which thereby gives them even greater power and influence over those at the bottom of the hierarchy. Thus, national economic growth can actually harm low-power members in these societies.

This helps explain why Egypt's Hosni Mubarak was overthrown (and many others ruling over and perpetuating similarly unequal societies). Mubarak ruled Egypt for decades, overseeing economic growth averaging nearly 5 percent in the ten years before the revolution[22] but also permitting or expediting a decidedly pyramidal power distance construct in which power was held primarily by a clique of military and business leaders close to the regime.[23] Economic indicators therefore appeared positive in Egypt, and many multinationals flooded into the fast-developing suburbs of Cairo. At the same time, however, a fury was building within the downtrodden masses of Egypt, accompanied by an ever-growing gap between those masses and the few at the top of the pyramid. The result in Egypt was, as we know, the revolution and overthrow of Mubarak in 2011, a nationalizing of many businesses, years of unrest and a society that still today is best described as fragile.

In highly unequal countries, consequently, the hierarchy is destabilizing as the elites devour the resources of the state in a race to pad their pockets. In more equal countries, hierarchy is stabilizing and mutually supportive. Understanding the difference is key to appreciating the role of outside managers in these societies – managers in the former may be thought corrupt, and employees may have little expectation, and therefore little motivation, for professional growth. By contrast, hierarchy in more paternal societies may be seen by those atop the pyramid and at the bottom as legitimate. Managers may be expected to uphold this system, in part by ensuring that employees are well-cared for and by considering their personal as well as professional interests. Employees, by contrast, may be eager followers of such leaders, presenting a vast opportunity for change management and innovation.

The strength of the middle class helps predict whether hierarchical cultures are likely to be paternalistic and mutually beneficial. It also helps predict whether a culture is hierarchical or egalitarian in the first place: as the middle classes gains strength, hierarchy tends to decrease. Japan and Korea, however, serve as two examples of how a middle class alone is not enough to explain hierarchy. To see the full picture, we must also understand religion and governance within a society. Let's uncover some of the roots of power distance.

Once the root is secured, the Way unfolds.

Confucius

Hierarchies have deep roots, and even the most egalitarian cultures probably were hierarchical at some point and are still hierarchical to a certain degree. It was during the agricultural age that the first-class systems began to arise, often based around the patriarchal family.[i] As the primatologist Frans de Waal put it: "Without agreement on rank and a certain respect for authority there can be no great sensitivity to social rules."[24]

Hierarchy is even coded into many languages. Writes Haidt, "In French, as in other romance languages, speakers are forced to choose whether they'll address someone using the respectful form (vous) or the familiar form (tu). Until recently, Americans addressed strangers and superiors using title plus last name (Mrs. Smith, Dr. Jones)."[25]

Furthermore, while early humans were relatively egalitarian and wary of alpha males, Haidt also notes that in times of threat or increased competition, groups quickly rallied around just such a leader.[26] He writes: "We all recognize some kinds of authority as legitimate in some contexts, but we are also wary of those who claim to be leaders unless they have first earned our trust. We're vigilant for signs that they've crossed the line into self-aggrandizement and tyranny."[27]

In prehistoric times, those who crossed the line risked a club to the head. A contemporary society's readiness to swing the (usually symbolic) club may indicate their relative level of hierarchy – the readier its people are to swing away, the less willing they are to accept a pyramidal power scheme, and thus the more egalitarian they are. In this we might see a transformation from tyrannical control – in which power is wielded without responsibility to those ruled – to that of hierarchical leadership in which a form of the social contract is at work.

Since those early days, however, culture has impacted power distance, creating pressures for less of it in some cultures, while in others perpetuating and entrenching those hierarchies. In many societies, it is believed that through hierarchy, society itself may be held stable. Confucius exemplified this correlation between hierarchy and stability when he said: "A man who respects his parents and his elders would hardly be inclined to defy his superiors. A man who is not inclined to defy his superiors will never foment a rebellion. A gentleman works at the root. Once the root is secured, the Way unfolds. To respect parents and elders is the root of humanity."[28]

The impact of this idea should not be underestimated given that large parts of the populations of China, Korea, Vietnam, Taiwan, and Japan are influenced by Confucian ideals. Confucianism is just one example of how ideology affects power distance. Analyses of other major philosophies of the world would, in many cases, be similarly informative. Along with ideologies and the relative strength of the middle class, religion, and governance are also driving forces that merit consideration.

Religion

Just as we found that Catholics tend to be more collectivist than Protestants, Catholicism also tends to correlate with greater power distance than Protestantism.[29] The Catholic Church, not unlike Confucius, historically stressed social stability and encouraged the "common man and woman to accept his or her own fate."[30] They were further governed by a pope who, for many, was prevaricating from afar.

Protestants, on the other hand, espouse a certain egalitarianism, a freedom from centralized control and hierarchy as demanded by Martin Luther and his sixteenth century adherents, the possibility of an individual relationship with God, and the advancement of a less hierarchical religion with no pope. Indeed, the original meaning of "Protestant" was to "protest" the centralized, hierarchical practices of the Catholic Church.[31] One possible result of these histories, although it is difficult to say who attracted whom, is that "societies that have been primarily Roman Catholic tend to be high in power distance, whereas Protestant societies prefer lower power distance."[32]

Indian and other South Asian societies in which Hinduism thrives have *historically* embraced a strict caste system.[33] The caste into which one is born is the primary, often conclusive determinant of one's relative power and position within society[34]; to be at the bottom is to be an "untouchable,"[ii] literally and figuratively left behind by society. This caste system thus speaks to an ascriptive and highly hierarchical society.

The Hindu creation story justifies these differences, using a decidedly hierarchical image in the process. *Sapiens: A Brief History of Mankind* author Yuval Noah Harari, a master at unraveling the puzzle of humanity, explains: "Hindus who adhere to the caste system believe that cosmic forces have made one caste superior to another. According to a famous Hindu creation myth, the gods fashioned the world out of the body of a primeval being, the Purusa. The sun was created from the Purusa's eye, the moon from the Purusa's brain, the Brahmins (priests) from its mouth, the Kshatriyas (warriors) from its arms, the Vaishya (peasant and merchants) from its thighs, and the Shudras (servants) from its legs. Accept this explanation and the sociopolitical differences between Brahmins and Shudras are as natural and eternal as the differences between the sun and the moon."[35]

The caste system was outlawed upon India's independence in 1947, but despite the best efforts of Mahatma Gandhi and his successors in government to foster a more egalitarian social life, the caste system is stubbornly refusing to die in India.[36] Part of the explanation for this resistance may be the Hindu religion's embrace of karma.[37] While the creation story justifies the caste system itself, karma says that the caste into which an individual is born is a product of one's behavior in a past life.[38]

So those at the bottom of the pyramid – or the bottom layers of the caste – might be said to deserve their inferior positions, while those at the top have earned in a past life the superior conditions into which they were born.

Paternalism in support of those at the bottom is therefore not nearly as common as in East Asian societies. Additionally, if those born into higher castes are considered superior, then it would stand to reason that these are the people who should take the lead in society as holders of great power and influence. Together, a complex but powerful combination of religious, moral and sociological justifications help adhere power distances to the hearts and minds of many Indians.

The impacts on business are real. Emerson's Jean Paul Montupet shares this story: "I was visiting an Indian customer and I was in the car with the local sales manager who was in charge of the customers, and he was briefing me on the meeting. He went into all kinds of details and I cut him off and I said, 'Okay, I understand the big picture, but when it comes to the details, you'll be there to take care of that.' And he said, 'No, no, no! I am not going to the meeting! The customer you are meeting with is of a caste that is different than mine and he won't talk to me. And if I am in the meeting it just won't be acceptable. So, you are on your own!' And I said, 'Okay! Give me all the details,' then [chuckles] ... I almost panicked. He clarified that he could deal with all the people in the company, but he simply could not deal with this top guy. I thought that was going away in India, but it unfortunately still exists sometimes."[39]

Buddhist-influenced South Asian and East Asian societies tend to have high power distances. We noted previously that East Asian societies tend to have high power distances but relative income equality, and while the poorer Buddhist countries of South Asia have less equality, they are also not nearly as unequal as we might expect of developing countries. Buddhism says that people should accept their position within the social hierarchy but also that people are judged not based on their position in the hierarchy but on their character or virtues.[40] Buddhism thus tends to uphold rather than discourage power distances, and this helps explain in part the high power distance that we see in both South and East Asian Buddhist societies.

In East Asian societies, as we saw, Confucianism stresses hierarchical, paternal relationships in which males and elders have power and obligations to those lower in the hierarchy. Confucianism identified five hierarchical relationships: the "ruler-subject; father-son; older brother-younger brother; husband-wife; and senior friend-junior friend."[41] Confucianism says that within a relationship, the senior person is responsible for, and should care for, the junior person, while the junior person should show loyalty and respect to the senior person. Buddhism also says that rulers should seek to provide for the basic needs of all citizens and should uphold a fair and equitable legal system.[42] This combination of religion (Buddhism) and philosophy (Confucianism) may help explain the sense of high but mutually beneficial power distances that make many East Asian societies unique.[43]

Broadly speaking, in the Muslim faith, every person has equal value before Allah. The Quran moreover stresses an egalitarian system in which Muslim leaders consult with followers, which, as we will see, is a hallmark of the egalitarian workplace. Additionally, the Muslim community is far more decentralized than, for instance, the Catholic Church, with a relatively flat leadership structure.

Nonetheless, we find that many predominantly Muslim societies of the Middle East, such as Egypt, have power distances with a distinct element of social and economic inequality. The reasons for this are not entirely clear. Within Middle Eastern Muslim societies, the contemporary state of affairs could derive from the confluence of law, religion, and politics, in which, historically, a "caliph" or leader took control of both the temporal (legal and political) and spiritual (religious) realms of society. The result was a leader with near all-encompassing power over his inhabitants.

The Muslim religion therefore has a mixed impact on power distance, at times advocating an egalitarian structure but tending to legitimize a political structure of high power distance.[44] Indeed, the history of the Middle East is one in which extreme hierarchy long prevailed, with absolute monarchies continuing to hold firm even as monarchs have been weakened or overthrown in most other parts of the world. Consequently, power distance became entrenched – power begetting more power – and the somewhat ambiguous stance of Islam on the subject did little to change this.

Ultimately, the case serves as a reminder against oversimplifying the role of religion or any other single factor on cultural dimensions. GLOBE contributors Dale Carl, Vipin Gupta and Mansour Javidan, for instance, posit that while religion is often the biggest driver of power distance within a culture, a small middle class and a lack of democracy of the sort seen in most Muslim Middle Eastern countries almost inevitably lead to (or result from) high power distance.[45]

Governance

Medieval European nations were largely feudal nations. They were typically ruled by a monarch with absolute power, and the monarch gave land to nobles and powerful families who then enlisted peasants to work the lands on behalf of the monarch.[46] To ensure the wealth of the harvest could be reaped, merchants worked as middlemen, delivering the goods to urban centers, and conducting trade sometimes to the far reaches of the known world.[47] In return for the wealth derived from these lands, the nobles would provide military soldiers to the realm in times of need.[48] Over time, however, the landed nobles – so central to the effectiveness of the monarch that they possessed influence if limited power – demanded greater power. They sought an end to absolute monarchism.[49] And as the merchants gained in wealth, they too sought greater say in the affairs of the realm.[50] Collectively, and gradually, these powers led to the crumbling authority of the monarchs, a process epitomized with the English Magna Carta of 1215.

Over a longer period still, this led to the rise of democracy. The hierarchy was in consequence flattened.

The late twentieth century bore witness to the rise of democracy throughout all regions of the world, a form of governance that in its classical iteration demands a certain egalitarianism. The early twenty-first century has seen the rise of what author and political analyst Fareed Zakaria terms "illiberal democracies."[51] This describes the process by which leaders, from Russia, Turkey, Venezuela, and elsewhere, use the levers of (often newly established) democracies to assert legitimacy, but they do so in environments with limited freedom of speech, association and space for political opposition.

While the term illiberal democracy is made real by its very existence, in many ways the term is an oxymoron; it is freedom of speech, association, and political opposition that facilitates free and fair elections and that are the foundation upon which democracy rests.[52] And despite this unnerving trend, it is accurate to say that democracies tend to allow greater expression for liberal social values than do non-democracies.[53] And these liberal values – values such as freedom of expression regardless of societal position, and one person, one vote, regardless of that person's wealth and power – help level the social playing field.[54] Therefore, traditional democracies tend to have lower power distances than non-democracies. Moreover, older democracies – with these liberal values more deeply entrenched – tend to have lower power distance than newer democracies.

What we see then is that hierarchy is relative, but also that it is a shifting concept much as we saw with individualism/collectivism. Just as Japan was more collectivist at one time than it is today,[55] the medieval history of absolute monarchy speaks to a time when even the most egalitarian of contemporary European nations were profoundly hierarchical.

What then separates a destructively high power distance in Egypt from a harmonious Japan? And high power distance Japan from more egalitarian America? We now know that power distance is driven largely by religion, governance and the strength of the middle class. Cross-cultural businesspeople can use these concepts to better understand how power distance differentials – whether high or low – are likely to play out. It is not difficult to determine whether a society has a strong middle class: reference either to Gini coefficients or even in-person observation may well suffice. And where the middle class is vibrant, so too does egalitarianism tend to thrive (with East Asia serving as a notable exception). We can look to religion, and governance too, to predict both the relative levels of power distance and whether power differentials are likely to be used in a harmonious way, or to subjugate those lower in power and further entrench those in power.

And once we have predicted the amount of power distance and the way in which power is used, then we can next ask ourselves: what does this mean for the business, for employees and for good leadership? (Table 6.1)

TABLE 6.1 Power distance onion diagram

Inner	Middle	Outer
Economics (equal) and/or political (democratic)	Egalitarian	All citizens have equal impact on election day; middle class demand equal rights; freedom of speech encouraged, even when this means disparaging those higher in status or dissenting with those higher in organization; delegative management thrives when managers rule by consensus, not fiat; employee autonomy flourishes, but at a risk that employees hold on to information rather than sharing with bosses
Economics (unequal) and/or political (non-democratic)	Hierarchical	Significant wealth and power held by the few (economic inequality, making in-group collectivism, and particularism more likely); little paternalism on the part of status holder, thus institutional collectivism unlikely; autocratic leadership thrives: employees unlikely to challenge boss, and boss likely to manage through orders, not consensus; employee autonomy restricted
Ideology (Confucianism)	Hierarchical	Bounded by status relationships; paternal relationship from high status to low – status persons; institutional collectivism more likely; employees unlikely to challenge boss, but even preference of the boss may give way if needed to maintain consensus of the group
Ideology (Protestantism)	Egalitarian	Aversion to centralized control, with leaders diminished in popular culture; delegative leadership likely
Ideology (Catholicism)	Hierarchy	Subservience to hierarchy (e.g., the papacy); subservience may extend to workplace in traditionally Catholic countries (e.g., southern Europe, Latin America); autocratic leadership likely, though political and democratic factors may moderate autocratic leadership
Ideology (Hinduism)	Hierarchy	Hierarchy determined by caste, an ascribed status; little paternalism on the part of status holder, and thus institutional collectivism unlikely

Power Distance and Business Decisions

Cross-cultural negotiation specialist Jeannie Brett tells the story of a US employee who asked his Chinese counterpart for a meeting in order to discuss the American's desire for a report to include some additional data.[56] His counterpart equivocated, and she later went to a superior, a boss of both individuals, to relay the request.[57] The boss then went to the American to tell him that no, the data requested would not be provided.[58]

Here we see different cultural characteristics colliding. On the one hand, the Chinese employee was bound by rules of hierarchy and collectivism. Collectivism precluded making the decision without the input of others. And hierarchical work spaces tend to exhibit highly structured environments in which responsibilities are made explicit. Information may not be readily provided to lower members of the hierarchy, and autonomy is similarly circumscribed.[59] Hierarchy in this case meant that any decision on the report would have to be approved by the boss who, unlike the employee at issue, saw the whole picture. The Chinese employee, in short, had no choice but to include her supervisor in the decision.

Secondly, the Chinese employee presumed the Westerner had a similar perspective. To her, to be told no by an equal is more offensive than to be told no by a person higher in the hierarchy, to whom one is used to deferring. And we can't know with certainty, but the boss may very well have seen his authority as challenged when the American did not directly raise the issue with him.

As for the American, his unfamiliarity with hierarchical environments left him embarrassed to be told no, not just by his counterpart, but by a higher-ranking member of the organization. Furthermore, coming from an egalitarian culture, he didn't understand that his Chinese counterpart was in an impossible position. The Western manager came from a culture that is more egalitarian than hierarchical,[60] which meant he expected his counterpart to have the autonomy to make their own decisions on such matters.

Egalitarian work spaces are often decentralized, more informal and can include extensive consultation with members of the workforce irrespective of status.[61] The matrix organization – in which employees may work on multiple projects with multiple teams under multiple managers – is thus a natural fit within egalitarian societies but undermines the natural "chain of command" expected in hierarchical cultures.[62]

We also return to our concerns with groupthink and the failure to dissent, first introduced in Chapter 3. Even if that Chinese employee thought the data should be included, she was in no position to publicly disagree with her boss.

Tim Nowak, for example, the executive director of World Trade Center St. Louis, notes his frustration in closing an air transit deal between the city of St. Louis and Chinese airlines. He noted that he and his team did not go first to the airlines, even though they knew it was the airlines that would ultimately have to agree. Instead, they started with the Chinese government. Says Nowak: "[We were] lamenting that none of these airlines will commit – we have all the [Chinese] airlines flying into and out of Chicago because Chicago is what they have always done – and we are trying to get one of them to break out of that cycle to do something different and build their own in St. Louis. And I remember this high-ranking Chinese official looking at me and laughing and says, 'Guys, you don't get it – the tallest blade of grass gets cut first.' [It's an] old saying they have, [and so] with these middle managers, the first one of them who might propose, 'Yeah, this is what we should be doing,' all of a sudden sticks out from the group, and if this deal goes bad, they will lose their job first. So it is so difficult for one to recommend a different course."[63]

This hesitation to speak up in hierarchical cultures is relayed as well by Sumitomo Chemical's executive Juan Ferreira, who offers this strategy to gain trust:

> You go into many of these meetings, and either because of respect or because of hierarchy, you see early on some people that actively participate and others that are quiet. And so, I make sure that any topic that we either want to advance or close, that we get everybody heard. People know that I am sitting in a meeting and they know that they are going to be asked and it doesn't matter if they are from Malaysia or Argentina, or if there is someone more senior to them in the meeting; they still know that I am going to ask them.
>
> The latest example is this guy from Argentina, a very smart, very quiet guy. His boss is in the room and his boss is American, and everybody had spoken and so I said, "I want to hear your opinion." Now, it's even harder for this guy, out of Argentina, because his boss is sitting in the room, and the principle that governs in Argentina is hierarchy. So his principle is not speaking out of respect, because he's thinking if what I say is in any way slightly different than what others that are superior to me are saying, I'd rather be quiet.
>
> ... [but] you can only get that feedback when you have built a relationship. I've been dealing with the international community for the better part of twenty years, and so I have interacted with these people many times. These are not one-time interactions: this is a multiplicity of interactions. So, the first time, the individual may not be entirely forthcoming, the second time there has been a short conversation in the hall, or a short phone call from me saying, "Look, I got your answer, but you were saying the exact same thing as your boss." You know it's not only about IP [intellectual property] here, but intellectual honesty. You need to tell me what you are thinking if you want to get promoted." So my work is to push them and say speak up, bring it up. It can be a bit disruptive, but because we do it constantly, they get used to it as the way it is.[64]

As we've seen with other cultural dimensions, however, behavior is rarely entirely homogeneous within a society. For instance, certain professions may be more likely to exhibit certain cultural traits worldwide. It may be that in hierarchical Malaysia, certain professionals in the modernizing capital of Kuala Lumpur are more egalitarian than their fellow citizens in more rural or lower-skilled positions.

This confluence is increasing given that so many professionals today are educated in the United States, and, increasingly, other centers of learning such as Europe and China. Says Emerson's Montupet: "You now have a generation of Asian managers that have studied in the United States, speak perfect English, and completely understand the American way of doing business. So they interface with American management very well, and then they have to translate back to their base and make it work with their people." This allows large multinational companies to hire cross-culturally, but with some expectation that the core values of the company will resonate across the world.

However, not all companies have the market power of Emerson and other similarly situated multinational companies to strike this balance between corporate and national cultures. And no company is entirely able to control the type of person it works with (and nor should it want to eliminate diversity). Sumitomo Chemical's Juan Ferreira, for instance, distinguishes between his internal and external approach to culture.

Ferreira deeply believes in engaging in repeated one-on-one interactions with his workforce in order to establish mutual trust and cooperation, and to forge a certain connection to Monsanto's corporate culture. But with external partners, such interactions may be more limited, and, perhaps more importantly, Ferreira cannot guarantee that these people will not face retaliation for disagreeing with their supervisors as he can when dealing with his own workforce. This is a return to the "tallest blade of grass gets cut first" mentality. Ferreira is therefore more inclined to pragmatically take a hands-off approach when engaged with external parties.

Ferreira paints a picture of a typical interaction with a hierarchical partner in a joint international venture. This interaction differs sharply from his strategy when dealing with employees from hierarchical cultures: "We're sitting at a meeting table, there's four of us, there's five of them. The head guy sits right in front of us, and he's the only one who talks. If anyone has a disagreement, they will lean over and whisper in his ear, and then he'll talk again. If I turn and say to another, 'How is this project working?' they will not share, so I've quit trying to break that. Even if he were to say something when you ask, then you may lose the trust of the senior guy. I would like inclusiveness to be brought into everything that we do, but in reality there is only so much that you can change."[65]

This cultural variability, which people like Nowak, Ferreira, and Montupet experience regularly, highlights that the cultural dimensions must not be absent-mindedly relied upon. The curious traveler, able to empathize with others and to take meaning from seemingly inconsequential details, is the astute leader.

As proof of this wide variability, Americans in general are relatively hierarchical within their business relationships. But what about Silicon Valley tech companies? These have some of the most egalitarian cultures on the planet. Let's explore how the expanded autonomy of very egalitarian cultures played out in a company we all know – Google's parent company, Alphabet, Inc.

Success in the Velocipedic Age

Bill Gates predicted that "As we look ahead into the next century, leaders will be those who empower others."[66] In the early nineteenth century, however, an aging Johann Wolfgang von Goethe predicted a world interconnected by communication networks, where people had all the most current news and information at their fingertips. He called this the velocipedic age.[67]

Goethe's velocipedic age is here, even if his name didn't stick: contemporaries refer to the time we live in as the Information Age. Writing in 2005, the University of Michigan's Kim Cameron explained the Information Age with these dramatic examples:

> ...more information was produced last year than was produced in the previous five thousand years. A weekday edition of the *New York Times* or the *International Herald Tribune* contains more information than the average person was likely to come across in a lifetime during the eighteenth century. The total amount of information available to the average person doubles every year.[68]

In this era, the dynamic between manager and employee is changing, and employee empowerment is particularly important for success in the twenty-first century's Information Age. In the twentieth century, executives had an informational advantage: they were privy to information that others were not – they may even have prevented others from accessing that information in order to maintain the informational advantage.[69] This control of information put managers in a position to make better decisions than less informed rivals.[70]

Pre-Information Age, corporate siloes and hierarchies facilitated this informational advantage.[71] A silo is often a vast, vertical structure, built of solid steel in the twentieth and twenty-first centuries. A siloed company might look something like this: you are one of a dozen mid-level managers in the finance department of a Fortune 500 company. You report to the vice president of finance. You have five employees that report directly to you. In this siloed world, you expect your employees to communicate with you – and only you. The idea that they would communicate with another manager is absurd; indeed, managers of other departments work in other parts of the building, and neither your employees nor you are likely to be familiar with these managers. As a result, your employees don't see the big picture or understand the scope of the business, so they are asked to provide you with all potentially relevant information rather than doing the job of sorting through information and determining the relevance themselves.

You, in turn, will report up to your vice president and wouldn't consider taking up problems, or ideas, with the vice president of any other department. Again, you're unlikely to see these other vice presidents very often or have a working relationship with them. At this level, you lack the big-picture perspective, so your boss expects you to send up vast amounts of information on which he or she can act. This continues all the way to the top, with eventually the highest-level executives receiving information that originated at the lower levels of the organization. With a limit to the total information available, this is manageable. Those atop the hierarchy are paid big bucks to, essentially, put the puzzle together: that is, make decisions on the basis of the collected information. The bureaucratic organization – with its deeply layered organizational structure – adequately facilitates this process.

Today, the world is more complex than ever, and thanks to technology, information is not only abundant, as Cameron noted, it is for the first time easily accessible to almost everyone. Even children in rural India can often access more information than could the well-informed in previous decades. This is a notably positive development, but the consequences of this revolution are still being processed. What we know with certainty is this: the informational advantage of the few, is, in most places, a distant memory.

Instead, managers must seek to identify the most relevant information in order to make better decisions faster.[72] But bureaucracies are notoriously *slow*, precisely because all that information flowing up the hierarchy can drown, rather than benefit, the manager of the twenty-first century. The puzzle becomes too complex to put together, not to mention that more pieces are always being added. It is the rare genius who is able to master the wide variety of subjects on which information is available (and useful). Analysis paralysis is the likely result.

And yet, as the *Harvard Business Review* relates, bureaucracies continue to grow long after their reason for being has passed, like a "cancer that eats away at economic productivity and organizational resilience."[73] Cameron similarly writes: "Large organizations and government agencies are generally dominated by a hierarchy culture, as evidenced by large numbers of standardized procedures, multiple hierarchical levels (Ford has seventeen levels of management), and an emphasis on rule reinforcement."[74]

Managers need their employees to see not only their pieces of the puzzle but those of their colleagues too, so they can help put together the puzzle, or at least help simplify the puzzle by recognizing which pieces are essential.

Consequently, the employee autonomy that comes in egalitarian and delegative cultures – and of the sort that Washington University's Mark Wrighton relayed at the beginning of this chapter – may be particularly well-suited for acting quickly to solve problems or grab opportunities.[75]

Consider this from Google chairman and former CEO, Eric Schmidt, and former SVP of products, Jonathan Rosenberg, in their book *How Google Works*:

> Larry Page was exploring the organic ads that pop up on Google when doing a search. As an example of how this should work, if one does a google search asking about the product quality of vintage wines, ads will populate showing such wines for sale, or perhaps wine glasses and other accoutrements. Instead, Page found the ads perfectly unrelated to the terms of his search. Instead of sending out an angry email or calling the ad team, he printed out the problem ads, put them on a bulletin board along with a note that said, "These ads *suck*!," calling out no one in particular and essentially inviting anyone to solve the problem. Then he went home for the weekend. That Monday at 5:05 a.m., an email was sent out by an engineer. He not only agreed with Page but identified the cause of the problem and provided a detailed solution. The engineer and a team of colleagues had worked through the weekend to come up with a solution to the problem. They understood the culture – that anybody could look into a problem or opportunity; if they failed, nobody would be angry; if they succeeded, then nobody would be jealous, not even the ads team.[76]

In this case, the "flat" (egalitarian) organization is helping Google succeed in this Information Age. The general sentiment, however, often seems to be that this is the only way to succeed in the twenty-first century and that we would argue is a step too far.[77] The egalitarian culture of Google certainly resulted in a quick solution, indeed by a team not even responsible for the adware. Note, however, that the problem was discovered by Page himself, almost by chance. How many other problems were not brought to his attention? The problem for flat organizations is that relatively egalitarian, highly individualistic, achievement-oriented Americans may hesitate to share information, seeing this as a relinquishment of power. In response, Page and Rosenberg recommend a focus on coherent and mutually loyal teams, for instance by minimizing the physical space between employees and increasing collaborative efforts.[78]

By contrast, researchers Inzerilli and Laurent note that in Italy, France and Japan, all traditionally home to hierarchical organizations, managers tend not to worry about those lower in the hierarchy holding on to pertinent information. Managers in these countries are expected to "know everything": to admit ignorance is a loss of face.[79] The "know-it-all" manager may, however, seek to become more knowledgeable in order to live up to his self-acclaimed reputation. In this way, we see a self-fulfilling prophecy in the same way we did with respect to the connection between seniority and competence (in attribution societies). Additionally, in paternalistic societies where the manager is akin to the father figure, "the supposition that your manager does know everything may require you to discuss everything with him, thus encouraging the upward movement of information."[80]

Hierarchical and egalitarian organizations may thus need to respond differently to the Information Age, with hierarchical organizations finding a way forward that does not rely on haphazard copying of organizational models from geographically and culturally distant places. Such an attempt goes against the "mental programming" of the workforce, and there is consequently a high risk of failure. Says Stella Sheehan, deputy director of the World Trade Center, St. Louis: "people in certain markets would just crumble apart if forced to operate in an egalitarian space. Even though people say they want egalitarian, I think people from many cultures gravitate towards the hierarchical." She's right, so there must be another way.

Egalitarian managers may follow the recommendation of Larry Page and Jonathan Rosenberg by decentralizing supervisory authority and employee responsibilities while encouraging – even demanding – the upward flow of information. The transition to more egalitarian organizational cultures will likely be well received by people living in societies that are already more egalitarian than their workplaces. Indeed, the gap between organizational hierarchical and societal culture may prove a source of resentment.

By contrast, hierarchical organizations where paternalism is strong may not need to *demand* the upward flow of information; it is likely to be voluntary, with the caveat from Chapter 3 that information potentially embarrassing to the manager may not flow quite so readily. The challenge for these organizations is to empower employees so that they have higher quality information to raise up the hierarchy, but without losing the built-in benefits of loyalty and teamwork that paternalistic hierarchy can bring. This is a fine balance that does not have a one-size-fits-all solution. Instead, it will require precision tailored to the culture and tailored to the specific organization and people within it.

We will see in the next section however that when employees are given greater discretion, those more empowered employees in hierarchical societies may be more satisfied and the organization more competitive than it would be in blindly following culturally inappropriate practices represented as "best practices." Empowerment – albeit more cautiously and gradually implemented than in the already egalitarian societies of the West – is a strategy worth exploring even for hierarchical organizations.

Leadership Styles and Power Distance

Autocratic leadership, participative leadership (also known as democratic) and delegative (also known as laissez-faire) leadership are categories often used to represent the spectrum of leadership styles.[81] Delegative leadership occurs when employees make decisions and the manager simply provides guidance or direction.[82] This is a natural fit in egalitarian societies. In participative leadership, managers seek the advice of their workforce, but ultimately, it is the manager who makes the decision.[83] In autocratic leadership, it is the manager who makes the decision and simply tells her employees what to do.[84] Structured environments and low employee empowerment, typical of hierarchical cultures, tend to follow the autocratic leader.

Many egalitarian societies and organizations reject visibly powerful leaders, which is often the result of historic memories of powerful and destructive leaders within the society or organization at issue. In other words, those with negative leader experiences are more likely to disdain leaders than those more familiar with heroic, accomplished leaders. For instance, cross-cultural researcher Robert J. House reported that in the Netherlands, Dutch children will not admit to their classmates if their father is a manager.[85] The negative Dutch experience with authoritarian leadership during the excesses of World War II, and more generally their historical rejection of centralized authority going back the middle ages, may help explain this sentiment.

Consequently, the more egalitarian the culture, the more likely that the somewhat passive, nonconfrontational style of delegative leadership will be the expected leadership style. For instance, egalitarian German, Austrian, and Swiss managers were found to regularly conform to delegative leadership.[86]

Additionally, managers may use the delegative leadership style when they have a high degree of trust in their employees.[87] This may occur even in otherwise hierarchical organizations or societies. A manager of a large public company for example may act rather authoritarian and hierarchical with respect to low skilled manufacturers but be more deferential within the corporate suite of upper-level executives.

The participative leadership style is common in the United States, which we will recall leans, though just slightly, toward egalitarianism.[88] French managers also tend to fall between these two styles.[89] Beyond cultural conditioning, the participative style is also drawn upon when managers have some of the information needed to make a decision, but employees have important parts of the answer as well. In this case, the manager is not able to be authoritarian – he needs input from others – but may feel he has enough knowledge or expertise to argue against a delegative leadership style. The more complex the organization, the more beneficial this leadership style may be vis-à-vis the authoritarian style of leadership.

Countries and organizations exhibiting higher levels of power distance may be more likely to support powerful leaders than those more egalitarian countries and organizations. Indeed, the United States is a place renowned for its admiration of leaders – in effect a reverse of what we see in Dutch society – which helps explain why the power distance within American *society* is relatively low but *organizational* power distance tends to be much higher. In the United States, even more hierarchical organizations are still somewhat moderate compared to other societies, which is why participative leadership is common while delegative leadership is widely seen within certain knowledge-intensive industries.

In truly hierarchical cultures, however, autocratic leadership may be considered acceptable or even desirable. In this area, Polish and Czech managers[90] were found to be the most autocratic.[91] Again, looking beyond cultural conditioning, we might also see autocratic management styles in situations where employees have limited skills and thus need greater direction, or where employees are new and thus temporarily lacking pertinent knowledge to act in more empowered ways.

It may be natural to look down on autocratic leadership – after all, who wants to be perceived as an autocrat, let alone work for one? Some writers have instead advised a hybrid approach in which participative and democratic leadership are drawn upon and autocracy downplayed.[92] Can we not see a place for autocratic leadership when a strong hierarchal culture prevails?

Autocratic leadership, in conjunction with the social contract theory in which managers care for employees, is the standard leadership style in many hierarchical societies.[93] As Eylon and Au note for example, "in hierarchical Mexico,[94] the ideal boss is viewed as a benevolent autocrat or a good father."[95] After all, we defined hierarchical work environments to include low empowered employees and high structure. The same characteristics are exhibited in hierarchical organizations. There is increasing evidence suggesting a misfit between a delegative leadership style – often imported by well-meaning outsiders – and a hierarchical culture.

Here's what Hofstede had to say on the matter:

> In countries with higher power distances – such as many third-world countries, but also France and Belgium – individual subordinates as a rule do not want to participate. It is part of their expectations that leaders lead autocratically, and such subordinates will, in fact, by their own behavior make it difficult for leaders to lead in any other way. There is very little participative leadership in France and Belgium.[96]

But Hofstede, unusually, did not have it entirely right! It is true that some people from hierarchical societies are content with low levels of empowerment.[97] But researchers Eylon and Au provide an interesting twist, suggesting that job satisfaction increases as empowerment increases.

The researchers worked with MBA students from both hierarchical and egalitarian countries. Half the students were randomly chosen to participate in a work scenario in which they were given very little access to information, and few responsibilities; the other half were given much more information and responsibility. Eylon and Au found that participants from *both* hierarchical and egalitarian countries were more satisfied when empowered with greater access to information and responsibility.[98] Put differently, when employees feel trusted, informed, supported, and in control, their job satisfaction increases.[99] This effect is stronger for egalitarian workers – in others words, they will be particularly dissatisfied if not empowered – but is seen for hierarchical workers as well.[100] Consequently, it may be that small levels of employee autonomy are driven less by the preferences of employees and more by managers that have a mentality akin to that of Hofstede. Research suggests managers do just that.[101]

They also found however that respondents from hierarchical countries performed "significantly less well" when provided with that greater autonomy.[102] This has important implications. It suggests that in hierarchical cultures, employee satisfaction and performance may be mutually exclusive. Perhaps more importantly, it suggests that a desire for autonomy may be pan-cultural but that the skill to use that autonomy in a productive manner may be less developed in hierarchical cultures.

Perhaps this should not surprise us. After all, employees in hierarchical cultures are given fewer chances to practice autonomy, so they do not have the benefit of experience. This structured work environment in which empowerment is the exception rather than the rule may even be enculturated from a young age. We know, for instance, that in classically hierarchical countries such as China, the educational systems have long been criticized for an overemphasis on highly structured learning to the detriment of critical thinking.[103] And strong critical thinking is the linchpin to the success of empowered employees. If skills are not developed, a sense of incompetence may even arise, which deflates the initial sense of satisfaction.[104] Consequently, managers may tepidly engage in activities to increase empowerment, but should do so in accompaniment with training and while maintaining a close eye on both satisfaction and employment.

This lack of experience in acting with empowerment suggests that the skills of autonomy need to be taught. The studies of Eylon and Au suggest that many employees would be keen learners, and the Age of Information indicates that managers should seriously consider providing such lessons.

Notes

i Exhibit visited by author, Bussen, at The National Museum of Kazakhstan.
ii Technically, these unfortunate people are not just at the bottom of the caste system; they are without a caste at all, and thus least valued in society.

References

1 J. Stuart Bunderson and Ray E. Reagans, "Power, Status, and Learning in Organizations," 22 *Organization Science* 1182–1183 (citing to R.M. Emerson, "Power-Dependence Relations," *American Sociological Review* 27 (1962): 31–41).
2 Wrighton, *supra* note 130.
3 Keuper, *supra* note 194.
4 Dale Carl, Vipin Gupta, and Mansour Javidan, *Power Distance, in Culture, Leadership, and Organizations: The GLOBE Study OF 62 Societies* 541 (eds. Robert House, Paul J. Hanges, Mansour Javidan, Peter W. Dorfman, and Vipin Gupta, Sage Publications) (2004).
5 Id.
6 Id. at 549 (exceptions to this finding were Germanic Europe, Nordic Europe, and Latin America, where organizational power distances were significantly lower than at the societal level).
7 Id. at 538.

8 Id.
9 Id. at 549.
10 Keuper, *supra* note 194.
11 Carl et al., *supra* note 313 at 556.
12 Gross Domestic Product, the World Bank (last accessed July 29, 2018), https://www.google.com/publicdata/explore?ds=d5bncppjof8f9_&met_y=ny_gdp_mktp_cd&idim=country:CHN:USA:IND&hl=en&dl=en.
13 GDP Per Capita (Current US$), the World Bank (last accessed July 29, 2018), https://data.worldbank.org/indicator/NY.GDP.PCAP.CD?year_high_desc=false.
14 Id.
15 Gini Index (World Bank Estimate), the World Bank, (last accessed July 29, 2018), https://data.worldbank.org/indicator/SI.POV.GINI?locations=CN.
16 Gini Index (World Bank Estimate), the World Bank, (last accessed July 29, 2018), https://data.worldbank.org/indicator/SI.POV.GINI?locations=KR-LU.
17 Gini Index (World Bank Estimate), the World Bank, (last accessed July 29, 2018), https://data.worldbank.org/indicator/SI.POV.GINI?locations=KR.
18 World, *supra* note 323.
19 Carl et al., *supra* note 313 at 539.
20 Id. at 547.
21 Daniel Bekele, "Equatorial Guinea: Why Poverty Plagues a High-Income Nation," Human Rights Watch (Jan. 27, 2017), https://www.hrw.org/news/2017/01/27/equatorial-guinea-why-poverty-plagues-high-income-nation.
22 GDP Growth (Annual %), The World Bank (last accessed July 29, 2018) https://data.worldbank.org/indicator/NY.GDP.MKTP.KD.ZG?end=2011&locations=EG&start=2000.
23 Osama Diab, "Egypt's Widening Wealth Gap," MADAMASR (May 23, 2016), https://www.madamasr.com/en/2016/05/23/feature/economy/egypts-widening-wealth-gap/. (While the Gini coefficient shows relatively equal incomes In Egypt, the actual wealth within Egypt is disproportionately held by a small number of people. In 2000, an already high 61% of wealth was held by 10% of the population; by 2007 this rose to 65.3%, and by 2014 to 73.3%.)
24 Haidt, *supra* note 98 at 119.
25 Id.
26 Haidt, *supra* note 98 at 186–187.
27 Id. at 140.
28 Confucius, *supra* note 239 at Chapter 1, 1.2.
29 Carl et al., *supra* note 313 at 520.
30 Id. at 519.
31 Id. at 520.
32 Id.
33 Id. at 522.
34 Id.
35 Harari, *supra* note 66 at 151–152.
36 Carl et al., *supra* note 313 at 522.
37 Id.
38 Id. at 521.
39 Montupet, *supra* note 10.
40 Carl et al., *supra* note 313 at 523.
41 Bruce Barnes, *Culture, Conflict, and Mediation in the Asian Pacific* 9 (UPA, 2006).
42 Carl et al., *supra* note 313 at 523.
43 Id.
44 Id. at 521.
45 Id. at 526.
46 Id. at 524.

47 Id.
48 Id.
49 Id.
50 Id.
51 Fareed Zakaria, "The Rise of Illiberal Democracy," *Foreign Affairs* (Nov./Dec. 1997), https://www.foreignaffairs.com/articles/1997-11-01/rise-illiberal-democracy.
52 Carl et al., *supra* note 313 at 524.
53 Id.
54 Id.
55 Hofstede, *supra* note 23 at 40.
56 Brett, *supra* note 81 at 80.
57 Id.
58 Id.
59 Dafna Eylon and Kevin Y. Au, "Exploring Empowerment Cross-Cultural Differences Along the Power Distance Dimension," 23 *International Journal of Intercultural Relations*, 373, 382.
60 *Power Distance Index*, Clearly Cultural, (last accessed July 28, 2018), http://www.clearlycultural.com/geert-hofstede-cultural-dimensions/power-distance-index/.
61 Eylon and Au, *supra* note 371 at 382 (citing Hofstede, 1993; Morris and Pavett, 1992).
62 Hofstede, *supra* note 4 at 85 (writing: "Taylor's work appeared in a French translation in 1913, and Fayol [a Frenchman] read it and showed himself generally impressed but shocked by Taylor's 'denial of the principle of the unity of command' in the case of the eight-boss-system." This system led to the Matrix organization.)
63 Nowak, *supra* note 82.
64 Ferreira, *supra* note 175.
65 Id.
66 Bill Gates Quotes, Brainy Quote (last accessed July 29, 2018), https://www.brainyquote.com/authors/bill_gates.
67 Robert Greene, *Mastery* 337 (Penguin Books) (2012).
68 Kim S. Cameron and Robert E. Quinn, *Diagnosing and Changing Organizational Culture* 8 (Jossey Bass: San Francisco, CA) (2005).
69 In 1980s China, for instance, managers were known to treat organizational problems as secret, and rarely consulted subordinates. Eylon and Au, *supra* note 371 at 377.
70 Eric Schmidt and Jonathan Rosenberg, *How Google Works* 36 (Grand Central Publishing: New York, NY; Boston, MA) (2014).
71 Id. at 39.
72 Collins, *supra* note 142.
73 Gary Hamel and Michele Zanini, "More of Us Are Working in Big Bureaucratic Organizations Than Ever Before," *Harvard Business Review* (July 5, 2016), https://hbr.org/2016/07/more-of-us-are-working-in-big-bureaucratic-organizations-than-ever-before.
74 Cameron and Quinn, *supra* note 380 at 38.
75 Carl et al., *supra* note 313 at 534.
76 Schmidt and Rosenberg, *supra* note 382 at 49.
77 Ed Catmull, *Creativity Inc.: Overcoming the Unseen Forces that Stand in the Way of True Inspiration* (Random House) (2014); see also Schmidt and Rosenberg, *supra* note 382; see also Carl et al., *supra* note 313 at 534 (writing "In the contemporary learning- and knowledge-driven environment, the mantra in several Western cultures is that lower power distance is more effective in organizational settings. Power sharing, empowerment, and, hence, lower power distance is the prescribed norm. The concept of empowerment and semi- autonomous teams has proved particularly striking in the societies at the forefront of the information technology revolution" (Gupta, 1998).

78 Schmidt and Rosenberg, *supra* note 382 at 52, 56.
79 Trompenaars and Hampden-Turner, *supra* note 12 at 164.
80 Id.
81 See "Leadership Styles," Mindtools (last accessed July 29, 2018), https://www.mindtools.com/pages/article/newLDR_84.htm.
82 Id.
83 Id.
84 Id.
85 Carl et al., *supra* note 313 at 554.
86 Peter W. Dorfman, "Prior Literature," in *Culture, Leadership, and Organizations: The GLOBE Study of 62 Societies* 61 (eds. Robert House, Paul J. Hanges, Mansour Javidan, Peter W. Dorfman, and Vipin Gupta, Sage Publications) (2004).
87 Leadership Style Quiz, Mindtools (last accessed July 29, 2018), https://www.mindtools.com/pages/article/leadership-style-quiz.htm.
88 Dorfman, *supra* note 396 at 61.
89 Id.
90 Poland and Czechia were not studied by GLOBE. However, Central European neighbor Hungary was found to be the most hierarchical European country studied. Culturally connected Germany was not far behind. See Carl et al., *supra* note 313 at 539.
91 Dorfman, *supra* note 396 at 61.
92 Leadership Styles (last accessed July 29, 2018), http://www.nwlink.com/~donclark/leader/leadstl.html.
93 Dorfman, *supra* note 396 at 61 (writing: "The researchers developed predictions of participation based on Hofstede's power distance scores and results were generally supportive for the prediction that participation scores would be higher for lower power distance cultures" (Jago et al., 1993)).
94 GLOBE did not study Mexico, but Latin American countries generally ranked amongst the most hierarchical. See Carl et al., *supra* note 313 at 539.
95 Eylon and Au, *supra* note 371 at 377.
96 Hofstede, *supra* note 13 at 87.
97 C. Robert, T.M. Probst, J. Martocchio, F. Drasgow, and J.J. Lawler, "Empowerment And Continuous Improvement in the United States, Mexico, Poland, and India: Predicting Fit on the Basis of the Dimensions of Power Distance and Individualism," 85 *Journal of Applied Psychology* 643–658 (2000) (finding that hierarchical India, but not hierarchical Mexico, hierarchical Poland, or egalitarian United States preferred less empowerment to more).
98 Eylon and Au, *supra* note 371 at 381.
99 Michael K. Hui, Kevin Au, and Henry Fock, "Empowerment Effects across Cultures," 35 *Journal of International Business Studies*, 46, 48 (2004).
100 Id. at 53.
101 Kabasakal and Bodur, *supra* note 44 at 584 (writing: "in paternalistic societies managers believe that employees by nature seek more supervisory guidance. Hence, jobs are designed in a way that does not give much autonomy to employees").
102 Eylon and Au, *supra* note 371 at 381.
103 Ben Blanchard, "Wen Says Rote Learning Must Go in Chinese Schools," *Reuters* (Aug. 31, 2010), https://www.reuters.com/article/us-china-education-idUSTRE67U18Y20100831.
104 Indeed, other research has found that high power distance employees may be uneasy with their expanded responsibilities. Hui et al., *supra* note 411 at 58 (citing to C. Robert, T.M. Probst, J.J. Martocchio, F. Drasgow, and J.J. Lawler, "Empowerment and Continuous Improvement in the United States, Mexico, Poland and India: Predicting Fit on the Basis of the Dimensions of Power Distance and Individualism," *Journal of Applied Psychology* 85 (2000): 643–658.

7

AVOIDING THE ELIXIR OF POWER

> Don't worry if people don't recognize your merits; worry that you may not recognize theirs.
>
> Confucius

Canadian anthropologist Richard Borshay Lee detailed his visit to the !Kung people in the 1960s in his article "Eating Christmas in the Kalahari."[1] The !Kung are a seminomadic people that survive by hunting and gathering and are perhaps best known for their use of clicking sounds to aid communication.

Lee recounts presenting the tribe with an ox as a gift.[2] The !Kung responded by insulting the ox and demeaning the gift, asking, "Do you expect us to eat that bag of bones? ... Everybody knows that there's no meat on that old ox. What did you expect us to eat off it, the horns?"[3] In point of fact, the ox was fat and the gift generous under the circumstances.[4]

Lee, being the inquisitive anthropologist he was, asked a member of the !Kung why the tribesmen would lodge insults in this situation: "Arrogance," was his cryptic answer. "Arrogance?" "Yes, when a young man kills much meat, he comes to think of himself as a chief or a big man, and he thinks of the rest of us as his servants or inferiors. We can't accept this. We refuse one who boasts, for someday his pride will make him kill somebody. So we always speak of his meat as worthless. This way we cool his heart and make him gentle."[5]

The !Kung thus found a way to avoid the "elixir of power," or the growing ego that follows success. In Chapter 3 we discussed the danger that egotistical leadership poses. Across cultures, employees desire leaders who support their needs and wants.[6] Peter Drucker seconded this notion when he wrote in his article "What Makes an Effective Executive" that great leaders "are focused on the needs and the opportunities of the organization before they think of their own needs and opportunities."[7] Egotistical leaders do just the opposite, promoting their own interests to the detriment of others.[8] As a result, egotistical leadership is associated with inferior company performance.[9]

But avoiding the elixir of power is harder than it sounds. Even people with a relatively selfless track record tend to become protective of prerogatives as they gain power.[10] As the famous proverb states and researchers have largely confirmed,[11] "All power corrupts; absolute power corrupts absolutely." We need look no further than the countless freedom fighters who went from risking their lives for their country to spending their lives accumulating riches and power as kleptocratic dictators, or the heads of companies who transformed from motivational leaders to quite unmotivating thieves of untold riches. The reason is that as power increases, acting with humility, acting to support employees and generally acting in a prosocial manner can become more difficult.[12] The problem, in short, is that power is an elixir that tastes good.

One implication of this loss of humility is a loss of perspective: those with less power tend to be better at understanding the perspective of others, to walk in their shoes.

A study by Columbia Business School's Adam Galinsky and colleagues[13] illustrated this:

> The researchers divided participants into two groups. Before the experiment began, one group engaged in an exercise that was intended to induce a feeling of power. The other group engaged in an exercise intended to emphasize their impotence. The participants were then asked to draw the letter E on their foreheads. Previous studies showed that those better attuned to others draw an E that reads correctly to others, but which from the participant's perspective would seem backward (readers can try this themselves and may find that the "natural" inclination is to draw the letter in a way that would read backward to anyone reading it). The exercise thereby provides a visible manifestation of the degree to which respondents take regard of others.

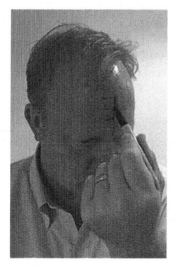
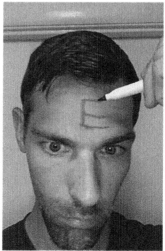

What the researchers found was that those primed before the study to feel powerful were three times more likely to draw a "self-oriented" E, such that the E appeared backward to everyone else, than were those for whom power was deemphasized.[14] The power, in short, reduced the ability or willingness of respondents to put themselves in the shoes of others. Other researchers too have found that those with fewer resources, or are lower in status, tend to do a better job of observing others, and being less self-oriented.[15]

Although most researchers conceptualize power as static – something you have or don't have, and which changes only slowly with major career events such as promotions – in reality, it is typically much more fluid.[16] For instance, you may be a follower when working on group tasks in which you have little experience, but in the next moment you may lead a team on a task in which you bring the most skills to bear. You may be a follower when meeting with your boss and a leader when meeting with your employees. You may be a leader when asking your children to do chores but a follower when doing the chores your spouse asks you to do.

An important implication of Galinsky's study is just how quickly the increase in power results in an increased self-orientation among the participants. This suggests that a self-orientation is not merely a gradual shift over time as one becomes increasingly isolated in a position of power, but instead, that orientation can change as rapidly as do shifts in one's relative power.

For those that prefer examples outside of the lab walls, this sort of transformation is also readily identifiable in the business world. In Roderick Kramer's "The Harder They Fall" (*Harvard Business Review*), he notes the flamboyance of Tyco's Kozlowski, the brazenness of Enron's Kenneth Lay and the excesses of WorldCom's Bernard Ebbers.[17]

For instance, WorldCom grew into one of America's largest companies under the leadership of CEO Bernard Ebbers. It also lost $200 billion in shareholder value under his excesses.[18] Coming from modest means, Ebbers was earning millions, but still he managed – and the board allowed him – to accumulate $400 million in debt to the company (with Ebbers's stock as collateral) to cover his lavish lifestyle.[19] He had another $400 million in personal loans from private lenders.[20] In a desperate effort to boost the value of company stock – which represented his primary source of earnings – Ebbers and his top executives facilitated a fraudulent reporting scheme.[21] As word leaked of the scandal, the stock value, once selling at almost $100 per share, plummeted to as low as twenty cents while tens of thousands lost their jobs.[22] For Ebbers, the fall reached its inevitable conclusion when he was sentenced to twenty-five years in prison.[23]

The changes seen in executives like these are often sudden, a reversal of the positive characteristics that led to the rise to power in the first place. Kramer termed this change the "genius to folly syndrome," in which leaders neglect the very characteristics that tended to support their rise.[24] This is not, Kramer notes, a mere quirk of personality.[25] Something deeper is at play.

As we saw in the Milgram studies, the tendency of people to follow those in positions of authority renders the behavior of leaders even more important. In the Milgram study, we saw how followers can almost blindly acquiesce to the demands of leaders, but in that experiment, the focus was on followers. The "leader" was an actor, an artificial creation.

We thus turn now to the famous Zimbardo experiment to see how power affects the behavior of leaders. Like the Milgram study, it is a sobering read in which the true dangers of power and its corrupting forces are most visible.

In 1971, Professor Philip Zimbardo, at Stanford University, randomly divided eighteen male college students into two groups. Half the students were randomly assigned to be prisoners and the other half guards. A simulation prison was built in the basement of the psychology building, which was the setting of the experiment that was to last two weeks. The guards wore uniforms and were told to maintain law and order, prevent prisoner escapes and avoid physical violence.[26]

The prisoners were stripped and hosed down and given a prisoner gown, ID number and had a chain bolted to their ankle. These served to dehumanize the prisoners. After just thirty-six hours, the first prisoner had a mental breakdown and was removed from the experiment. For the rest, the show went on: the guards increasingly used dehumanizing tactics such as forced pushups, buckets as toilets and paper bags over the prisoners' heads. Within two days the first rebellion took place in which the prisoners barricaded the cells as they attempted to regain their identities. The guards called in backup and intervened by stripping the prisoners – thus doubling down on the dehumanization – and creating a more comfortable "privilege" cell for better behaved prisoners, which had the effect of creating distrust among the prisoners.[27]

The "fight" of the prisoners was effectively smothered, along with their sense of humanity. Within only a few days, the prisoners' sense of reality shifted, and they no longer felt they could leave. The show had become reality. The guards continued to use more and more degradation on prisoners who, let's not forget, were actually their fellow students. Professor Zimbardo even proved oddly taken by his own experiment, frantically moving the prisoners to another floor after a rumor of a raid from the outside world.[28]

Six days into the planned two-week experiment, the interactions escalated so much that the experiment was brought to a premature conclusion (and only after outside intervention).[29]

A few years later, professor Zimbardo made the comment: "Evil deeds are rarely the product of evil people acting from evil motives but are the product of good bureaucrats simply doing their job."[30] As with the obedience experiments, the prisoners here had an authority figure (Dr. Zimbardo) against whom to defer responsibility to.

There was also, however, something undeniably powerful about the uniforms. Wearing the uniform of authority figures creates a sense of power within the bearer, as well as increased obedience from others. Leonard Bickman showed in a study in 1974 that people are twice as likely to follow a command if it comes from someone in a uniform, and another study on physicians shows that people are more likely to trust a doctor wearing professional attire.[31] This result is similar to the obedience experiment conducted by Dr. Milgram, where people are more likely to give painful shocks to another participant when the experimenter giving the instructions is wearing a lab coat.

On the flip side, what you wear influences how you act. Wearing a white doctor's coat improves focused attention. Interestingly, when the same coat is labeled as a painter's coat, this effect is no longer present, suggesting that it is your own perception and the identification with the role the clothing depicts that is of importance.[32] Additionally, in the 1990s, many Western business organizations shifted to a more casual dress style at the workplace. This seems to be linked to a more open, friendly organizational culture, which is less hierarchical.[33] These changes are often thought of in terms of how we perceive others, such as our boss and our colleagues. We also feel friendlier when we wear casual attire, our creativity more increased, but some studies suggest that people wearing casual attire feel less productive.[34] By contrast, when we wear business attire, we feel authoritative, trustworthy and competent.[35]

This shows us that the roll we are assigned, born with or simply see ourselves as holding is important for the way we act. We have to mentally remove the uniform and see things for how they are. We have to unshackle our own psyches and hold ourselves responsible, rather than deferring to others. And as leaders, we have to recognize that to lead is, in a very real way, a responsibility. Employees may well follow the leader to the proverbial ends of the earth, so the leader must set the right direction. The elixir of power, however, can make this difficult, leading us in directions that may benefit the leader but few others.

Combating the Elixir of Power

The WorldCom board failed to restrain Ebbers, failed to evince proper oversight within Enron, and proved disinterested as Tyco collapsed. The !Kung of the Kalahari may therefore be on to something by preventing the undue accumulation of ego. The Dutch similarly take pains to avoid unduly elevating leadership and to avoid associating it with heroism and greatness, as is so common in the American mind-set. Certainly, it is not that Dutch leaders are immune to the elixir of power – all individuals must be wary of the inclination to grasp for, and abuse, power, even at the expense of others. This is indeed the very reason the !Kung insulted the anthropologist. However, Dutch society and the !Kung created cultural constraints – or taboos – in which leaders seen as too powerful are subject to more criticism from their fellow citizens. Not only is this sense of ostracism painful to us as highly social humans, but without followers, a leader is leader of nothing at all. Consequently, these cultural norms go far in restraining behavior.

Companies can likewise leverage cultural norms by forging shared organizational values, such as promulgating the shared belief that the greatness of the company is explained by the vast contributions of all employees, or by celebrating the careers and contributions of its most humble.

Organizations can also do as regulators and lawmakers around the world do, by imposing certain structural restraints on the unbridled exercise of power, which has been the downfall of many companies, not to mention governments. For one, they can demand greater accountability. At Emerson Electric, for instance, the fear is that regional leaders of their far-flung empire will float under the radar. Communication is key, and the company consequently asks for employees to provide annual reviews, called opinion surveys, about their managers. Says Montupet, "In Europe it takes a while to get the feedback, and in Asia, they are sometimes hesitant, but it always gets done."[36]

Where wrongdoing is uncovered, policing must follow – penalties, even termination of employment. Conversely, those exhibiting the values of the company should be rewarded. These structural constraints play a role analogous to the state: the greater the likelihood of getting caught when trying to aggrandize power, and the greater the penalty if caught for doing this, the less likely one will be to engage in this behavior. Furthermore, the greater the likelihood of being noticed and rewarded for exhibiting desired behavior, the more employees will follow this path.

More importantly than even these structural and cultural restraints, individuals must take responsibility for inhibiting their own egos. One antidote to this psychological reaction to power, for instance, is to actively seek to reduce your power perception. Recall that in the Galinsky study, using the E-test, those primed to take a less powerful perspective become more oriented toward others. In other studies, people primed to think about honesty became more honest.[37] The takeaway is that we can consciously minimize the degree of power we perceive ourselves as holding by actively considering the limitations to our power through, for example, recognizing the importance that others have had in our success. This can also be accomplished simply by reflecting on the importance of compassion and humility.

Galinsky found in another study that consciously thinking about the needs of others does in fact improve perspective-taking. In the study, Galinsky asked participants to take part in a fictional negotiation in which a gas station was being sold. The participants were divided into three groups: one group was asked to imagine what the other side was *feeling*. The second group was asked to imagine what the other side was *thinking*. A third group was not given any instructions at all. The third group performed worst of all in the negotiation, suggesting that conscious awareness of others is a valuable business skill, at least in terms of negotiation. The group that performed best in this area was the first group in which participants imagined what the other side was thinking.[38] In so doing, they considered their needs and thus sought to respond to those needs in a way that made mutually beneficial settlement more likely. Managers can reduce their self-orientation by consciously asking themselves, "What are my employees/partners/customers thinking?" To do so, perversely, may enhance power far more than the unreflexively general instinct to consider only one's own needs and feelings as valid input for improved performance.

Finally, we tend to blame our failures on external factors and attribute our successes to our own greatness. Studies indicate it is a far better strategy to take the opposite approach: be your own harshest critic, thereby subjecting yourself to an attack similar to that parsed out by the members of the !Kung. Mark Zuckerberg and Warren Buffett, for instance, minimize their perceptions of power by refusing to assert that their greatness is the result of personal brilliance; instead, they attribute their success to the decidedly humble factor of "luck."[39] By contrast, Tyco's Kozlowski and Ebbers acted to enhance their power perceptions, acting contrary to Zuckerberg and Buffett and in contradiction to the best practices set forth by Jim Collins in *Good to Great*.[40] Kozlowksi, for instance, "reigned as the archetype of avarice," living his life not unlike kings of old.[41] Ebbers was a "cowboy-wearing, larger-than-life personality" that "bragged about his high-flying stock price."[42] More pointedly, Ebbers refused to take responsibility for his company's failures during his own criminal trial, with the *New York Times* writing that "Mr. Ebbers displayed a folksy innocence that was part of the defense effort to cast him as someone who relied on others with greater expertise to handle the details of running WorldCom."[43]

And if all that is not enough, perhaps you can take a note from the !Kung and ask your countrymen to lob a few insults your way (Figure 7.1).

FIGURE 7.1 Avoiding the elixir of power.

References

1. Richard Borshay Lee, "Eating Christmas in the Kalahari," *Natural History* (1969).
2. Id. at 1.
3. Id.
4. Id. at 3.
5. Id. at 3–4.
6. Kabasakal and Bodur, *supra* note 44 at 588.
7. Peter Drucker, "What Makes an Effective Executive," *Harvard Business Review* (June 2004).
8. Jon K. Maner and Nicole L. Mead, "The Essential Tension between Leadership and Power," 99 *Journal of Personality and Social Psychology* 482, 483 (2010) (citing to Galinsky et al., 2008; Guinote, 2007; Smith and Trope, 2006).
9. Collins, *supra* note 142 at 29.
10. Maner and Mead, *supra* note 425 at 483 (citing to e.g., McClelland, 1975; Tiedens et al., 2007).
11. Id. at 482. (citing to Kipnis, 1972, 1976).
12. Id. at 483.
13. Daniel PinK, *To Sell Is Human: The Surprising Truth about Moving Others* 59 (Riverhead Books) (2013) (citing to Adam D. Galinsky, Joe C. Magee, M. Ena Inesi, and Deborah H. Gruenfeld, "Power and Perspectives Not Taken," *Psychological Science* 17 (2006): 1068–1074).
14. Id. (citing to Galinsky at 1070).
15. Id. (citing to Michael W. Kraus, Paul K. Piff, and Dacher Keltner, "Social Class as Culture: The Convergence of Resources and Rank in the Social Realm," *Current Directions in Psychological Science* 20 (4) (2011): 246–250).
16. See generally, Federico Aime, Stephen Humphrey, D. Scott Deure, and Jeffrey B. Paul, "The Riddle of Heterarchy: Power Transitions in Cross-Functional Teams," 57 *Academy of Management Journal*, 327 (2014).
17. Roderick Kramer, "The Harder They Fall," *Harvard Business Review* 2 (2003).
18. Clarke, *supra* note 136 at 331.
19. Id. at 337.
20. Id.
21. Id. at 334, 337.
22. Id. at 331
23. Id. at 348.
24. Kramer, *supra* note 434 at 3.
25. Id.
26. C. Haney et al., *supra* note 2.
27. Id.
28. Id.
29. Id.
30. P.G. Zimbardo, "Obedience to Authority," 29 *American Psychologist*, 566–567 (1974).
31. For the study on following commands of those in uniform, see L. Bickman, "The Social Power of a Uniform," 4 *Journal of Applied Social Psychology* 47–61 (1974). For the physician study, see S.U. Rehman, P.J. Nietert, D.W. Cope, and A.O. Kilpatrick, "What to Wear Today? Effect of Doctor's Attire on the Trust and Confidence of Patients," 118 *The American Journal of Medicine*, 1279–1286 (2005).
32. H. Adam, and A.D. Galinsky, "Enclothed Cognition," 48 *Journal of Experimental Social Psychology*, 918–925 (2012).
33. K.A. Karl, L.M. Hall, and J.V. Peluchette, "City Employee Perceptions of the Impact of Dress and Appearance: You Are What You Wear," 42 *Public Personnel Management*, 452–470 (2013).

34 Finding that productivity is affected by casual clothing: see, J.V. Peluchette, and K. Karl, "The Impact of Workplace Attire on Employee Self-Perceptions," 18 *Human Resource Development Quarterly*, 345–360 (2007). Finding that productivity is not affected by casual clothing: see Karl et al., *supra* note 450.
35 Peluchette and Karl, *supra* note 451.
36 Montupet, *supra* note 10.
37 Ariely, *supra* note 102 at 211–213.
38 Pink *supra* note 430 at 61 (citing Adam D. Galinsky, William W. Maddux, Debra Gilin, and Judith B. White, "Why It Pays to Get inside the Head of Your Opponent: The Differential Effects of Perspective Taking and Empathy in Negotiations," 19 *Psychological Science* no. 4 (2008).
39 For Warren Buffett on luck, see Joe Welsenthal, "We Love What Warren Buffett Says about Life, Luck, and Winning the 'Ovarian Lottery,'" *Business Insider* (Dec. 10, 2013), http://www.businessinsider.com/warren-buffett-on-the-ovarian-lottery-2013-12; for Mark Zuckerberg on luck, see Catherine Clifford, "Billionaire Mark Zuckerberg: Success like Mine Only Happens with Luck, and That's a Huge Problem We Need to Fix," *CNBC* (July 24, 2017), https://www.cnbc.com/2017/07/24/billionaire-mark-zuckerberg-success-like-mine-only-happens-with-luck.html.
40 See inter alia, Collins, *supra* note 142 at 24.
41 David A. Kapaln, "Tyco's 'Piggy,' Out of Prison and Living Small," *The New York Times* (Mar. 1, 2015) https://www.nytimes.com/2015/03/02/business/dealbook/dennis-kozlowskis-path-from-infamy-to-obscurity.html.
42 Frank Ahrens, "Ebbers, One in a Long Line of Egos," *The Washington Post* (Mar. 16, 2015), http://www.washingtonpost.com/wp-dyn/articles/A38401-2005Mar15.html.
43 Ken Belson, "Ebbers Mounts an 'I Never Knew' Defense," *The New York Times* (Mar. 1, 2005), http://www.nytimes.com/2005/03/01/business/ebbers-mounts-an-i-never-knew-defense.html.

8
UNCERTAINTY AVOIDANCE

The chameleon looks in all directions before moving.

Ugandan Proverb

Think about the future – say, five years from now. Did a tingle of excitement just course through your body, or was it something closer to anxiety, fear or maybe even dread? As with all these dimensions, your answer may vary depending on where you call home. Some societies are made more anxious by the future than others and seek to avoid the risk of uncertainty in their lives. These people are said to have a strong uncertainty avoidance (UA).

A good example of this can be seen in a study done on American, Chinese and Japanese graduate students. The participants were presented with two options. Under the first option, the participants would gain an immediate reward; under the second option, they could potentially receive a bigger reward, but that larger amount had a payout probability ranging from 5 to 95 percent. The participants had to indicate which option they would choose. Rational people, of course, discount the value of that larger payout as the probability of getting it decreases, but the amount of discounting varies by culture. In this case, Japanese and American students discounted very similarly, whereas the Chinese students showed less discounting, suggesting they were less risk averse.[1]

It may be that nature coded some of us to be more risk averse than others. Susan Cain's research illustrates how a population's variant risk seeking and risk avoidance behaviors can actually benefit a species' survival, "From fruit flies to house cats to mountain goats, from sunfish to bush baby primates to Eurasian tit birds, scientists have discovered that approximately 20 percent of the members of many species are 'slow to warm,' while the other 80 percent are 'fast' types who venture forth boldly without noticing much of what's going on around them. [Researchers believe] that both types of animals exist because they have radically different survival strategies, each of which pays off differently at different times. ... 'Shy' animals forage less often and widely for food, conserving energy, sticking to the sidelines, and surviving when predators come calling. Bolder animals sally forth, swallowed regularly by those farther up the food chain but surviving when food is scarce, and they need to assume more risk."[2]

A similar survival mechanism may help explain the diversity of risk aversion in human societies. Our level of risk aversion, however, is not just a natural occurrence. Just as animals would over time learn to be more adventurous when food levels fall – and less adventurous when predators rise – so too is our risk aversion likely to be higher where the future is objectively dangerous than in situations where it is safer. It is clear, for example, that a poor farmer has more to fear of the future than a wealthy aristocrat. If the crops were to fail next year, the farmer and not the aristocrat would suffer more. The best way for the farmer to reduce his exposure to this risky future may be increasing his stockpile of food – in short, by becoming wealthier. If the best way to do this is to install new machinery, the farmer will likely be prompt to do just that. If the stockpile remains too small for comfort, he may advocate a study of the sciences, perhaps by pushing his child to study in the university or by willingly paying taxes for a stronger educational system. If the farmer is prone to having his food stolen by the aristocrat, he may call upon the courts to provide greater legal protections.

These actions – the embrace of the rule of law, technology, and science – are precisely those taken by many societies that have a strong desire to minimize future uncertainty. Over time, these are likely to make the society quite stable and wealthy, just as the farmer had hoped.[3] Thus the descendants of this farmer are unlikely to give much thought to the possibility of a crop failure – the granaries of the local Walmart are full, and they can even afford to enjoy their favorite delicacies at French bistros, Italian joints and steakhouses. They are furthermore more likely to be educated and thus employable in a variety of fields, perhaps even in a variety of countries, in the event the proverbial crops fail and one's immediate employer goes out of business. Their fear of the future, therefore, is greatly minimized relative to that of their great-great-grandfather. With this greater cushion, they may be willing to take greater risks in their own lives.

If, however, the state is too weak to staff the universities with scientists and collect taxes for the educational system, and it's too fractious to impose restrictions on the rogue aristocrat, then the farmer is likely to rely on self-help mechanisms. He may band together with other precariously situated farmers to uphold justice and perhaps use this force to steal from others during times of scarcity. In this scenario the great-great-grandchildren of this farmer will be in much the same position as their ancestor and still rather at risk for their future.

This idea that the environment in which we live affects our risk tolerance is more than speculation. Adam Grant, in his work *Originals*, noted that researchers Frank Sulloway and Richard Zweigenhaft made a surprising statistical finding involving professional baseball players. As it happens, the most prolific base stealers in history are predominantly younger brothers. They found that younger brothers attempt to steal a base 10.6 times more often than major leaguers that are older brothers, and when the attempt is made, they are 3.2 times more successful.[4] The correlation was so strong that numerous studies have been extended to determine whether younger children were less risk averse than older siblings not just on the baseball field, but in all facets of life.

Researchers found that, indeed, younger children are more likely to take risks in their personal and professional lives: they are more likely to go against the status quo as scientists and more likely to take risks as politicians.[5] They are also more likely to use drugs or alcohol, to perform poorly on standardized tests, and to disdain prestigious occupations.[6] We would expect that this risk-taking would carry over into the world of business decisions, causing the younger born to be more open to risk. If the statistics on base stealing are any indication, we might expect that these individuals will in fact take better chances than others, if for no other reason than because they have more experience taking risks.

Why would this happen? The reason may be that parents are more likely to coddle younger children, which leads those children to view the world around them as less threatening than older children. This may contribute to positive risk-taking behavior. Less favorably, parents may alternatively pay less attention to younger children, leading to a worldview in which there are few consequences for wrongdoing and which may lead to negative risk-taking behavior. Just like the farmer and his descendants, children are an evolving, ever learning product of their environments.

The desire to take risks by doing things differently is thought to be further exacerbated by a need for uniqueness such as noted earlier with our beer drinking individualists. If one's older siblings have already taken prestige careers in law and medicine, that younger sibling may decide instead to carve out a niche as a cook or an actor.[7]

Indeed, standup comedian Amy Poehler provides an anecdote that corroborates these findings. Poehler, for those not familiar, spent years performing in Chicago comedy clubs – in a most uncertain, high risk, low-paying environment – before succeeding in spectacular fashion on *Saturday Night Live*.

As you read Poehler's reflections on childhood, note her emphasis on her safe foundation and supportive parents and the ways in which she indicates this led to both positive and negative risk-taking:

> We never locked our door [growing up]. I had a younger brother whom I loved, but also liked. I thought my mother was the most beautiful person in the world, and my father was a superhero *who would always protect me* [emphasis added]. I wish this feeling for every child on earth. Because of this safe foundation, I had to create my own drama. … I was dealt two loving parents, and they encouraged me to be curious. This *safety net* [emphasis added], combined with the small drumbeat inside of me, meant that I did a lot of silly things to try to make life seem exciting.[8]

This suggests nature alone is not responsible for our risk tolerance. Our environments, and this certainly includes our societies, also play an important role. This helps us understand in part why societies of the world are so diverse when it comes to risk tolerance.

A Contradictory Result: High Societal UA Means Low Individual UA

Societies with historically high levels of uncertainty avoidance have at times acted in such a way as to reduce uncertainty through the accumulation of greater wealth and stability. As a result, the people of these historically high UA countries can become quite open to uncertainty. A manifestation of this openness to uncertainty is that which is different is more readily accepted in these countries, so tolerance and a willingness to accept differences of opinion tends to be higher.[9] However, the structures that facilitated an openness to risk and embracing the future – the machinery to produce more crops, the belief in science to ever improve and the rule of law to protect – all stay in place. The result is that people with *low* UA live in societies organized around systems maximizing orderliness and predictability. Perversely, this orderliness and predictability is often brought about by historically *high* UA, which resulted in the embrace of laws, technology and science in earlier ages.

We can see this contradictory phenomenon with a glance at Singapore. Singaporeans are rated as having the lowest uncertainty in all the world,[10] but more than almost any other country they have taken steps to reduce their risk exposure.[11] The reason may be Singapore's historically precarious position: Singapore faced an uncertain beginning when it became independent from Malaysia in 1959. With few natural resources, a tiny land mass, low economic development and surrounded by larger neighbors, Singapore's very existence was precarious, and much like the farmer fearing crop failure, there was little margin for error.

Singaporeans responded with an extraordinary period of development, characterized by very strong institutions and legal systems and culminating in one of the most stable, developed and wealthy countries in the world.[12] Consequently, the rules and law that have reduced uncertainty live on, but they do so in a country where the average Singaporean lives quite the stable life. Thus, many Singaporeans now welcome fewer rules and more independence in order to achieve greater self-actualization, a level in one's hierarchy of needs that Maslow terms the pinnacle of human happiness.[13] Other countries that have acted to reduce the risk of an uncertain future, and which now have low uncertainty avoidance, include mostly Nordic or Germanic European societies, including Switzerland, Sweden, Denmark, Germany, Austria, and Finland.[14]

Not all countries, however, have effectively implemented these risk-reducing institutions or for that matter any other forms of protection. Those with high levels of uncertainty avoidance, therefore, often live in less-developed countries in which the future remains a riskier proposition. They in turn may react in profoundly different ways.

They may *desire* greater science, technology and rule of law to minimize the uncertain dangers of the future, but in the absence of a viable path toward implementation, they are forced on minimizing risk much like the farmer who recruited a posse to reduce his risk. Don't, for instance, plant a new crop if you are not sure it will grow or if it could attract thieves, even if it would potentially be of greater value. They may also resist outsiders, exhibiting higher levels of racism and prejudice, ethnocentrism and intolerance for differing opinions.[15] The reason is probably that anything different is seen as potentially dangerous, and, thus inclusion is not worth the perceived risk. That which is known, by contrast, is predictable. This has important implications for international business, as such exchanges can be likely perceived as presenting greater transactional uncertainty. Countries exhibiting this quality include Thailand, Nigeria, Albania, Iran, Egypt, El Salvador, and Morocco,[16] and more generally the South Asian, Middle Eastern, Sub-Saharan African and Eastern European regions.[17]

The consequences for businesses are myriad but include the possibility that in countries that have acted to reduce the risks of the future, the people of those countries may have long forgotten the reasons those protections were first put in place. The walls may be seen not as defensive, but as oppressive. Assured of relative safety within this world, they may seek to knock down those walls, reducing rules and increasing flexibility. By contrast, those in less developed countries and with less stable environments may welcome greater clarity and formalization in their work and everyday lives but may resist the predictably unpredictable nature of international business transactions and relationships (Table 8.1).

TABLE 8.1 Practicing uncertainty avoidance (from highest to lowest)[18]

1. Switzerland	21. Hong Kong	41. Costa Rica
2. Sweden	22. Ireland	42. Italy
3. Singapore	23. Nigeria	43. Slovenia
4. Denmark	24. Kuwait	44. Ecuador
5. Germany (West)	25. Namibia	45. Iran
6. Austria	26. Mexico	46. Kazakhstan
7. Germany (East)	27. Indonesia	47. Morocco
8. Finland	28. Zimbabwe	48. Argentina
9. Switzerland (French speaking)	29. India	49. Turkey
10. China	30. United States	50. Poland
11. Malaysia	31. Zambia	51. El Salvador
12. New Zealand	32. South Africa (white sample)	52. Brazil
13. Netherlands	33. Japan	53. Colombia
14. England	34. Egypt	54. South Korea
15. South Africa (black sample)	35. Israel	55. Georgia
16. Canada (English speaking)	36. Qatar	56. Venezuela
17. Albania	37. Spain	57. Greece
18. France	38. Thailand	58. Bolivia
19. Australia	39. Portugal	59. Guatemala
20. Taiwan	40. Philippines	60. Hungary
		61. Russia

Reducing Risk

Hofstede writes that there are three common reactions when a society, like Singapore, is anxious about an uncertain future. The first is to bring safety through technology; the second is to use laws to restore predictability; and the third is to seek the comforts of universal scientific truths, spirituality or religion. Additionally, a further response to uncertainty avoidance may be to work hard and therefore try to "beat the future," as Hofstede puts it.[19] This need to work hard was explored in the "Need for Achievement" section of Chapter 5. It is no surprise then that countries like Singapore with historically high uncertainty avoidance eventually reach higher levels of prosperity.[20]

Technology

While countries with low uncertainty avoidance are more likely to be technological innovators, countries with high uncertainty avoidance practices are most ready to adopt new technologies. This may appear counterintuitive, but technology can bring security from the elements, as well as security against outside aggressors. Hofstede writes: "We build houses, dikes, power stations, and ICBMs which are meant to give us a feeling of security."[21] Additionally, more mundane things like "product warranties, insurance policies or investment markets and plans" can serve to reduce uncertainty.[22] Countries with high levels of UA tend to be more technologically advanced than those low on the spectrum. As discussed above, it may be that these societies' steps to tame uncertainty have worked, leading many members of these societies to actually feel less anxiety about the future.

Japan has the eighth strongest aversion to uncertainty under Hofstede's findings.[23] They may have good reason to fear the future, as recurrent earthquakes, tsunamis and volcanoes mark the island nation as seventeenth most at risk of natural disasters and first among developed countries.[24] Perhaps as a result Japan has taken to building infrastructure such as railways with a resistance to environmental hazards like no other country.[25]

While countries with high UA quickly *adopt* new technologies, researchers have found that countries with low UA tend to *invent* many of those technologies, as they are willing to take the risks that are inherent in new ventures.[26] For instance, entrepreneurship thrives in the United States, which may be indicative of Americans' willingness to embark on high risk ventures. So too, is the US stock market plagued occasionally by dramatic swings in value that do not seem to significantly deter US investors over the long-term, a system further supported by a legal and economic system that focuses on growth, rather than the minimization of future risks.[27] While the uncertainty avoidance index of the United States is moderate or even high overall, it is among the lowest of the developed countries.[28]

In more risk-averse countries, the precise opposite is often true. Innovation tends to lag, but when new products or technologies are developed, these societies tend to be the most effective implementers.[29] For instance, Germany is relatively risk averse.[30] There, the economy is buoyed by deeply established organizations such as DaimlerChrysler, Allianz, Volkswagen, Bayer, and Siemens Group, with a stock market growth that is modest yet relatively steady.[31]

In 1997, the German government sought to increase innovation, so a stock market for young companies and high-risk tech businesses – akin to NASDAQ in the United States – was opened to much fanfare.[32] Unfortunately, this market was a disaster and shut down only five years later.[33] As usual, the reasons were complex,[34] but it is fair to suggest that a disdain for risk proved in part the culprit. For instance, the German legal system and banking system both favor established firms over startups.[35] High-risk, high-reward technology firms in particular often struggled to gain the attention of lenders.[36] As a result, the old, classic German companies continued to thrive, but very few new names were added to the mix.[37] The *Financial Times* blamed the failure of tech companies on a lack of available capital funds and quoted a former senior engineer at Twitter and Airbnb as saying, "German business culture was less tolerant of risk-taking and failure, noting that it took less time to create a company in the US than it did to open a bank account for our business in Germany."[38]

By contrast, Germans have been rapid adaptors of renewable energy sources. They lead the world in solar energy use and generated more than one-third of their energy needs through alternative sources in the first half of 2017.[39]

And if we return to Japan, we can see that it too has historically done better in adopting new technologies than in developing its own. For example, its car companies gained a reputation for replicating the best features of foreign automobiles but without much in the way of technical advances. And in the postwar years, Sony, Panasonic and others took the world by storm after adopting W. Edward Deming's management principles, which emphasized quality and efficiency through improved management rather than innovation.[40] Although Deming had found little success in the United States, Japanese companies were at this time seeking strategies to succeed in a postwar world.[41] They found in Deming a path to global success and were surprisingly receptive to his ideas even though he was an outsider.

Finally, Hofstede speaks of the adoption of infrastructure and particularly military hardware. The legacy of World War II for Japan means that it is not the militarized power it once was. But what about North Korea? While we don't have statistics on the hermit nation, it's fair to conclude that the country's uncertainty avoidance is quite high. Evidence suggests that the people of North Korea are constantly bombarded with propaganda suggesting an invasion of the country is imminent. Additionally, the people of culturally similar South Korea statistically feel particularly vulnerable concerning their future.[42] How, then, does North Korea use technology to reduce uncertainty? As any watcher of current events might surmise, they do so through promotion of military technology such as their nuclear weapons and ICBM capabilities much as Hofstede's studies predicted. The North Korean regime seems to believe, and only time will tell if this is a correct belief, that in military hardware they can buy protection from the perceived dangers of the world.

Religion and Ideologies

Religion too can help ease the anxiety that an uncertain future brings.[43] We see religion throughout the world, but countries in which leaders have taken few steps to reduce uncertainty tend to have higher levels of religiosity, as the citizenry seek security through mechanisms outside the governmental framework.[44] Hofstede notes that the term "religion" is quite broad and can include "ideologies, such as Marxism, dogmatic Capitalism, or movements that preach an escape into meditation. *Even science is included*"[45] (emphasis added). Scientists, for instance, and indeed scholars of all stripes, attempt to explain the world in a way that is coherent and therefore reduces uncertainty.[46] In looking to the science programs of high UA countries, we see the Austrians with the ninth most science, technology, engineering and math (STEM) graduates as a percentage of their population and the second most PhDs per capita, the Finns ranking fourth in STEM graduates, the Swedes third, the Germans second, and the South Koreans first.[47]

A relevant byproduct of the search for predictability in high uncertainty avoidance societies is a desire to avoid the unknown and a desire to find "ultimate, absolute truths" through either religion or science.[48] These absolute truths imply that what is true in one place is true in all places, at all times. This is a mindset that is often anathema to successful cultural integration. Cross-cultural actors should beware of this possible bias when meeting people from high risk avoiding countries and should be prepared to meet one's counterpart more than halfway to help reduce anxieties.

Rules and Laws – Universalism versus Particularism

> For my friends everything, for my enemies the law.
> Óscar R. Benavides
> *Former President of Peru*

Laws and other formal rules also increase predictability. Hofstede wrote: "[Uncertainty avoidance] can be defined as the degree to which people in a country prefer structured over unstructured situations. Structured situations are those in which there are clear rules as to how one should behave. These rules can be written down, but they can also be unwritten and imposed by tradition."[49]

This preference for, or reliance upon, rules and systems is reflected in a related cultural dimension, which Fons Trompenaars calls "universalism." Universalists are driven by the idea that there are certain rules and ways of doing things from which deviation is undesirable, even unethical. These ways of doing things, for better or worse, hold true for everyone: the self and one's family, friends, strangers and even enemies.[50] A particularist, by contrast, may hold that relationships with family, with friends and other personal relations, bring obligations that justify deviations from the general rules or special treatment. With some exceptions, institutions in these particularist societies are often less developed and consequently less relied upon.[51] This preference for, or willingness to deviate from, formal systems of rule and law is closely related to uncertainty avoidance.

Countries in which respondents indicate a preference for particularist values include Venezuela, Nepal, South Korea, Russia, and China.[52] More moderate forms of particularism are seen in countries such as Belgium, Singapore, Japan, France, and Spain.[53] By contrast, Central European, Anglo countries including the United States and Nordic European countries exhibit a preference for universalist systems.[54] These results generally align with the uncertainty avoidance results, which saw Russia, South Korea, and Venezuela with low UA, Central European and Nordic countries with high UA, and Anglo countries with relatively high UA.[55] China is an outlier, with high UA scores but low particularist preferences.[56]

What of the visible manifestations – the outer layer of the onion – of particularist and universalist cultures? In fact, there are many. For instance, do drivers speed and obey traffic laws? Do they stop for pedestrians (and do pedestrians stop at traffic lights)? Anyone who has traveled to a Scandinavian country can attest that even when no cars are in sight, the locals will not cross when the pedestrian light is red. The odd tourist may do so, and disapproving frowns will mark the faces of the rule-abiding locals. In many countries, pedestrian lights are merely "advisory." In some, they practically lack all relevance. Try crossing a street in urban India, or Cairo, Egypt or Ho Chi Minh City in Vietnam for example, a treacherous experience where the life-preserving urge to dodge vehicles quickly overtakes any sense of righteousness about the state of the pedestrian light.

Question Often, Judge Slowly

The crucial point is that particularism and universalism are both responses to our environments, in the same way that jay walking is a necessary reaction to a particular environment.

Just as with UA more generally, universalism and particularism have developed in response to dramatically different political, social and even religious systems. Catholics, for instance, with their history of absolution for breaking the rules, tend to be more particularist than do Protestants.[57]

Universalists may justify this standardized behavior. They may ask: If you make a small exception for your friend, will you tomorrow make a big exception for your sister? And what of the people that are disadvantaged by those "exceptions"? Isn't that unfair to them? They might even channel Emmanuel Kant's categorical imperative in asking: What if everyone behaved in this way? Would not the rule of law itself collapse? But of course this presumes that the present rule of law is adequate and desirable.

Equality in universalist countries is often upheld by a strong rule of law and other institutional support that provides some semblance of fairness.[58] The United States, for example, is considered a highly universalist country and also the most litigious.[59] In particularist countries, there may be less institutional support, demanding that individuals – rather than courts or other institutions – take a stand to uphold the rights and interests of their in-group.

Trompenaars asked people from a variety of cultures whether they would testify against a friend who had accidentally injured a pedestrian while driving too fast.[60] What he found was that universalists were more likely than particularists to report the facts honestly and expose even their friends to punishment. What is perhaps most interesting about this study, however, was that for the universalists, the smaller the injury to the pedestrian, the less likely they were to report honestly. In this case, they believed, their moral obligation to the law and to this stranger was small and so might give way to their obligation to their friends.[61] But for particularists, the opposite was true: the more serious the injury to the pedestrian, the less likely they were to report the friend.[62] In this case, the severity of the injury meant there was a higher probability of the friend facing serious punishment, so the moral obligation to the friend was that much higher.

This study is important for two principal reasons. First, it shows that universalists believe they have an obligation to friends and family (as long as that does not take away from the rights of others), just as particularists believe that even strangers have rights (as long as those rights do not demand causing harm to one's relations). In this way, we see that even at the far ends of the spectrum, there are shared values. It is the relative weight of the values that varies.

Secondly, we can begin to see in this study a relative respect, or lack thereof, for the "rule of law." In many cases, particularist behaviors are a reaction to corruption in the given society that erodes the moral authority of the government. Indeed, the more particularist a country, the more corrupt the society tends to be,[63] and the legal systems of corrupt societies, by their corruption, are essentially by definition forfeiting any claim to legitimacy. Where the laws do not reflect the values of society, the obligation to respect those laws is more easily denied. Indeed, if one believes the punishment his friend will face for injuring that pedestrian would be meted out unfairly, then it becomes much easier – perhaps even moral – to lie. In this way, we can see how universalists and particularists may each consider themselves the moral actor, and each may indeed be moral given the environment.

Just as universalists tend to view particularists as corrupt or unethical, the particularist tends to view the universalist as unethical or coldhearted. Ultimately, both sentiments may be undergirded by some misunderstandings. The relationship-oriented behavior of particularists may be a core component of the particularist's worldview. The particularist may find it unfathomable that a universalist wouldn't give his child a push toward that dream job, or that he would turn a friend in for breaking the law. What are friends and family for, if not to help one another? But the particularist may fail to recognize that strong and legitimate institutions decrease the need of giving one's favored relations that extra push; the rules, in theory, make the playing field more equal. The universalist, by contrast, may label the particularist as corrupt by his exceptionalism, without asking whether the rules being broken are themselves legitimate or sufficient. This is not to advocate nepotism or corruption, but rather to note that the so-called "right" decision may not be the same in all places at all times.

The car accident scenario reveals that there is often a visible component to particularism, or what we might term for consistency in our work here the outer layer of the onion. But what we see here is that there is a strong inner layer too, representing a worldview and even an ethos. This is therefore the first of many cases where the cross-cultural participant must observe carefully, question often and judge slowly.

This rule-based orientation applies not just at the governmental level, but within the organization as well. For instance, the reader will recall that the hierarchical society seeks to maintain social order through clearly delineated positions of power and limited empowerment of nonmanagerial employees. In this case, employee behavior is circumscribed such that their range of behavior is relatively predictable. The egalitarian country, by contrast, gives significant autonomy to employees. This in turn makes the behavior of individuals less certain than in highly structured environments of hierarchical organizations, and so these dimensions would seem to conflict.[64] In countries that have both high UA and are egalitarian, organizations may seek to minimize uncertainty by establishing more rules and structures to increase predictability of otherwise rather autonomous employees.

For instance, Austria is ranked as the most egalitarian country on earth, but the society practices very high levels of UA. The practical result is that Austrian employees are given autonomy, access to information; they work well in groups, and they are comfortable with unstructured work environments.[65] Organizations operating in high UA countries, including Austria, also seek to facilitate open channels of feedback, as communication serves as a warning beacon of coming risks.[66] But at the same time, rules and norms may establish the parameters of behavior for the fast changing work groups and for the organization as a whole. Consequently, the rules are used not to establish hierarchy and lines of reporting but instead to establish a mutually agreed upon set of rules and norms upon which the behavior of empowered employees may be made more predictable.[67]

All these rules can restore a certain level of predictability and may result in greater stability, but these organizations and societies may also be less responsive to sudden changes. In high uncertainty avoidance organizations for example, change to the mission or objectives of organizations where employees and leaders have high uncertainty avoidance often requires changing the rules, which can be a slow process.[68] "For this reason, the [uncertainty avoiding] culture does not adapt well to turbulent environments."[69] This is exacerbated by a tendency to respond to changes in the environment by resisting those changes and holding fast to the status quo rather than adapting.[70] Consequently, high UA may increase stability but also render the society unprepared when change does inevitably occur.

The proper response is to recognize that, as Hofstede posited, rules can be either good or bad. Good rules are of the sort that foster economic growth in the many countries with high UA; bad rules are those that stymie innovation, miss new opportunities and fail to respond to change. This is as true at the organizational level as at the societal level. Managers must identify the "goldilocks" principle – the "just right" number and intensity of internal rules – needed to respond to the cultural environment and other factors specific to the organization.

Consider this famous experiment as an example of a "bad" rule:

> Gneezy and Rustichini carried out research at day-care centers in Israel. The management had a problem: parents were supposed to pick up their children at four in the afternoon but often arrived late, so that the staff had to wait. The managers decided to introduce a penalty. When a parent arrived more than ten minutes late, three dollars extra per child was added to the monthly bill of $380. The penalty was introduced at six of the ten day-care centers. The four day-care centers where the penalty was not introduced acted as a control group. ... In these four day-care centers, the percentage of late parents remained the same. The managers hoped that the penalties would solve the problems at the six day-care centers where they were applied. Unfortunately, instead of the number of late parents dropping, it actually grew. In short order, the percentage had actually doubled.[71]

Before the penalty, people were only showing up on time to respect the social norms of the society in which they lived, but the financial penalty wiped out the other motives. The punishment for arriving late added a financial contour, introducing a whole new human calculus. Under the new system, "[a]rriving on time was an economic consideration: 'Shall I pay the price of the penalty for being late, so that I can finish my work first?' This placed moral and social motives in the background."[72] The economic motive might have worked, but not at these small levels. Conversely, too high of a penalty for late arrivals would have deterred parents from using the day-care center at all. Thus, a balance was needed.

The new rule at the Israeli day-care center also failed to account for the existing social norms, or values, of parents. By leveraging the social norm in a more effective way, it is possible that the center could have decreased late arrivals even without a financial incentive. Conversely, where the law reflects values, compliance quickly follows. Where the laws fail to reflect values, however, there is a disconnect or a "destabilizing tension," which reduces compliance.[73] Managers must therefore understand and respect the values that people hold, such as the cultural dimensions addressed here.

Contractual/Legal Implications of Universalism and the Role of Trust

In universalist countries, the reliance on formal arrangements extends to include legal institutions. This means that there is a reliance on contracts, among other things. Universalists tend therefore to operate with clearly defined employee contracts inclusive of a well-defined set of responsibilities. Employees may be evaluated against these preestablished responsibilities, and both employee and employer – comfortable with the "fairness" inherent therein – submit to the process.

Managers must recall that in particularist cultures, however, the organizational or institutional framework ensuring fairness is more often lacking. Reliance on the manifestations of those institutions, such as legal contracts, is often fruitless. After all, where legal institutions are weak or corrupted, the enforceability of contracts is equally weak.

As something of a proxy for this, the World Bank's Ease of Doing Business Index includes details on the enforceability of contracts in countries, including detailed time, cost and quality indicators.[74] In Venezuela, for example, the most particularist of countries, the average contract requires 620 days in court to enforce, while legal fees amount to almost 50 percent of the value of the claim. The quality of contractual enforcement in Venezuela is thus ranked 137th out of 190 countries.[75] Given its current political instability and rampant inflation, that ranking is probably still worse. India, another particularist country, scores even lower at 172nd.[76]

While contracts in countries like Venezuela may be fruitless, Trompenaars writes that in other countries "[w]eighty contracts are a way of life in universalist cultures." As noted above, this is particularly true in the United States, where this is heightened by a relatively assertive culture that emphasizes competitive behavior (see Chapter 10 for more on assertive cultures).[77] In relationship-oriented particularist cultures, however, "if you introduce contracts with strict requirements and penalty clauses, the implied message is that one party would cheat the other if not legally restrained from doing so. *Those who feel they are not trusted may accordingly behave in untrustworthy ways*" (emphasis added).[78]

This is an important point. While Trompenaars does not elaborate further, there is an abundance of behavioral science research that confirms this belief.

Researchers Robert Rosenthal and Lenore Jacobson conducted an experiment in an American elementary school. Students took an IQ test at the beginning of the year. Teachers were then provided with a list of students who were likely to make an intellectual leap throughout the year. In reality, the students were randomly chosen. At the end of the year, another IQ test was performed. The IQs of the students labeled "promising" increased by at least 12 percent more than those of the other students. As the researchers explained, "when teachers expected that certain children would show greater intellectual development, those children did show greater intellectual development."[79]

The teachers had established a warmer relationship with the children they believed were more gifted, providing more learning materials, more opportunities to respond to problems, and higher-quality feedback on their work.[80] The children who were trusted and believed in responded accordingly.

Researchers Rosenthal and Jacobson further showed us that there is a tendency to live up or down to expectations, and if that legal contract is seen to indicate a lack of trustworthiness, that just may be a self-fulfilling prophecy. Instead, seek to learn the legal best practices in your country of business. For example, in parts of Asia, Latin America, the Middle East, and North Africa, it may be that a flexible contract, subject to renegotiation with broader terms, is the price of admission.[81]

The particularist, by contrast, should determine whether fairness is built into the organizational or institutional system. She should try instead to understand that thick legal contracts with onerous terms are not meant to offend – they are meant to provide a foundation upon which trust can be built. Particularist cultures, lacking or abstaining from ironclad contracts, first seek trust and only then move on to finalize agreements. They do this because without legal guarantees, one must establish trust prior to expending resources on new business relationships. As Trompenaars writes: "This process takes a considerable amount of time, but for particularists, the time taken to grow close to your partner is saved in the avoidance of trouble in the future. If you are not willing to take time now, the relationship is unlikely to survive vicissitudes."

When entering a new country, look to where the country falls on this scale. Then ask how the trait is exhibited – what are the outer, observable parts of the onion – and what does this signal at a deeper level? Ask furthermore what is expected not just of the manager but of the *person* in her daily interactions; ask whether behavior is a response to a corrupted or weak institutional system, and whether trust is established in conjunction with, or through avoidance of, the institutional system (Table 8.2).

TABLE 8.2 Uncertainty avoidance onion diagram

Inner	Middle	Outer
Economics (poor)	High UA	Few institutions to minimize risks, with insufficient technologies, rule of law, and higher levels of religiosity; weak rule of law results in particularist tendencies, e.g., nepotism, rule-breaking, corruption, reliance on relationships (not contracts); people long for greater stability
Economics (wealthy)	Low UA	Many institutions to minimize risk, including robust technologies, strong rule of law, and scientific or political ideologies partly in place of religious ideology; strong rule of law results in universalist tendencies, ready resort to litigation, reliance on contracts; stability may increase, while ability to innovate or react to change may decrease; people become relatively numb to the risks of the future

References

1 Wanjiang Du, Leonard Green, and Joel Meyerson, "Cross-Cultural Comparison of Discounting Delayed and Probabilistic Rewards," 52 *The Psychological Record* 479–492 (2002).
2 Cain, *supra* note 87 at 157.
3 Mary Sully de Luque and Mansour Javidan, "Uncertainty Avoidance," in *Culture, Leadership, & Organizations: The GLOBE Study of 62 Societies* 630 (eds. Robert House, Paul J. Hanges et al., SAGE Publications) (2004).
4 Related in Grant, *supra* note 72 at 140 (citing to Frank J. Sulloway and Richard L. Zweigenhaft, "Birth Order and Risk-Taking in Athletics: A Meta-Analysis and Study of Major League Baseball," *Personality and Social Psychology Review* 14 (2010): 402–416).
5 Id. at 141 (citing to Frank J. Sulloway, *Born to Rebel: Birth Order, Family Dynamics, and Creative Lives*. New York: Vintage, 1997; "Birth Order and Evolutionary Psychology: A Meta-Analytic Overview," *Psychological Inquiry* 6 (1995): 75–80; and "Sources of Scientific Innovation: A Meta-Analytic Approach (Commentary on Simonton, 2009)," *Perspectives on Psychological Science* 4 (2009): 455–459; Frank J. Sulloway, "Born to Rebel and Its Critics," *Politics and the Life Sciences* 19 (2000): 181–202, and *Birth Order and Political Rebellion: An Assessment, with Biographical Data on Political Activists* (2002), www.sulloway.org/politics.html.
6 Id. at 144 (citing to Dean Keith Simonton, *Greatness: Who Makes History and Why*. New York: Guilford Press, 1994).
7 Id. at 146 (citing to Sulloway, *Born to Rebel*; Helen Koch, "Some Personality Correlates of Sex, Sibling Position, and Sex of Siblings among Five- and Six-Year-Old Children," *Genetic Psychology Monographs* 52 (1955): 3–50; Frank Dumont, *A History of Personality Psychology: Theory, Science, and Research from Hellenism to the Twenty-First Century*. Cambridge: Cambridge University Press, 2010; *How Is Personality Formed? A Talk with Frank J. Sulloway*, EDGE (May 17, 1998), https://edge.org/conversation/how-is-personality-formed-.).
8 Amy Poehler, *Yes, Please* 87 (Dey Street Books) (2014).
9 Hofstede, *supra* note 13 at 81.
10 "Uncertainty Avoidance," *Clearly Cultural* (last accessed July 28, 2018), http://www.clearlycultural.com/geert-hofstede-cultural-dimensions/uncertainty-avoidance-index/.
11 As a country, Singapore practices the third *highest* amount of uncertainty avoidance of the sixty-two societies studied by GLOBE. See de Luque and Javidan, *supra* note 462 at 623.
12 Ping Zhou, "Singapore's Economic Development," *Thoughtco* (April 16, 2018) https://www.thoughtco.com/singapores-economic-development-1434565.
13 Sunil Venaik and Paul Brewer, "Avoiding Uncertainty in Hofstede and GLOBE," 41 *Journal of International Business Studies* 1294, 1309 (2010).
14 De Luque and Javidan, *supra* note 462 at 623.
15 Id.
16 Id. (showing low UA practices and high UA values).
17 Id. at 636 (low UA practices and high UA values).
18 Id. at 622.
19 Hofstede, *supra* note 13 at 81.
20 House, *supra* note 45 at XVII.
21 Hofstede, *supra* note 13 at 83.
22 De Luque and Javidan, *supra* note 462 at 607.
23 Uncertainty Avoidance, *supra* note 471.
24 *WorldRiskReport 2015*, United Nations University 64 (2015), https://collections.unu.edu/eserv/UNU:3303/WRR_2015_engl_online.pdf.

25 Elena Holodny, "The 11 Countries with the Best Infrastructure around the World," *Business Insider* (October 2, 2015), http://www.businessinsider.com/wef-countries-best-infrastructure-world-2015-9/#5-japan-7.
26 De Luque and Javidan, *supra* note 462 at 613.
27 Clarke, *supra* note 136 at 135 (noting the "minimally intrusive system" of corporate governance; noting also that times of regulatory reform take place only rarely, and at that, following financial scandals); see also Id. at 170 (noting the cooperative relationships and consensus seeking in continental European markets).
28 See de Luque and Javidan, *supra* note 462 at 622.
29 Id. at 613.
30 "Country Comparison," Hofstede Insights (last accessed July 29, 2018), https://www.hofstede-insights.com/country-comparison/germany/.
31 See Kim Iskyan, Stransberry Churhouse Research, "China's Stock Markets Have Soared by 1,479% Since 2003," *Business Insider* (November 6, 2016), http://www.businessinsider.com/world-stock-market-capitalizations-2016-11 (showing that German companies' market capitalization has growth since 2003 by 91 percent, whereas the average in the top ten largest market cap countries is 122 percent and in the world overall, 133 percent).
32 Clarke, *supra* note 136 at 182.
33 Id. at 181.
34 The more complex explanation includes factors such as the global tech crash, and scandals that plagued the market. Id. at 181–182.
35 Id. at 182.
36 Id.
37 Id.
38 Chris Bryant, "German Companies Struggle to Rise to Silicon Valley Challenge," *Financial Times* (September 4, 2014), https://www.ft.com/content/3fe29cce-2846-11e4-9ea9-00144feabdc0.
39 Markus Wacket, "Germany Breaks Green Energy Record by Generating 35% of Power from Renewables in First Half of 2017," *Independent* (July 3, 2017), http://www.independent.co.uk/news/world/europe/germany-green-technology-record-power-generation-35-per-cent-renewables-solar-wind-turbines-a7820156.html. See also Guest Contributor, "How 11 Countries Are Leading the Shift to Renewable Energy," *Clean Technica* (February 4, 2016), https://cleantechnica.com/2016/02/04/how-11-countries-are-leading-the-shift-to-renewable-energy/.
40 John Holusha, "W. Edwards Deming, Expert on Business Management, Dies at 93," *The New York Times* (Archives, 1993), http://www.nytimes.com/1993/12/21/obituaries/w-edwards-deming-expert-on-business-management-dies-at-93.html?pagewanted=all.
41 Id.
42 South Korea practices a low "as is" uncertainty avoidance, but its people desire significantly more steps be taken to reduce the risk of an uncertain avoidance. See de Luque and Javidan, *supra* note 462 at 622, 623.
43 Id. at 607.
44 Id. at 634.
45 Hofstede, *supra* note 13 at 83.
46 Id. at 603.
47 Rebecca Harrington, "These Are the 10 Smartest Countries in the World When it Comes to Science," *Business Insider* (December 4, 2015), http://www.businessinsider.com/most-technological-countries-lag-behind-in-science-2015-12/#2-germany-31-had-the-third-highest-average-annual-raw-number-of-stem-graduates-at-about-10000-right-behind-the-us-and-china--despite-those-countries-much-larger-populations-9.
48 Hofstede, *supra* note 13 at 83.
49 Hofstede, *supra* note 4 at 90.

50 Trompenaars and Hampden-Turner, *supra* note 12 at 31.
51 Id. at 33, 36.
52 Id. at 35.
53 Id. at 37, 39.
54 Id. at 35.
55 De Luque and Javidan, *supra* note 462 at 622.
56 Id.
57 Trompenaars and Hampden-Turner, *supra* note 12 at 35.
58 Id. at 36.
59 Henrich et al., *supra* note 1 at 75.
60 Trompenaars and Hampden-Turner, *supra* note 12 at 34.
61 Id.
62 Id.
63 The five most particularist countries are Venezuela, Nepal, South Korea, Russia, China, and India. See Trompenaars and Hampden-Turner, *supra* note 12 at 35. Out of 176 countries, these countries rank 166th, 131st, 52nd, 131st (tied with Nepal); 79th and 79th (tied with China) in the Transparency International Corruption Perceptions Index. The five most universalist countries, Switzerland, United States, Canada, Ireland, and Sweden, are ranked 5th, 18th, 9th, 19th, and 4th in the index. See Corrupt Perceptions Index 2016, *Transparency International* (January 25, 2017), https://www.transparency.org/news/feature/corruption_perceptions_index_2016#table.
64 De Luque and Javidan, *supra* note 462 at 606 (stating that organizational rules are suggested as a way of maintaining a stable environment given that the behavior of organizational members may be unpredictable).
65 Ashkanasy et al., *supra* note 60 at 323.
66 De Luque and Javidan, *supra* note 462 at 604; see also Gobe 182.
67 Ashkanasy et al., *supra* note 60 at 323 (stating: "They work rather independently of their teams, with whom they coordinate through well-planned standardized rules and systems").
68 Trompenaars and Hampden-Turner, *supra* note 12 at 170.
69 Id.
70 De Luque and Javidan, *supra* note 462 at 607 (writing: Innovation tends to introduce unanticipated changes for the employees and cause uncertainty that may lead to resistance to innovation [Shane, Venkataraman, and MacMillan, 1995; Van de Ven, 1986]).
71 Muel Kapstein, "Why Good People Sometimes Do Bad Things: 52 Reflections on Ethics at Work" 50 (last accessed July 29, 2018), http://www.ethicsmanagement.info/content/Why%20good%20people%20sometimes%20do%20bad%20things.pdf.
72 Id.
73 Trompenaars and Hampden-Turner, *supra* note 12 at 22.
74 Doing Business: Economy Rankings, The World Bank (last accessed July 29, 2018), http://www.doingbusiness.org/rankings.
75 Doing Business: Enforcing Contracts, The World Bank (last accessed July 29, 2018), http://www.doingbusiness.org/data/exploretopics/enforcing-contracts.
76 Id.
77 Hofstede, *supra* note 23 at 41.
78 Trompenaars and Hampden-Turner, *supra* note 12 at 40.
79 Nitish Singh and Thomas J. Bussen, *Compliance Management: A How-To Guide for Executives, Lawyers, and Other Compliance Professionals* 80 (Praeger) (2015) (citing to Robert Rosenthal and Lenore Jacobson, *Pygmalion in the Classroom: Teacher Expectation and Pupils' Intellectual Development*. Holt, Rinehart, and Winston 1968, 16).
80 Id.
81 Trompenaars and Hampden-Turner, *supra* note 12 at 40.

9

THE LOSS AVERSION BIAS

> Because no one's opinions are quite what he wills them to be, no one's beliefs are quite what he wills them to be.
>
> Giovanni Pico della Mirandola

We don't have the luxury to thoroughly process every detail that passes before us: many events that are missed by our conscious selves are absorbed by our subconscious minds, but even those things that we are conscious of are often subject to mental shortcuts. To be able to make sense of the world, we use our previous experiences and opinions to make quick judgments and choices. These mental shortcuts are called heuristics. A few examples are

- *The availability heuristic*: We determine the likelihood of events based on how easily examples come to mind rather than actual statistics. For example, we tend to think that terrorist attacks or airplane crashes are more likely than they really are, and in contrast drowning less likely, because these are more commonly before us on the nightly news.
- *The representativeness heuristic*: Judging a situation based on how similar it is to a mental prototype. For example, if we know a muscular person who is a "meathead" or a person with glasses who is smart, we may ascribe these characteristics to all muscular people or people with glasses.
- *Familiarity heuristic*: Familiar situations are preferred over new ones since they seem safe (even though this might not necessarily be the best or safest choice).

Even though heuristics are necessary and useful, these are biases and can often lead to systematic errors in judgments. A cognitive bias is the subconscious tendency to draw incorrect conclusions or make logical fallacies based on heuristics.

The risk-aversion bias is one such heuristic. While risk aversion differs slightly among cultures – for example, some cultures are more resistant to risk based on the expected size of the loss, while others are more resistant based on the probability of the loss – seeking to avoid risk nonetheless approaches a universal truth.[1] Indeed, it is a survival mechanism: there is good reason to be cautious about the future, and such caution translates to higher degrees of prosperity in the modern world. This inclination is so deeply ingrained however that in some cases it results in a bias that leads to suboptimal decision-making.

The risk aversion bias means that we often prefer a "sure thing" to an uncertain outcome with a higher expected value. For example, the expected value of receiving a guaranteed $100 is the same as a 10 percent chance of receiving $1000. Economics tells us that we should be indifferent between these two options if given this choice enough times, because eventually the outcomes are the same. But the risk aversion bias means that most people will choose the certain $100. Even if you increase the chance of receiving the $1000 to 15 or 20 percent, in which the expected value now goes to $150–$200, double the certain outcome, many still stick to the "safe" choice.

Ultimately, the risk aversion is caused by a fear of loss, and thus loss-aversion bias is closely related to risk-aversion bias. The loss-aversion bias says we try to avoid losing money or other things of value that we already have, more than we seek to gain money or things of value. Moreover, we value something we own more than something we don't, even when they have the same value and even when lacking sentimental value. Said in another way, we are more motivated to avoid losing $100 than we are to earn that $100. Mathematically, not losing $100 is no different from earning $100, so we should be equally motivated by both.

Researcher Dan Ariely, in *Predictably Irrational*, further demonstrates how this loss aversion bias causes us to act irrationally. Ariely notes that at Duke University, basketball is king. However, the stadium is small, and demand for tickets far exceeds supply. To address this, rather than selling tickets through a traditional first-come, first-served system, Duke makes its fans *work* to earn tickets to games, and for a long time.

Ariely explains the systems:

> Even before the start of the spring semester, students who want to attend the games pitch tents in the open grassy area outside the stadium. Each tent holds up to ten students. The campers who arrive first take the spots closest to the stadium's entrance, and the ones who come later line up further back.
>
> … an air horn is sounded at random times. At the sound, a countdown begins, and within the next five minutes at least one person from each tent must check in with the basketball authorities. If a tent fails to register within these five minutes, the whole tent gets bumped to the end of the line. This procedure continues for most of the spring semester and intensifies in the last forty-eight hours before a game.

At that point, forty-eight hours before a game, the checks become "personal checks." ... [W]hen the air horn is sounded, every student has to check in personally with the basketball authorities. Missing an "occupancy check" in these final two days can mean being bumped to the end of the line. Although the air horn sounds occasionally before routine games, it can be heard at all hours of night and day before the really big contests. ...

But that's not the oddest part of the ritual. The oddest part is that for the really important games, such as the national titles, the students at the front of the line still don't get a ticket. Rather, each of them gets a lottery number. Only later, as they crowd around a list of winners posted at the student center, do they find out if they have really, truly won a ticket to the coveted game.[2]

In this, Ariely and his colleague Ziv Carmon saw a natural experiment that might prove the loss aversion theory. After the lottery was completed, he obtained the names of all lottery participants, including winners and losers. Then he called all the losers and asked how much they would be willing to pay one of the winners to turn over their tickets to the game. The average "loser" (for lack of better word) offered $170. Ariely notes: "The price they were willing to pay ... was tempered by alternative uses for the money (such as spending it in a sports bar for drinks and food)."[3]

Ariely then called the "winners." Would any of them accept $170 for the tickets? Both the winners and the losers had stood in the same lines and shown the same commitment to getting the tickets. Rationally, therefore, the value of the tickets should be about the same. This is not what happened. Instead, the average "winner" demanded $2,400. That's right – nearly fifteen times the amount the "losers" were willing to pay. "Not a single person was willing to sell a ticket at a price that someone else was willing to pay."[4] In considering their selling point, the winners cited the lifelong memories that they would gain from attending the game.[5]

However, "from a rational perspective, both the ticket holders and the non-ticket holders should have thought of the game in exactly the same way. After all, the anticipated atmosphere at the game and the enjoyment one could expect from the experience should not depend on winning a lottery. Then how could a random lottery drawing have changed the students' view of the game – and the value of the tickets – so dramatically?"[6]

It is entirely possible that the "losers" would have liked to pay more for the tickets but were limited by their student budgets. But note the emphasis of the students. While the "losers" focused on alternative uses for the money, the winners cited the lifelong memories that they would gain from attending the game.

Loss aversion explains this difference in perspective and thus the difference in offers.[7] Once the "winners" had the tickets, the loss of the ticket was felt more psychologically than the gain of money. The "losers," however, didn't have the tickets, but they did have money in the bank. Thus, instead of thinking about the memories they would gain from the tickets, they thought about the lost opportunities from the money. Both parties focused on what they would lose – the money or the tickets – rather than what they would gain. This ensured that the winners valued the tickets more than the losers, and the losers valued the money more than the winners. Loss aversion prevented a meeting of the minds, and we can't help but wonder how many negotiations fail for similar reasons.

The loss aversion bias has been replicated in young children as well as nonhuman primates, suggesting it is a robust and innate bias related to our survival. We hold on to what we have and avoid losses to an irrational degree. This, however, does not mean there are no differences between people. A study comparing loss aversion related to buying or selling a coffee mug that Western and East Asian participants had just been given showed a larger loss aversion in the Americans. The study showed further that there was an increase in loss aversion in the Americans as they got more attached to the cup but the opposite in the Asian participants.[8]

The reasoning behind this is that owning an object creates an association between the object and the self, and the mug becomes a part of one's self-image. And how we value the self is different across cultures. The more individualistic, Western cultures view the individual (and with that the objects that are owned) as of high importance. In contrast, in eastern, more interdependent cultures, there is an emphasis on self-criticism, and the individual is deemphasized. Consequently, individualistic people may be more likely to hang on to those basketball tickets – or even that coffee mug – than collectivists.

Loss Aversion and Your Behavior

Loss aversion has personal implications as well. Ariely argues, "we have an irrational compulsion to keep doors open."[9] For instance, we may spend time socializing with friends that we know we will never be close with; we may work extra hours to merit a promotion, even though we know we will probably change professions or jobs; we may keep a bar license, an accounting license or a Realtor's license even though we long ago ceased to practice in these areas. Why? In all these cases, the answer is essentially "just in case." These are classic attempts that speak to our fear of losing out on a possibility. However, we waste energy keeping these doors open in our personal and professional lives, and in that preoccupation, we avoid walking through the doors that offer the most opportunity. Ariely argues that we would be better served in committing to a smaller set of opportunities and forgetting about those that are not crucial to our future plans or goals. While jumping between opportunities may keep many doors open, only by having the courage to close doors are we able to focus on the things that will truly allow us to excel.

For example, Sheryl Sandberg relates the story of an unhappy young lawyer that was interested in a career change: "A friend of mine had been working as a lawyer for four years when she realized that instead of shooting for partner, she'd rather join a company in a sales or marketing role. One of her clients was willing to hire her in this new capacity but wanted her to start at the ground level. Since she could afford the temporary pay cut, I urged her to make the jump, but she decided against taking a job that would put her 'back four years.'"[10]

This is a classic case of loss aversion. The years of effort toward the partnership were a "sunk cost," and she would never get those years back. However, she could make sure her future years were put to a happier, more fulfilling purpose. Instead, torn between a partnership in a career she didn't care for and an uncertain position in a new industry she found exciting, she chose the more predictable path. Adam Grant writes: "When we have a certain gain, we like to hold on to it. ... But when presented with a guaranteed loss, we are willing to do anything to prevent it – even if it means risking a bigger one."[11]

In this case, we could also be seeing the lawyer friend's individualism making the change harder. It is possible that her self-worth was tied up in the idea of a prestige job such as law, or the high salary that came along with it. While her individualism would leave her ready and able to shift jobs *within* the industry without much concern for obligations to the company itself, giving up the profession entirely was akin to giving up that coffee mug: it had become a part of who she was (or at least, how she saw her herself).

Our loss aversion and our preference for "sure things" (risk aversion) reduce our willingness to change, which in some scenarios is a wise defensive posture. In other scenarios, however, it can keep us from our full potential. Studies on brain activity have indeed shown that the brain areas involved in the loss-aversion bias are related to negative emotions, suggesting that these "irrational decisions" are driven by fear and anxiety.[12]

Kahneman and Tversky use a different classification system that captures part of this, which they call type 1 and type 2 thinking. Under type 1 thinking, we quickly respond through emotion and instinct, which is what drives most of our biases. We can, however, combat this through the slower type 2 thinking, which is driven through the more effortful logic and conscious thought.

We don't necessarily suggest quitting your job or giving up those well-earned basketball tickets – but perhaps the coffee mug can go? All of this requires making an honest appraisal of your choices, aware of your possible psychological biases. In this way, our decisions can become driven more by objective factors rather than these subconscious biases.

Loss Aversion and Your Business

This bias gets all the more interesting when you take into account what has been termed "the framing effect." Adam Grant addresses this when he relates the following study.

> Imagine that you're an executive at a car manufacturer, and due to economic challenges, you need to close three plants and lay off six thousand employees. You can choose between two different plans:

> Plan A will save one of the three plants and two thousand jobs. Plan B has a one-third chance of saving all three plants and all six thousand jobs, but a two-thirds chance of saving no plants and no jobs.
>
> In the original study, 80 percent chose to play it safe rather than take a chance.
>
> But suppose we gave you a different set of options:
>
> Plan A will lose two of the three plants and four thousand jobs. Plan B has a two-thirds chance of losing all three plants and all six thousand jobs, but a one-third chance of losing no plants and no jobs.
>
> In the latter option, 82 percent of people prefer plan B. Their preferences reverse.[13]

What changed? Nothing, in substance. Just the use of the word "loss." How amazing is that? This study reveals not just the deeply layered aversion we have to loss, but also how such aversion can result in truly irrational behavior. So the next time you propose a new business strategy, make sure you avoid words like "lose," "loss" and "give up," and focus on the gains, savings and growth.

This shows us how deeply irrational both the loss-aversion bias and the risk-aversion bias can make us.[i] Let's then explore how loss aversion can actually be leveraged to the benefit of an organization, or person.

> At the pharmaceutical giant Merck, CEO Kenneth Frazier decided to motivate his team of executives to take a more active role in leading innovation and change. He asked them to do something radical: generate ideas that would put Merck out of business.
>
> For the next two hours, the executives worked in groups, pretending to be one of Merck's top competitors. Energy soared as they developed ideas for drugs that would crush theirs and key markets they had missed.[14]

What was Frazier thinking? Market leaders like Merck have a lot to lose, and thus the loss-aversion bias is particularly resonant. This can result in a tendency to play it safe.[15]

But Frazier knew that large companies often decline as loss aversion sets in, and maintaining an established position becomes more prized than growth and innovation. Frazier thus reframed the issue by asking them to first view themselves as pursuing a hypothetical market leader. From this perspective, they had less to lose, so they were ready to take risks. Moreover, they were ready to act in a way that they had not been before: the participants were ready to "consider many creative possibilities, but then drill down into one or two plans of attack."[16]

Frazier wasn't quite done with this exercise. They were challenged next "to reverse their roles and figure out how to defend against these threats. When they considered how their competitors could put them out of business, they realized that it was a risk not to innovate."[17] Thus, the loss aversion bias *forced* them to try not just to avoid losing but to avoid loss through gain.

TABLE 9.1 Heuristics overview

- The risk-aversion bias means that we often prefer a "sure thing" to an uncertain outcome with a higher expected value.
- Loss-aversion bias says we avoid losing money or other things of value that we already have more than we seek to gain money or things of value. We saw this with the Duke University experiment.
- This is a pan-cultural bias, but stronger for individualistic Westerners than collectivist easterners.
- Framing effect: You are faced with the option of a certain but incomplete loss or a gamble in which you could lose nothing or everything. If the loss is emphasized in the first option you are likely to gamble. If the amount that you will not lose is instead emphasized you are unlikely to gamble. The scenario is identical but the loss is framed in the first scenario but not the second.
- Managers can use this to advantage. Emphasize the losses that will derive from undesired actions even more than the gains that could result from desired actions.

Taking risks is, yes, *risky*. Americans start businesses in record numbers, and American businesses fail in record numbers. But risk aversion does not necessarily eliminate risk either, as we saw from the Merck case, and as the Germans learned through their failed *Neuer Markt* stock index. The key is to make decisions as objectively as possible, seeking to at least be aware of the risk-aversion and loss-aversion biases, and to help our workforces avoid the psychological traps they pose.

So too should we seek to respect the varying levels of comfort each of us has with the unknown, levels that vary for both environmental and genetic reasons (Table 9.1).

Note

i Of course, this isn't always true. Maybe if you lose some money you can't pay a bill; if you gain some money you can buy a TV. The bill is more important. But the point is that on average, it balances and so should be considered equally. After all, the opposite should also be true just as often – if you gain money you can pay the bill; without it, whether you lose money or stay the same, you can't pay that bill. Either way, you need the money.

References

1 See Robert N. Bontempo, William P. Bottom, and Elke U. Weber, "Cross-Cultural Differences in Risk Perception: A Model-Based Approach," 17 *Risk Analysis: An International Journal* 479–488 (1997).
2 Ariely, *supra* note 102 at 127–129.
3 Id. at 132.
4 Id.
5 Id.
6 Id.
7 Id. at 134.

8 William W. Maddux, Hajo Adam, and Adam D. Galinsky, "When in Rome ... Learn Why the Romans Do What They Do: How Multicultural Learning Experiences Facilitate Creativity," 36 *Personality and Social Psychology Bulletin* 731–741 (2010).
9 Ariely, *supra* note 102 at 150.
10 Sandberg, *supra* note 301 at 59.
11 Grant, *supra* note 72 at 233.
12 Benedetto De Martino, Dharshan Kumaran, Ben Seymour, and Raymond J. Dolan, "Frames, Biases, and Rational Decision-Making in the Human Brain," 313 *Science* 684–687 (2006).
13 Grant, *supra* note 72 at 233 (citing to Amos Tversky and Daniel Kahneman, "The Framing of Decisions and the Psychology of Choice," *Science* 211 (1981): 453–458; Max Bazerman, *Judgment in Managerial Decision Making*. New York: John Wiley & Sons, 1994).
14 Grant, *supra* note 72 at 233.
15 Id. at 234 (citing to Anita Wooley, "Playing Offense versus Defense: The Effects of Team Strategic Orientation on Team Process in Competitive Environments," *Organization Science* 22 (2011): 1384–1398).
16 Id.
17 Id.

10
ASSERTIVENESS

> The man who has confidence in himself gains the confidence of others.
> Hasidic Proverb

In this chapter, we explore the "assertiveness" cultural dimension, as well as the related but distinct concept of gender egalitarianism. GLOBE's authors define assertiveness as follows:

> Broadly speaking, cultural assertiveness reflects beliefs as to whether people are or should be encouraged to be assertive, aggressive, and tough, or nonassertive, nonaggressive, and tender in social relationships.[1]

Gender egalitarianism is described this way:

> At its core, this measure reflects societies' beliefs about whether members' biological sex should determine the roles that they play in their homes, business organizations, and communities. Societies with greater gender egalitarianism rely less on biological sex to determine the allocation of roles between the sexes.[2]

Hofstede too described cultural dimensions pertaining to gender. He described these as masculinity versus femininity. His findings are conceptually and statistically correlated with the assertiveness dimensions of GLOBE, as men tend to be more assertive than women.[3] However, we primarily focus on the statistically stronger GLOBE findings, with Hofstede's findings playing more of a supporting role.[i]

Assertiveness: The So-called "Masculine" Dimension

Are you ambitious? If so, are you ambitious for your own advancement, or are you ambitious for the success of your organization? Or would you prefer to work as little as possible, spending more time with your children, your spouse and your friends?

If you're assertive, chances are you are also ambitious as assertiveness tends to result in a higher need for achievement.[4] If you come from a society in which ambition is lauded, the hard work that accompanies the need for achievement is likely to result in a prosperous society.[5]

If you are assertive but collectivist, you're more likely to direct your ambitions toward some greater good – that of your extended family, community or organization. For instance, at Emerson Electric, employees are rewarded with personal incentives for achieving their goals, but Montupet notes that the Chinese workforce is additionally driven by a fear of losing face if they do not make their goals.[6] In this case, we have ambitious-types drawn to the performance-oriented Emerson culture, but this ambition overlaps with the employees' traditionally collectivist culture. Nonetheless, we know that most assertives are individualistic,[7] and these people are more likely to be ambitious for their own gain and the welfare of their immediate family.

If you reach a leadership position, how are you going to manage your workforce? Will you be direct and demanding of your workforce, or understanding and compassionate? Will you put yourself in the corner office, highlighting your standing above rather than with the workforce, or out in an open-air cubicle with your employees?

Assertive societies tend to prefer lower-context, or direct, communication[8] and relatedly, handle confrontational interactions better. By contrast, unassertive people exhibit greater compassion, and one way of showing this compassion is through the use of high-context or indirect communications that can soften the blow of criticism. Countries with high levels of assertiveness tend also to be more hierarchical,[9] as more assertive countries tend to be more supportive of authoritative leaders.[10] Managers of this stripe may put themselves in that corner office and make heavy demands on their workforce. People from less assertive countries, by contrast, prefer more consultative and agreeable leaders[11] and tend to exhibit greater levels of tolerance.[12] These people are more likely than their assertive counterparts to choose the open-air floor format, seek consensus in decision-making and embrace a more diverse team.

If you gain material success, are you likely to show off that success by purchasing a large home, a fancy car or designer clothes? Would you invest some of that money to make yet more money, or would you be content with what you have and consider an early retirement?

Assertives tend to be more extroverted[13] and are more likely to flaunt their success and manifest their wealth. In Western countries that extroversion interestingly makes it somewhat more likely that professional success will follow.[14] By contrast, non-assertives tend to exhibit greater modesty. For example, Norway is one of the least assertive societies.[15] The country has a GDP/capita of nearly $70,000, which is the eleventh highest in the world.[16] Paired with large oil reserves that drive up that GDP/capita, one might predict the streets to be filled with gas-guzzling sports cars and ego enhancing SUVs. Instead, as of 2017, the second best-selling car in Norway was a Tesla Model X.[17] At one point, Norway was the second biggest purchaser of the Tesla Model S in the world. These are expensive cars,[18] but they are cars that make a rather humble statement about the owner's respect for the environment more than any need for show.

Finally, both men and women may act in nonassertive ways. This is particularly true in Nordic Europe, but it is nonetheless still the exception to the rule. In a few countries, both the men and women act with assertiveness, but in many societies, women are expected to act in a nonassertive manner and men to act assertively. While no doubt many women are highly assertive and many men are nonassertive in these countries, on the whole, the statistics show significantly greater assertiveness from men.[19] Consequently, assertiveness often closely resembles a certain "machismo" – or as Hofstede termed it, "masculinity."

These behaviors have accumulated over the centuries, and in some cases are evolving, responding to the rapidly changing conditions of the modern world. In some societies, for example, assertiveness is a more modern response to real or perceived external challenges.[20] In other countries, less assertive nations have a stiffer resolve against competition and aggressiveness due to a history in which this behavior led to uncooperative disharmony and even general failure.[21]

The GLOBE study found that the United States is the eleventh most assertive country out of sixty-two countries surveyed. Albania, Nigeria, Hungary, Germany, Hong Kong, and Austria were rated as the most assertive countries overall, while Sweden, New Zealand, Switzerland, Japan, Kuwait, Thailand, Portugal, Russia, and India ranked as the least assertive.[22] Germanic Europe and Eastern Europe were rated as the most assertive regions, while nearby Nordic Europe was the least assertive, followed closely by Southern Asia.[23]

However, Anglo, East Asian, and Latin regions exhibit the most assertiveness in organizational life, meaning that they show the highest levels of assertiveness in the workplace.[24] Because the United States already is rather high on societal assertiveness, this finding implies that American employees exhibit a remarkably high level of assertiveness generally. Indeed, this mostly aligns with the above findings, as Americans tend to exhibit more power distance in business than in societal life, great individualism, a high need for achievement and lengthy work weeks, a rather materialistic culture and a great deal of extroversion. All this assertiveness brings great societal advantages from an economic perspective, but as the next section will show, this also has potential drawbacks (Table 10.1).

TABLE 10.1 Practicing assertiveness (from highest to lowest)[25]

1. Albania	22. Australia	42. Taiwan
2. Nigeria	23. Israel	43. Namibia
3. Hungary	24. Argentina	44. Egypt
4. Germany (East)	25. Brazil	45. Guatemala
5. Hong Kong	26. Colombia	46. Malaysia
6. Austria	27. Georgia	47. Indonesia
7. El Salvador	28. Singapore	48. Finland
8. South Africa (white sample)	29. England	49. Denmark
9. Greece	30. France	50. Bolivia
10. Germany (West)	31. Qatar	51. China
11. United States	32. Ecuador	52. Costa Rica
12. Turkey	33. Zambia	53. India
13. Morocco	34. Italy	54. Russia
14. Switzerland	35. Zimbabwe	55. Portugal
15. Kazakhstan	36. Poland	56. Thailand
16. Mexico	37. Canada (English speaking)	57. Kuwait
17. Spain		58. Japan
18. South Korea	38. Iran	59. Switzerland (French speaking)
19. South Africa (black sample)	39. Philippines	
20. Venezuela	40. Slovenia	60. New Zealand
21. Netherlands	41. Ireland	61. Sweden

Assertiveness, Charisma, and Narcissism

In the above section, we defined some of the common characteristics of assertive types. These characteristics – ambition, directness, hierarchy, and "masculinity" – are seen in many cultures as descriptive of the prototypical leader. The evidence, however, does not support such a finding.

Here are psychologists Alice Eagly and Jean Lau Chin – using "masculine" in place of "assertive," and "feminine" in place of "nonassertive" – reporting on studies that suggest it may be time to adjust our stereotypes:

> People generally believe that leaders are ambitious, confident, self-sufficient, and dominant … (Powell, Butterfield, and Parent, 2002; V. E. Schein, 2001). For example, the role of business executives is thought to require attributes such as being action-oriented, decisive, and competitive (e.g., Martell, Parker, Emrich, and Crawford 1998). Management theorists have regarded behaviors such as competing with peers, imposing wishes on subordinates, and behaving assertively as prototypical of the managerial role (Miner 1993). Despite the inclusion of some expectations about considerate and supportive qualities, most managerial roles are strongly infused with cultural masculinity, especially as these roles are construed by men (e.g., Atwater, Brett, Waldman, DiMare, and Hayden 2004; V.E. Schein 2001).[26]

In short, assertive behavior has historically been seen as the benchmark, not only within organizations but by managerial scholars. Eagly and Chin warn, however:

> In most contexts, top-down, command-and-control leaders no longer provide the most effective or admired type of leadership (Eagly and Carli 2004, 2007; Kanter 1997). In response to these changes, scholars of leadership have increasingly emphasized that effective leadership emerges from inspiring, motivating, and mentoring followers. ... in which both followers and leaders take responsibility for adapting to challenges (e.g., Graen and Uhl-Bien 1995; Spillane 2006).[27]

In fact, the transformational model of good leadership (Avolio, 1999) appears to be infused with a good deal of cultural femininity, especially in its inclusion of support and mentoring that leaders provide to followers (Duehr and Bono 2006; Hackman, Furniss, Hills, and Patterson 1992).[28]

In short, nonassertive types are better at subordinating their own ego to that of their employees and the organization, which bodes well for effective organizational performance. As noted in Chapter 3, ego reduces the dissent needed to prevent groupthink. More generally, humble leaders are, on average, more effective. This was a fundamental finding for Jim Collins in *Good to Great*, and other researchers have made similar findings.[29] Sumitomo Chemical's Juan Ferreira for his part suggests that successful cross-cultural managers are those who are open-minded and humble, rather than closed-minded and overconfident.[30] These leaders are more successful for their ability to create highly collaborative environments, to hear feedback and to consequently more realistically appraise their own strengths and weaknesses.[31]

Humility is key, but we don't do a very good job at identifying humble leaders. Instead, the most charismatic people are the ones likely to catch our attention and rise through the ranks, and the confidence needed to show outstanding charisma means that the charismatic amongst us are, on average, more egotistical. *Harvard Business Review's* Margarita Mayo goes even further, writing that charismatic people are more likely to be narcissists, promoting "highly self-serving and grandiose aims."[32] These "leaders tend to abuse their power and take advantage of their followers."[33]

It isn't necessarily that all charismatic leaders are narcissistic. It tends actually to be the contrary – that narcissistic people tend to act in a charismatic way after fully realizing how this helps them promote their own interests.

Again, assertiveness has some benefits at the individual level, but at the managerial level it can be counterproductive. While both men and women can act humbly and less assertively, studies show that women are already doing this considerably more often than men. Indeed, women are more likely to view consensus and collaborative behaviors as positive leadership characteristics.[34] By contrast, men are more likely to affirm leadership behaviors that we know are ineffective, including self-serving behavior, and participating in conflict-inducing behavior.[35]

Men are perfectly capable of less-assertive management behavior, as shown in Nordic Europe, where this is already the norm, and as shown in Jim Collins's profiles of the men who ran the most successful companies of his era and who commonly shared a striking humility.

The point is relatively simple: stop with the machismo. To care about one's employees, to collaborate and be open to new ideas – these are (or should be) gender-neutral characteristics. Assertive types are likely to be more ambitious for their own personal material gain and not for the company writ large. Instead it is non-assertives who make for better leaders (Table 10.2).

Introversion/Extroversion

We noted that extroverts tend to be more assertive than introverts.[36] We see that many nonassertive Nordic Europeans, for example, are more introverted and more neutral communicators than the global averages. It's worth discussing the extroversion-introversion dimension, a concept that is often misunderstood.

We turn to Susan Cain, whose book *Quiet: The Power of Introverts in a World That Can't Stop Talking* sheds much-needed light on the power of introversion and the qualities of the introvert. She relates that extroverted people tend to be "ebullient, expansive, sociable, gregarious, excitable, dominant, assertive, active, risk taking, thick-skinned, outer directed, lighthearted, bold, and comfortable in the spotlight."[37] By contrast, introverts may be "reflective, cerebral, bookish, unassuming, sensitive, thoughtful, serious, contemplative, subtle, introspective, inner-directed, gentle, calm, modest, solitude-seeking, shy, risk-averse, thin-skinned." Introverts thus behave in a way that is relatively neutral, a term discussed in Chapter 13, which predicts one will outwardly exhibit low levels of emotion.

What introversion is exactly, it should be noted, varies across nations. In fact, it is believed that around 50 percent of a person's place on the introversion-extroversion spectrum can be explained by nurture, rather than nature. For example, Cain cites to American cultural behaviors that may reward greater extroversion: "we [Americans] rank fast talkers as more competent and likable than slow ones."[38] Even the seemingly stuffy world of academia is affected: "Scientists

TABLE 10.2 Assertiveness onion diagram

Inner	Middle	Outer
Static gender positions	Men assertive	Ambitious, aggressive, materialistic
	Women unassertive	Relationship-oriented, humble
	Overall effect	More economic growth at the societal level, but more stress for assertive types and less effective managers
Gender-neutral positions	Society may be assertive or nonassertive, but men and women within the society are likely to exhibit similar levels of assertiveness	

whose research gets funded have confident, perhaps overconfident personalities."[39] Indeed, approximately 50 percent of Americans are extroverted, making it "one of the most extroverted nations on Earth."[40]

In Asia, introversion is much more common, and again, cultural norms may perpetuate this. In Japan and other parts of Asia, for example, "you don't need charisma or to talk fast to get ahead."[41] Instead, "quiet and introspection are signs of deep thought and higher truth."[42] A simple walk down the street of any of Japan's major cities will reveal this, where one is tempted to whisper so as to not break the silence.[ii] Consequently, if you are a Japanese child, you learn from a young age the value of quiet, and your default interactive mechanism may be a more introspective one.

Additionally, and perhaps more provocatively, Cain cites research showing that the amount of extroversion we exhibit "is in our DNA – literally."[43] The researchers found that Europeans and Americans exhibit the extroversion trait more than Asians and Africans.[44] Americans in particular tend to be recent descendants of migrants, a prospect that may be more attractive to those with extroverted personalities.[45] Additionally, the migrants' need to make friends with new people in a new environment may reward extroverts and make it more likely they will succeed in their new country.

By contrast, Finland, one of the most neutral countries on Earth, is also one of the most introverted. Finland, and indeed most of Northern Europe, is a mostly homogeneous place in which meeting new people – and thus being extroverted – is not a social necessity. Consequently, Cain relays this self-effacing Finnish joke: "They ask, 'How can you tell if a Finn likes you? He's staring at your shoes instead of his own.'"[46] We can't help notice that we have heard versions of this joke stated for both accountants and actuaries as well, but it certainly makes the point (Table 10.3).

We discussed the trade-off theory in the section on risk aversion, finding that species survival may incline toward a mix of risk-averse and risk-seeking humans. It is believed that the trade-off theory applies also to extroversion.

Says Cain: "Human extroverts have more sex partners than introverts do – a boon to any species wanting to reproduce itself – but they commit more adultery and divorce more frequently, which is not a good thing for the children of all those couplings. Extroverts exercise more, but introverts suffer fewer accidents and traumatic injuries. Extroverts enjoy wider networks of social support but commit more crimes."[47] It is more likely that people from some cultures – Asia and Northern Europe, for example – will be introverted and that others (such as Americans and Latin Americans) will be extroverted. But as with all of these dimensions, we are speaking only to the law of averages. No doubt there are many Finns and Japanese that are far more extroverted than many Americans. And in all societies, both introversion and extroversion are present, and it is the manager's challenge – indeed obligation – to respect those differences.

TABLE 10.3 The Extroverted - Introverted spectrum across the world

Most extroverted countries	Most introverted countries[48]
1. Oman (61.66%)	1. Japan (59.88%)
2. Yemen (59.44%)	2. Lithuania (55.85%)
3. Saudi Arabia (58.95%)	3. Portugal (54.25%)
4. Jordan (58.41%)	4. Czech Republic (53.67%)
5. United Arab Emirates (58.01%)	5. Barbados (53.32%)
6. Kuwait (57.81%)	6. Slovakia (53.3%)
7. Bahrain (57.08%)	7. Puerto Rico (52.87%)
8. Syria (56.61%)	8. Latvia (52.68%)
9. Palestine (56.37%)	9. Estonia (52.5%)
10. Qatar (56.01%)	10. Bahamas (52.33%)

Here's just one example that shows how people react very differently to stimuli depending on their place in the spectrum:

> "robots interacted with stroke patients during physical rehabilitation exercises...introverted patients responded better and interacted longer with robots that were designed to speak in a soothing, gentle manner... Extroverts, on the other hand, worked harder for robots that used more bracing, aggressive language. 'You can do more than that, I know it!'"[49]

Cain offers advice for teachers to improve the learning experience of introverts in the classroom. We provide this excerpt above for our readers, with the understanding that many of these same recommendations apply equally to the office and the classroom (Table 10.4).

> "Many schools are designed for extroverts, and introverts need different kinds of instruction..."[50] The "person-environment fit" shows that people flourish when, in the words of psychologist Brian Little, "they're engaged in occupations, roles or settings that are concordant with their personalities. The inverse is also true: kids stop learning when they feel emotionally threatened."[51] Therefore, "balance teaching methods to serve all the kids in your class. Extroverts tend to like movement, stimulation, collaborative work. Introverts prefer lectures, downtimes, and independent projects. Mix it up fairly.[52] Have introverts do some group work, but in pairs or groups of three. And carefully structure the work so that each child knows her role." Introverts are "very comfortable talking with one or two of their classmates to answer a question or complete a task but would never think of raising their hand and addressing the whole class. It is very important that these students get a chance to translate their thoughts to language."[53]

TABLE 10.4 Introversion/extroversion onion diagram

Inner	Middle	Outer
Philosophical values and genetic makeup	Extroversion (typically Western)	Value charisma, fast-talking, sociability, assertiveness, risk taking
Philosophical values and genetic makeup	Introversion (Eastern, Nordic)	Value contemplation, quiet, risk aversion, unassertiveness

Notes

i Hofstede's findings would fail to distinguish a society in which all members tend to exhibit middling-levels of assertiveness from those in which men are very assertive and women hardly at all. GLOBE is also able to identify nations that are, on average, more or less assertive as a whole. But by examining the degree to which nations highlight or conflate gender differences in a separate study, GLOBE also provides an idea of whether certain characteristics – including but not limited to assertiveness – are held by men more so than by women. Thus, GLOBE results are qualitatively superior and at least quantitatively equivalent.

ii The author (Bussen) visited a campground over a popular national holiday in Japan. Though every site was sold out and the grounds were full of families and games, the site was almost eerily quiet in evenings. By nine or ten p.m., apparently by tacit understanding, total silence enveloped the camp.

References

1 Deanne N. Den Hartog, "Assertiveness," in *Culture, Leadership, and Organizations: The GLOBE Study Of 62 Societies* 395 (eds. Robert House, Paul J. Hanges, Mansour Javidan, Peter W. Dorfman, and Vipin Gupta, SAGE Publications) (2004).
2 Cynthia G. Emrich, Florence L. Denmark, and Deanne N. Den Hartog, "Cross-Cultural Differences in Gender Egalitarianism: Implications for Societies, Organizations, and Leaders," in *Culture, Leadership, and Organizations: The GLOBE Study of 62 Societies* 347 (eds. Robert House, Paul J. Hanges, Mansour Javidan, Peter W. Dorfman, and Vipin Gupta, SAGE Publications) (2004).
3 Hartog, *supra* note 562 at 413.
4 Emrich et al., *supra* note 563 at 344.
5 Javidan *supra* note 42 at 253.
6 Montupet *supra* note 10.
7 Emrich et al., *supra* note 563 at 344; see also Javidan, *supra* note 42 at 245.
8 Hartog, *supra* note 562 at 404 (citing Schneider and Barsoux, 1997).
9 Id. at 414.
10 Id. at 428.
11 Id.
12 Id. at 399.
13 Id.
14 Id. at 399–400.
15 Norway was not included in the GLOBE study, but because it shares much in common culturally with the other Nordic countries that collectively ranked the least-assertive on Earth, we can hypothesize that Norway, too, exhibit a relatively non-assertive culture. Hofstede, moreover, found Norway to be the second least masculine societies, after its neighbor, Sweden. See "Cultural Dimensions, Cleary Cultural" (last accessed July 29, 2018), http://www.clearlycultural.com/geert-hofstede-cultural-dimensions/masculinity/.
16 The World Factbook, Central Intelligence Agency (last accessed July 29, 2018), https://www.cia.gov/library/publications/the-world-factbook/rankorder/2004rank.html.

17 https://electrek.co/2017/07/04/electric-car-norway-tesla-model-x/.
18 It retails in Norway for more than $100,000, but numerous governmental subsidies diminish the bite. See Fred Lambert, "Electric Cars Reach Record 42% of Norway's Total New Car Sales with Boost from Tesla Model X," *Electrek* (July 4, 2017), http://jalopnik.com/heres-why-the-tesla-model-s-is-the-1-selling-car-in-no-1651261025.
19 Hartog, *supra* note 562 at 401.
20 Id. at 412.
21 Id.
22 Id. at 410.
23 Id. at 423.
24 Id. at 427.
25 Id. at 410.
26 Alice H. Eagly and Jean Lau Chin, "Diversity and Leadership in a Changing World," 65 *American Psychologist* 216, 217 (2010).
27 Id. at 219.
28 Id. at 221.
29 Margarita Mayo, "If Humble People Make the Best Leaders, Why Do We Fall for Charismatic Narcissists?" *Harvard Business Review* (April 7, 2017). https://hbr.org/2017/04/if-humble-people-make-the-best-leaders-why-do-we-fall-for-charismatic-narcissists (citing to A.Y. Ou et al., "Do Humble CEOs Matter? An Examination of CEO Humility and Firm Outcomes," *Journal of Management*, 2015. See also Inclusive Leadership: The View from Six Countries, Catalyst Report, 2014. http://www.catalyst.org/knowledge/inclusive-leadership-view-six-countries).
30 Ferreira, *supra* note 175.
31 Mayo, *supra* note 592.
32 Id.
33 Id. (citing to Daniel Sankowsy, "The Charismatic Leader as Narcissist: Understanding the Abuse of Power," *Organizational Dynamics* 23 (4) (1995): 57–71; citing also to Jay Conger and Rabindra Kanungo, *Charismatic Leadership in Organizations*. SAGE Publications, 1998).
34 Emrich et al., *supra* note 563 at 384.
35 Id. at 385. See also House and Javidan, *supra* note 8 at 14 for the definition of "self-protective leadership."
36 Hartog, *supra* note 562 at 399.
37 Cain, *supra* note 87 at 273.
38 Id. at 23.
39 Id. at 25.
40 Id. at 22.
41 Id. at 202.
42 Id. at 194.
43 Cain, *supra* note 87 at 46.
44 Id. at 46.
45 Id.
46 Id. at 33.
47 Id. at 159.
48 Based on personality quizzes with a minimum of one thousand member-country responses. See World Personality Map, 16 *Personalities* (last accessed July 29, 2018), https://www.16personalities.com/country-profiles/global/world.
49 Id. at 231.
50 Id. at 234.
51 Id. at 256.
52 Id. at 259.
53 Id. at 258. Cain offers a handy, albeit simple, way to test your introversion and that of others, available here: https://www.quietrev.com/the-introvert-test/.

11
PAN-CULTURAL MOTIVATION

Nothing can be made from nothing.

Lucretius

We've discussed how assertive types tend to have a high need for achievement. Let's explore now how people around the world are motivated. We can begin with what we already know – the most engaged workers are 50 percent more likely to exceed expectations than unengaged workers, while companies with engaged workers see 54 percent higher retention, 89 percent higher customer satisfaction and *400 percent greater revenue*.[1] However, a mere 13 percent of employees worldwide are engaged at work,[2] so the opportunity loss is substantial. This leads us to the all-important question: how can we better motivate our employees?

In 1943, Abraham Maslow offered a hierarchy of needs as a measurement of human happiness.[3] His model, though slightly modified and critiqued over the years, is still largely in use today. Maslow argued that humans have lower-level existential needs, such as food and water, which must be first satisfied.[4] However, once these lower level needs are satisfied, "*at once other (and 'higher') needs emerge. And when these in turn are satisfied, again new (and still higher) needs emerge and so on. This is what we mean by saying that the basic human needs are organized into a hierarchy.*"[5]

At the middle level of this hierarchy, we demand and pursue safety, stability and health.[6] We aim to satisfy these needs in several ways: (1) through health care or exercise; (2) by punishing murderers and other criminals; and (3) by seeking stable jobs but being ready to go on strike until satisfactory pensions are secured. Once all this is achieved, we are still not satisfied – we turn now to the next level of pursuits: the pursuit of love, and the need for affection and a sense of belonging (or "social relationships").[7]

Finally, resting atop Maslow's pyramid are the themes that dominate this chapter: the need for achievement (or "mastery"), for esteem and reputation, for autonomy and independence.[8] Esteem and reputation result in being treated with respect, and respect is often given as a result of accomplishment, background or status.[9] Autonomy refers to the ability to choose how one's time is spent and to the perception that one experiences intellectual and physical freedom.[10] Finally, one feels a sense of mastery when learning something new.[11] Mastery is also felt when one is able to realize and achieve at work what she perceives as her strongest ability.[12] When these outcomes are achieved, people tend to have positive feelings about their lives (Figure 11.1).[13]

> "Liberty," he cried in what was later described as his most glorious speech, "is the most precious possession of all mankind. Food and water are nothing; clothing and shelter are luxuries. He who is free stands with his head held high, even if hungry, naked and homeless."
>
> Victor Hugo[14]

Only once we achieve satisfaction of the higher levels is true happiness achieved, or, as Maslow writes, "feelings of self-confidence, worth, strength, capability and adequacy of being useful and necessary in the world."[15] But without first satisfying the lower levels of the hierarchy, we cannot hope to achieve full satisfaction of the higher levels. Researchers Louis Tay and Ed Diener note that "[p]eople require all ... needs to be fulfilled for higher evaluation of life, but it is not enough – additional factors are relevant."[16]

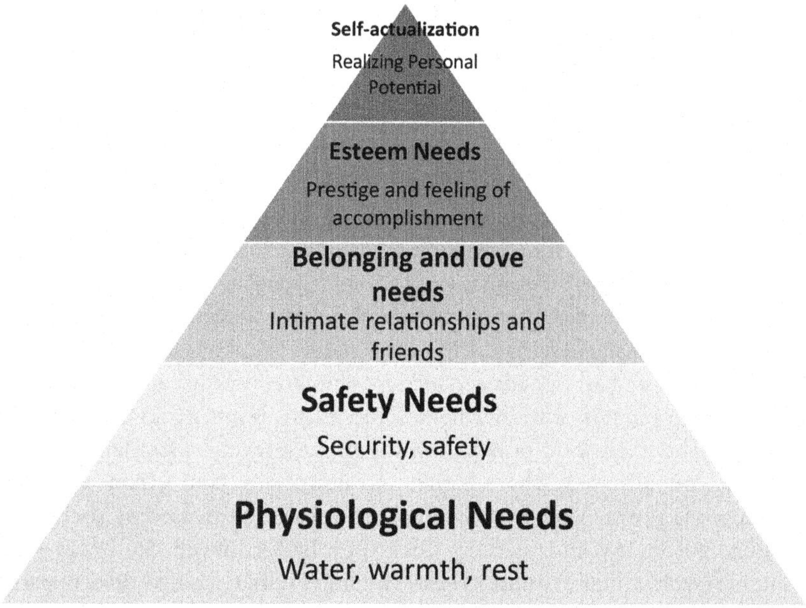

FIGURE 11.1 Maslow's hierarchy of needs.

The essence of Maslow's hierarchy is that we are motivated *intrinsically* to aspire toward the highest levels of that hierarchy. Ryan and Deci (2000), in refining the top of Maslow's hierarchy, referred to mastery, autonomy and social relationships as the "three needs of *self-determination*" (emphasis added).[i] To be intrinsically motivated means that, without the push of others (such as employers), we will pursue certain actions that we understand from experience or observation are likely to result in happiness. As Steve Jobs said, "If you are working on something that you really care about, you don't have to be pushed. The vision pulls you."[17] Organizations then should at worst get out of the way, but optimally they should create the conditions for our natural, intrinsic motivation to drive us forward beyond the middling levels of the hierarchy.

Intrinsic Motivation – Cross-cultural Implications

For decades, motivational theory in the United States seemed to neglect these ideas, focusing instead on extrinsic motivations – bonuses, compensation and other benefits.[18] It was thought that the individualistic nature of Americans made this form of motivation particularly effective, even as cross-cultural researchers sought to explain motivation for more collectivist peoples. The idea of universal explanations for well-being, and relatedly motivation, were considered decidedly out of fashion.[19] As a result, corporations focused on paying employees a little more, giving a higher bonus, pushing toward that next promotion. It turns out, however, that compensation is not as all-explanatory as we once thought, even for individualists. Compensation, after all, satisfies only the middle level of the hierarchy, leaving the need for mastery, autonomy and social relationships unaffected.

Tay and Diener found that across 123 countries, *people everywhere desired and aspired towards these happiness indicators.* Their findings indicate that these drivers of happiness – social relationships, autonomy and mastery – are "wired into humans."[20] It is important to note that one's country of origin and domicile substantially affect the likelihood of satisfying the lower-level needs, without which little else matters.[21] Tay and Diener add that their findings "do not preclude the possibility that cultures might emphasize some needs more than others, with this leading to certain differences" in behavior.[22] For instance, we might speculate that need for achievement mediates the strength of motivation with respect to mastery, doing what one does best at work.

However, once basic needs are met, people are almost equally motivated to continue in pursuit of higher needs, and at this point geography has little bearing on the likelihood of reaching the highest levels of satisfaction.[23] Put differently, people everywhere – rich and poor, rural and urban, and in all world regions – were consistently and intrinsically motivated by social relationships, autonomy and mastery once they had achieved the lower levels of the hierarchy. These studies therefore suggest that choice of occupation will be a stronger predictor of satisfaction across Maslow's hierarchy than culture.[24]

We are motivated for example by "the rewarding pursuit of nontrivial challenges,"[25] the satisfaction of which brings a sense of mastery. The implication is that pursuing these nontrivial goals is only "rewarding" if reaching them is yes, challenging, but also *possible*. Unskilled laborers, for instance, may deal with tasks that are possible, but not particularly challenging, while bankers, lawyers and IT technicians may regularly face challenges but can lose sleep wondering whether the challenges are solvable.

Hofstede found that unskilled workers were motivated by the lowest goals in Maslow's hierarchy – security and physical comfort, along with sufficient compensation to meet basic needs.[26] He found that "[u]nskilled workers in present-day society in the countries surveyed are not likely to attain work goals like [mastery] and autonomy," so they were less motivated by these benefits.[27] By contrast, managers and professionals took these lower-level needs for granted, so they most valued higher-level needs.[28] Finally, clerks were surveyed and found to have their lower-level needs met, but obtaining autonomy and mastery proved unlikely given their current positions. Therefore, they might have been happy to receive more autonomy and mastery, but like the unskilled workers, they most aspired for the achievable. In this case, that meant the middle of the hierarchy: satisfying their need for social support and love through cooperation and friendly relationships with coworkers.[29]

A similar dynamic helps explain our uncertainty avoidance findings. There we saw countries that have taken steps to reduce uncertainty tend to desire fewer rules and greater independence. These countries tend to be economically developed, and thus the people of these countries have reached the lower levels of Maslow's hierarchy. As a result, they desire fewer rules and greater independence in order to fully pursue autonomy and mastery. By contrast, those countries where the future is most uncertain tend to be undeveloped, and people there desire greater structure in a hope that this will bring economic development. Until such development is achieved and their lower-level needs are met, they are rather unconcerned about obtaining mastery and autonomy.[30]

Consequently, while all people would be *happy* to reach the top of the proverbial pyramid, people in some professions and some countries have, in effect, given up on this dream. The implications are that only highly skilled employees require autonomy, mastery and social relationships to be fully motivated. For others, something less might suffice. However, imagine how motivated your middle- and lower-level workers will be if they are given access to levels of the hierarchy that they previously considered out of reach. The satisfaction of those low-skilled workers would dramatically increase if their middle-level needs were satisfied along with their basic needs, and the clerks' satisfaction would increase if they were given greater autonomy and mastery while still maintaining that social support from coworkers. The organization would, after a fashion, literally exceed expectations. Anytime a manager is able to help an employee reach some or all of these higher forms of life experience, the employee's motivation is likely to dramatically improve.

These findings also suggest that where we are already intrinsically motivated – that is, when our activities allow us to achieve some combination of social relationship, autonomy and mastery – employers need not extrinsically motivate through additional compensation and other benefits so long as our basic needs continue to be met (this assumes that the existing compensation is considered fair). For instance, the professionals and managers in the above studies are likely to be less motivated by additional compensation than are low-skilled workers. Admittedly, this has something to do with the fact that they are already sufficiently paid to meet their basic needs, but the fact remains that they were able to find satisfaction in their work – satisfaction from the process of mastering knowledge and exercising autonomy over their lives – in a way the low-skilled workers were not. Research has long showed that once an income sufficient to meet basic needs is met, increased levels of income no longer increase satisfaction levels.[31]

The implications go still further. What recent research has revealed is that where extrinsic rewards are given for activities that are already satisfying our higher-level needs, we can actually *lose* our intrinsic motivation. Our minds play a trick on us and seem to say, "Well, if I'm being paid for this, then I'm doing it for the money rather than for mastery, autonomy or social support, and if I'm only doing this for the money, then it must not be very satisfactory on its own." Suddenly, that activity is performed not for intrinsic reasons, but for extrinsic reasons. And what happens if we stop receiving those extrinsic benefits? We lose interest in the activity.

When Extrinsic Rewards Discourage Intrinsic Motivation

When we see someone else performing a task for which there is no apparent extrinsic motivation, we presume this person is intrinsically motivated[32] – in short, that he or she receives some pleasure from the task, and consequently wonder if we too would feel this positive emotion.

This urge is famously represented in Mark Twain's Tom Sawyer, when Tom is charged with painting a fence as punishment. Initially, when Tom surveys the task before him "all gladness left him and a deep melancholy settled down upon his spirit."[33] When his nemesis Ben comes along, "the very boy of all boys, whose ridicule he had been dreading," Tom pretends he is fascinated by painting his fence, indeed "surveying his last touch with an artist's eye." When Ben taunts him, noting that Tom will have to work while he swims, Tom responds "what do you call work?" He continues to "daintily brush back and forth – step back to note the effect – add a touch here and there – criticize the effect again," and Ben becomes "more and more absorbed."[34] Tom quickly sees that by pitching whitewashing as a special talent, he can turn the tables. As all familiar with the story know well, in the end, Tom is not only able to get Ben to paint his fence for him but to make him and others pay for the opportunity![35]

Of course, we don't just decode others' motivations on the basis of the extrinsic rewards they're receiving for tasks. We also do this for ourselves.[36] If there is no extrinsic reward for a task we're engaged in, how do we justify our participation in an activity? After all, we're reasonable beings, and doing a task for no reward seems irrational. Our subconscious minds bridge the gap, saying, in essence, "Oh, I must be doing this because it's fun (or rewarding in some other way)!" In this way, our subconscious brain convinces us that in the absence of an extrinsic reward, we are receiving an intrinsic reward: enjoyment perhaps, or esteem if the task helps others, or mastery if it involves solving a difficult task.

This is wonderfully illustrated in a study involving participants that were asked to spin a peg and take part in other mundane activities for an hour's time.[37] Half the participants were told they'd be paid $20 for the task, while the other half were given just one dollar.[38] Upon completing the mind-numbing task, they were asked to speak to future participants and encouraged to communicate that the task was enjoyable.[39] For the most part, both the dollar and $20 recipients did just that.[40] Thereafter, the original respondents were surveyed to determine how enjoyable they actually found the task.[41]

Those paid $20 found the task dreadfully boring.[42] Why then did they tell others to take part? They were able to justify the lie by reminding themselves of that tidy $20 bill awaiting them.

But those paid a dollar? Why would they possibly lie to someone about a task, knowing that such a small sum was on the line? Unable to rationalize their behavior on the basis of the compensation – but still wanting to help out the researchers – they instead convinced themselves that the task was actually enjoyable.[43] They had no trouble convincing others to take part because all they had to do was tell the truth! The disconnect – the "cognitive dissonance" – was resolved.

We suspect that the apparent joy of those spinning the peg would have worn off relatively quickly, and if they hadn't been asked to encourage others to join, they certainly would not have found the task so interesting.[44] Consequently, reducing pay to increase motivation is not a likely winner for employers.

What the findings really suggest is an unexpected interplay between extrinsic rewards and intrinsic motivation. As we see in the next two cases, this is especially true in situations where extrinsic rewards are given when people are engaged in tasks for which – unlike the peg spinning exercise – we would expect high levels of intrinsic motivation. Consider:

> [Researcher Edward] Deci hypothesized that rewarding subjects with money and "closely related tangible rewards" for engaging in an intrinsically interesting task would decrease their subsequent interest in that task in the absence of such external rewards. To test this proposition, Deci asked college subjects to solve a number of inherently interesting puzzles during three experimental sessions. Following an initial base-line session for all subjects, one group of subjects was paid for solving a second series of puzzles, while a second group was not paid. In a third session, neither group was paid. During a break in each session, subjects were left alone for a few minutes to do whatever they

wished, including continuing work on the puzzles. During this time, the subjects' behavior was observed and recorded from behind a one-way mirror. Subjects who had been paid during the second session tended to show a greater decrease in intrinsic interest from the first to the third session than subjects who had not been paid.[45]

Other researchers extended this study to children, asking preschool children to take part in a drawing activity. Initially, all children showed an interest in drawing.[46] Then some of the students were told they'd receive a certificate with a gold seal and ribbon for their activities, and these students spent less time drawing than children that did not expect a reward.[47]

Both studies indicate that extrinsic rewards can actually *diminish* intrinsic motivation, and the fact that it appeared in both children and adults suggests the effect is quite strong and pervasive. Erasmus University's Muel Kapstein puts it as follows: "Rewards ... remind us of unpleasant things we were forced to do. This begins at a young age, when children are rewarded for leaving an empty plate (for instance with dessert or being allowed to leave the table sooner), for doing housework and tidying their room. This leads us to associate rewards with activities for which we are not intrinsically motivated. By coupling rewards to work, work is associated with boredom, monotony and annoyance, even if this is not really the case. Rewards are only effective when it comes to activities which people do not wish to do, and for which they cannot be intrinsically motivated."[48]

In short, our autonomy is stolen – or at least that is our perception – when extrinsic rewards are made contingent on the performance of certain tasks. This behavior is known as the "over-justification" hypothesis. It holds that intrinsic motivation can be reduced by providing certain extrinsic rewards.[49]

We could go on – an abundance of studies now show that poorly implemented external rewards diminish intrinsic motivation.[50] There is, for example, the story of blood donations dropping by half when financial compensation was introduced,[51] as well as the case where 50 percent of the people in Switzerland once willing to store nuclear waste in their local vicinity withdrew their support once compensation was offered.[52] Even in the field of intellectual property, it has been argued that the extrinsic principle used to motivate creative production needs profound rethinking, given the flourishing of non-extrinsically motivated outlets such as fan fiction and YouTube.[53] In all these cases, "the intrinsic motive for contributing to a social problem (a shortage of blood or the need for nuclear waste storage) disappeared."[54]

These results do not, however, mean that compensation cannot be offered to employees functioning with intrinsic motivation. It turns out that there are some ways in which compensation tends to undermine intrinsic rewards and other ways in which it does not.

For certain tasks, motivation is most undermined when compensation (or any reward) is made contingent on completing the task according to certain standards.[55]

Under such a construct, the individual must act in a certain way in order to receive the reward, so in a literal sense, autonomy is diminished.[56] Motivation is somewhat less undermined – but still adversely affected in a significant way – when the reward is not contingent on quality but is contingent simply on completion of the task.[57] Motivation is again undermined, albeit somewhat less, when rewards are contingent not on completing the task but on at least undertaking the task or making an effort toward completion.[58] All of these forms of reward, therefore, may be said to be counterproductive in situations where intrinsic motivation already exists.

What kind of reward is consistent with intrinsic motivation? An entirely unexpected reward has no measurable effect on intrinsic motivation.[59] An unexpected reward is, as the reader might guess, a reward that is provided for task completion but which the recipient did not realize was coming. In this case, the individual completed the task without expecting compensation, so he had to justify the completion of the task on the basis of intrinsic motivators (enjoyment, esteem, mastery, etc.).[60]

Of course if a reward is paid once, the individual may come to expect these supposedly "unexpected" rewards, so over time intrinsic motivation can be lost. When rewards come to be expected, they should at least be noncontingent.[61] Expected but noncontingent rewards are those given regardless of whether the individual completes or even undertakes the task. Autonomy is thus in no way threatened, so intrinsic motivation is left untouched.[62] Accountability is admittedly minimal in this case. However, if your employees truly are intrinsically motivated, they're not likely to underperform even with this relative lack of oversight. Compensation for the intrinsically motivated is consequently best thought of as a means to an end – a means to continue producing high quality work rather than as a reward for doing that work. Unfortunately, many organizations do not fully grasp how this works and often inadvertently undermine the very motivation they seek to engage.

Those resources that were previously spent on expanding the middle levels of the hierarchy – providing greater stability through compensation, pensions and the like – may at some point be better spent on the higher levels. For example, employers may increase mastery through more employee training and mentoring opportunities. They may also facilitate greater cohesion through team building exercises in order to create social support[ii] and leverage this increased trust to facilitate greater employee autonomy. As we will see, even praise can go far in supporting a sense of mastery, while conversely, even well-meaning comments can at times undermine those same things.

When Extrinsic Rewards Encourage Intrinsic Motivation

At India Hicks, the until recently thriving fashion company, 2,500 ambassadors worked almost entirely independently – from their homes and essentially without oversight. Employees were provided a commission of 25% on their own sales, but also received an 8% commission on sales made by the "ambassadors" that they had brought in. They then received a slightly smaller commission on those ambassadors' ambassadors (5%) and even received a commission on those ambassadors' ambassadors' ambassadors (3%)!

India Hicks' former national director Tracy DeLisle veritably gushed with enthusiasm for the community that was created from this autonomy, allowing ambassadors to work independently, but working to validate their achievements and make them feel a part of a larger community:

> I have worked to engage my team in a collaborative recognition process. I personally make it a point to send hand-written notes of appreciation and recognition each week or month and include callouts and highlights in a monthly newsletter I publish. However, our group at large is great about posting congratulatory (and motivational!) messages in our social media outlets. I can't specifically speak to any ROI [return on investment], but I do know that people are always commenting to me about the cards that they receive, and I believe that whether or not it is motivating them to do more, it is making them feel loved, and that is good enough for me![63]

In the fall of 2018, however, Delisle would leave the company—along with a host of others – when India Hicks shifted to a new, less group-oriented approach, removing all ambassador-related commissions and providing instead a flat percentage on sales.

This purely financial approach to motivating – albeit still autonomous – proved fatal As this book goes to press, India Hicks has decided to close its doors, stating officially it can no longer continue in the face of "too many obstacles."

Used correctly, nonfinancial extrinsic rewards, including verbal affirmation, can actually bolster intrinsic motivation by furthering that sense of mastery and building social relationships. Used incorrectly, however, autonomy is undermined just as surely as when compensation is used in a misguided way. In an autonomy-undermining scenario, the verbal rewards are used as a controlling mechanism. For instance, "keep up the good work" may sound like a nice compliment, but what's the hidden message here? The recipient may interpret this as a warning to not let up on her hard work, which in turn diminishes her sense of autonomy.[64]

Similarly, so-called "backhanded compliments" may reduce a sense of mastery. For instance, "You really seemed to know what you were talking about in that meeting," suggests you normally don't, and "That presentation was *actually* pretty good" suggests it normally isn't.[65]

By contrast, unambiguous appreciation has a positive impact on confidence – bolstering one's sense of respect, contributing to a feeling of mastery and even contributing to social connectedness – and without impacting autonomy.[66]

The following study by R.E. Kraut exemplifies this:

> A collector for the American Heart Association went from door to door in different neighborhoods of the city of New Haven. When anyone donated, the collector gave him a leaflet. In half of the cases the collector also said some words of appreciation: "You are a generous person. I wish more of the people I met were as charitable as you." To half of those who donated nothing, the collector said the following: "Let me just give you one of our leaflets anyway. We've been giving them to everyone, even people like you who are uncharitable and don't normally give to these causes." This was the first part of the experiment.
>
> The second part followed approximately a week later. A collector called again, this time to collect money for multiple sclerosis. At each house the collector noted what was donated. Did the previous collector's reaction affect what people gave this time?
>
> This was indeed the case: of those who had given money the first time and only received the leaflet, 47 percent gave again; of those who had also received words of appreciation, 62 percent gave again – and the sum given rose by as much as 70 percent! The reverse also appeared to apply: of the people who had given nothing and received a negative response, significantly fewer people gave compared to those who had given nothing but received no negative response. This experiment illustrates the effect of appreciation: a few simple words can make people feel valued, rightly or wrongly, and therefore put in more, or indeed less, effort.[67]

What we see here is that the positive words were not loaded in the way a phrase like "keep it up" is, nor was it a backhanded compliment as it might have been if the collectors said something like, "Well, I guess every little bit helps," when receiving modest sums. Instead, the words used by the collectors showed unambiguous appreciation for the generous act without seeking to control future behavior. The negative words, by contrast, threatened the recipient's sense of social connectedness and by implying they should have behaved differently, in a certain way, their autonomy.

A famous series of studies on IQ and verbal rewards sheds further light on the negative effect of even well-intentioned communications. These studies examined how children behaved when told they were smart or otherwise praised for intelligence and compared this behavior to children who were praised for their efforts but not for their intelligence.[68]

Those praised for intelligence were later found to care less about learning than the children praised for effort; they were instead more concerned about completing the task with little effort in order to show that the praise-giver was correct about their intelligence.[69] They took fewer risks as well, afraid that in making mistakes their intelligence – which adults had implied was the most important trait to which they could aspire – would be questioned.[70] They thus avoided the most challenging tasks. In this way, they might be said to have lost the autonomy to make mistakes while learning, and as a result, intrinsic motivation decreased.

The children praised for effort were, by contrast, willing to work hard to master subjects, because this confirmed the compliment. They were in essence subtly rewarded for learning, which bolstered their preexisting intrinsic desire for mastery. Children from a variety of ethnicities have conformed to these results, suggesting a pan-cultural application to the findings.[71] Managers should therefore consider their praise carefully and specifically ask whether the words chosen are likely to encourage mastery, autonomy and social support.

This may be the time for some of you to say, "That's all well and good, but I can't feed my family on compliments and intrinsic motivation." Fortunately, that's not the only option. Where there is already intrinsic motivation, the non-contingent compensation discussed above can ensure financial security without undermining intrinsic motivations.

As it happens, not all activities are intrinsically motivating, and they probably never will be – even as more and more roles automate, grunt work and mundane activities will remain for humans to do. The overall takeaway however is that where the job responsibilities of employees do not allow them to reach the upper ends of the needs hierarchy, employee performance can be dramatically improved through extrinsic motivation.

When compensation is offered, we know that the closer the connection between the activity performed and the reward given, the more motivating the reward.[72] It is more motivating, for example, to receive a paycheck at the end of the workday than at the end of the month. We also tend to assume that the larger the size of the rewards, the greater the motivation. As it turns out, this is only true up to a point. For nonmechanical or cognitive tasks, large monetary rewards can have a surprisingly negative effect. This is true regardless of whether one is intrinsically motivated or not.

Dollar Signs and Task Performance

Rats – yes, rats – are our starting point for this component of motivation. In *The Upside of Irrationality*, Dan Ariely relates an early twentieth century study involving the performance outcomes of rats in navigating a maze.[73] The researchers found that when the rats were given a slight shock for making incorrect decisions in the maze, they ended up doing a better job of successfully completing the maze.[74] When the shocks increased to a moderate intensity, performance increased yet more.[75] As the shock intensity increased to very high levels, however, performance declined.[76] At a certain point, the shocks were so severe as to shock both the body and the mind – the rats become frozen by fear, unable to recall the right and wrong turns, unable to navigate the maze to any discernable degree.[77]

These are more like punitive incentives – so they motivate differently than compensation. That said, they certainly do incentivize in their own way! Ariely writes that this experiment "clearly showed that incentives can be a double-edged sword.

Up to a certain point, they motivate us to learn and perform well. But beyond that point, motivational pressure can be so high that it actually *distracts* an individual from concentrating on and carrying out a task – an undesirable outcome for anyone."[78] Ariely wondered whether this held true for humans as well, and that is precisely what he found. Ariely stuck with compensation, however, as a motivator for humans, and he found that just as punishments can be too severe to bring about better performance, rewards can be so large as to blind one to the outcome sought.

Ariely's team traveled to India to carry out the study. Once there, the researchers gathered members of a village to take part in a series of intellectual tasks involving creativity, concentration, memory and problem-solving skills.[79] The better the participants did, the greater the reward would be,[80] although not every participant was eligible for the same reward. Before the tasks began, participants were assigned to one of three bonus groups: the small bonus group, the mid-level bonus group or the high bonus group.[81] They were told to which group they were assigned and given a breakdown on exactly how much money they stood to gain for high levels of performance.[82]

The reason this small Indian town was chosen was that the favorable exchange rate, low cost of living and high levels of poverty made it possible for the researchers to reward the high bonus people with amounts that, by local standards, were astronomical.[83] Even the small bonus was the equivalent of one day's pay by local standards, and the middle level was equivalent to two weeks' pay. The high bonus, meanwhile, was equivalent to five months' pay.[84]

The results, as Ariely relates, were as follows: "Those who could earn a small bonus ... and the mid-level bonus ... did not differ much from each other. We concluded that since even the small payment was worth a substantial amount to our participants, it probably already maximized their motivation. But how did they perform when the very large bonus ... was on the line? ... the data from our experiment showed that people, at least in this regard, are very much like rats. Relative to those in the low or medium-bonus conditions, they achieved good or very good performance less than a third of the time. The experience was so stressful to those in the very large-bonus condition that they choked under the pressure, much like the rats...".[85]

Cognizant that the results had questionable cross-cultural applicability given the narrow subject set – that of rural India – the researchers took their test to a wholly different group: MIT students. Here, they included both cognitive and noncognitive (or mechanical) activities. In this case, the higher the compensation, the higher the participants performed on the mechanical tasks.[86] However, "once the task required even some rudimentary cognitive skills," performance did in fact decline with the higher bonuses just as seen with the Indian villagers.[87] Ariely speculates that the reason for this is that the reward recipient is distracted from the task – they are blinded, not by fear as were the rats, but by all those money signs dancing across their line of vision.[88] In the case of mechanical tasks, by contrast, little if any mental acuity is required, so no such distraction takes place. Ultimately, the experiment would be performed nine times throughout the world, with similar results occurring in eight of the cases.[89]

Thus, the findings suggest that for mechanical, mundane tasks, higher compensation does indeed tend to result in higher performance. In essence, Henry Ford was right when he more than doubled the salaries of his Model T line workers.[90] However, when it comes to compensating people for intellectual activities – the kinds that professionals around the world perform and which are increasing with each passing day – higher is not always better and can, in fact, be worse.

Ariely specifically questioned the relevance of these findings for high-end professionals of the sort raking in millions of dollars in performance bonuses. Would they behave like the rats? he wondered. Indeed, the intellectual tasks that the MIT and Indian participants performed were meant to generally replicate the type of tasks that bankers performed. Though the big earners are understandably reluctant to take part in his experiments, Ariely hypothesizes that they too are subject to this effect. Jim Collins, similarly, at least confirmed that salaries don't seem to increase performance as we once thought, writing in *Good to Great*: "we found no systematic pattern linking executive compensation to the process of going from good to great" as a company.[91]

So while the results do not tell us exactly how much is too much, we know from the studies that there is a point where rewards become inefficient and indeed counterproductive, and we know too that the monetary amount at which this occurs is dependent on the relative wealth of the individual in question.

On the opposite side, we know that compensation must be at least high enough to meet basic needs. This, however, is rarely a challenge for professionals in the contemporary world. The bigger challenge is ensuring that compensation does not demotivate. This can occur when some people are paid more for the same or similar work, which results in a sense of outrage.

In fact, many many cross-cultural organizations do pay some workers more for the same type and quality of work. This happens most commonly when employees from wealthy nations relocate to poorer countries. In these cases, the relocated employees may be paid the same salary as they would have earned at home – after all, why would they relocate if it involved a dramatic pay cut? For the local employees, however, they are often paid a lower currency that is locally, but not internationally, competitive. After all, why would the company pay locals more money than the market demanded? Through this market-driven logic, local employees find themselves feeling underappreciated and marginalized.

Emerson's Montupet speaks to this issue. He says that at the lower levels, Emerson more often pays locals based on local wages, but at the higher levels of the corporate structure, the salaries become more homogeneous. The reason for this is, again, practical. Montupet says: high-level employees are often employable at an international level. If Emerson doesn't pay the international wage to high level workers, these internationally competitive employees will depart for "greener" pastures.[92] The lower-level employees are not likely to be able to move from one country, so they're unlikely to quit if their salaries are locally competitive.

They will, however, resent the double standard. As a result, Montupet notes that increasingly at Emerson, this wage structure is being extended to entry-level professional jobs.

He explains: "We hired Chinese MBAs, so they were employees who had done their Engineering studies in China and then their business studies in the US. For the US MBAs, we give them a US salary, and if we send them abroad, we are going to give them an excellent package, we are going to pay for their kids to go to private school, and so forth. And then you take a Chinese person graduating from the United States and send them back to China and give them a Chinese salary. Now that guy that was sitting next to you at the university and got the same job is making three times what you are making! And he gets the international school for his kids, and you're asking, 'Why not me?' So what do you do as a company? Companies have not perfectly solved that problem, but the main thing with compensation is that employees need to feel they are not mistreated and are paid similarly for similar work. If you don't do it, not only don't you motivate, but you demotivate people really quickly."[93]

Bringing It All Together

In this chapter, we found that once basic needs are met, people are intrinsically motivated to achieve social connections, autonomy and mastery, while respect and esteem from others also tends to motivate.

Secondly, we found that when our professions allow us to further these interests we are intrinsically motivated, and badly timed external rewards such as compensation can actually reduce our intrinsic motivation. Without intrinsic motivation, we will *only* carry on if external benefits are forthcoming, so if ever those rewards are discontinued, so too does our performance cease or decline in quality. We have, in essence, diminished motivation by attempting to ignite it. However, we found that when tangible rewards are given to the intrinsically motivated employee they should either be unexpected (such as a bonus), or noncontingent (i.e., guaranteed regardless of quality or even completion). Rewards should also be fair such that similar compensation is paid for similar work regardless of nationality.

Additionally, we found that managers have more in their toolkit than just monetary rewards: increasing employee autonomy and facilitating greater mastery over a subject is likely to pay dividends, while increasing cohesion of the organization will provide greater social connectedness. Moreover, verbal rewards such as compliments and other votes of confidence can effectively promote intrinsic motivation by increasing one's sense of mastery, as long as those rewards are unambiguously positive. If, however, the language used is such as to control behavior (keep it up), or is a backhanded compliment (you did better than expected!), then intrinsic motivation declines.

Finally, we have seen that regardless of whether one is or is not intrinsically motivated, compensation for cognitive activities should be in the "Goldilocks" range – not too large, not too small. If too small, basic needs go unmet and motivation drops precipitously; if too large, the dollars signs distract and performance declines (Table 11.1).

TABLE 11.1 Motivation

Intrinsically motivated for social connections, autonomy, and mastery.
Extrinsic rewards should be focused on increasing these forms of intrinsic motivation.
Extrinsic compensation demotivating if unfair (for example, differing levels of compensation for the same work), but not necessarily motivating just because they are fair.
Extrinsic compensation demotivating if there was intrinsic motivation, and rewards are expected and contingent on performance.
Extrinsic compensation not demotivating if there is intrinsic motivation, and the rewards are unexpected or noncontingent.
Extrinsic compensation is distracting if too large and provided for performance that requires cognitive capacity.
Extrinsic compensation is motivating if there is not intrinsic motivation, and if the performance does not require cognitive capacity then this motivation only increases as the compensation increases.

Notes

i This is the known as the "three needs of the self-determination theory.," See Id.
ii And also, in this case, derive the benefits of cohesion set forth in the chapter on groupthink and free-riding.

References

1 Rob Goffee and Gareth Jones, "Creating the Best Workplace on Earth," *Harvard Business Review* (May 2013) (citing to the Hay Group data), https://hbr.org/2013/05/creating-the-best-workplace-on-earth.
2 Steve Crabtree, "Worldwide, 13% of Employees Are Engaged at Work," *Gallup* (Oct. 8, 2013), http://news.gallup.com/poll/165269/worldwide-employees-engaged-work.aspx.
3 A.H. Maslow, "A Theory of Human Motivation," 50 *Psychological Review*, 370–396 (1943).
4 Id. at 373.
5 Id. at 375.
6 Id. at 376–377.
7 Id. at 380.
8 Id. at 381–382.
9 Louis Tay and Ed Diener, "Needs and Subjective Well-Being around the World," 101 *Journal of Personality and Social Psychology* 354, 355 (2011).
10 Id. at 356.
11 Id. at 355.
12 Id.
13 Id. at 357.
14 Samuel Edwards, *Victor Hugo: A Tumultuous Life*, D. McKay Co. (1971), loc 3825.
15 Maslow, *supra* note 621 at 382.
16 Tay and Diener, *supra* note 627 at 359.
17 56 Motivational and Inspirational Quotes about Success, *supra* note 461.
18 Gelfand et al., *supra* note 32 at 455.
19 Id. at 354.

20 Id.
21 Id. at 363.
22 Id. at 362 (citing to S. Oishi, E.F. Diener, R.F. Lucas, and E.M. Suh, "Cross-Cultural Variations in Predictors of Life Satisfaction: Perspectives from Needs and Values," *Personality and Social Psychology Bulletin* 25 (1999): 980–990. doi:10.1177/01461672992511006).
23 Id. at 363.
24 Geert H. Hofstede, "The Colors of Collars," 7 *The Columbia Journal of World Business* 72, 79 (1972).
25 Guy Claxton, "What's the Point of School?" *Oneworld Publication* 221 (2008) (citing to Jonathan Haidt, *The Happiness Hypothesis*. William Heinemann: London, 2006, 221).
26 Hofstede, *supra* note 641 at 78.
27 Id.
28 Id.
29 Id. at 77–78.
30 Venaik and Brewer, *supra* note 474 at 1309.
31 http://content.time.com/time/magazine/article/0,9171,2019628,00.html.
32 Mark R. Lepper, David Greene, and Richard E. Nisbett, "Undermining Children's Intrinsic Interest with Extrinsic Reward: A Test of the 'Overjustification Hypothesis,'" 28 *Journal of Personality and Social Psychology* 129 (1973).
33 Mark Twain, *Adventures of Tom Sawyer*, loc 168 of 3202 Amazon Classic.
34 Mark Twain, *Adventures of Tom Sawyer*, loc 168 of 3202 Amazon Classic 218 of 3202.
35 Indeed, as Twain puts it, Tom "gave up the brush with reluctance in his face, but alacrity in his heart." *Adventures of Tom Sawyer* 224 of 3202.
36 Lepper et al., *supra* note 649 at 129.
37 Festnger and Carlsmith, 204.
38 Ibid, 205.
39 Ibid.
40 Ibid, 206.
41 Ibid.
42 Ibid, 207.
43 Ibid.
44 Festinger 207.
45 Lepper et al., *supra* note 649 at 130 (citing to E.L. Deci, "Effects of Externally Mediated Rewards on Intrinsic Motivation," *Journal of Personality and Social Psychology* 18 (1971): 105–11S).
46 Id. at 131.
47 Id. at 131, 134.
48 Kapstein, *supra* note 532 at 160.
49 Lepper et al., *supra* note 649 at 130.
50 Kapstein, *supra* note 532 at 159.
51 Id.
52 Id. at 159–160.
53 Biggs, *supra* note 215.
54 Kapstein, *supra* note 532 at 160.
55 Edward Deci, Richard M. Ryan, and Richard Koestner, "A Meta Analytic Review of Experiments Examining the Effects of Extrinsic Reviews on Intrinsic Motivation" 125 *Psychological Bulletin* 627, 644 (1999).
56 Id.
57 Id. at 640, 641.
58 Id. at 641.
59 Id. at 640.
60 Id.
61 Id.

62 Id.
63 DeLisle, *supra* note 207.
64 Deci et al., *supra* note 672 at 640 (citing to Ryan, 1982).
65 Maddy Foley, "6 Backhanded Compliments You Didn't Realize You Were Giving," *Bustle* (Feb. 8, 2016), https://www.bustle.com/articles/140405-6-backhanded-compliments-you-didnt-realize-you-were-giving-your-coworkers.
66 Deci et al., *supra* note 672 at 629 (citing to E.L. Deci, "Effects of Externally Mediated Rewards on Intrinsic Motivation," *Journal of Personality and Social Psychology* 18 (1971): 105–115).
67 Kapstein, *supra* note 532 at 150–151 (citing to R.E. Kraut, "Effects of Social Labeling on Giving to Charity," *Journal of Experimental Social Psychology* 9 (1973): 551–562).
68 C.M. Mueller and C.S. Dweck, "Praise for Intelligence Can Undermine Children's Motivation and Performance," 75 *Journal of Personality and Social Psychology* 33 (1998).
69 Id.
70 Id. at 34 (citing to Elliott and Dweck 1988).
71 Id. at 39.
72 Deci et al., *supra* note 672 at 627.
73 Ariely, *supra* note 96 at 18.
74 Id. at 19.
75 Id.
76 Id.
77 Id.
78 Id. at 20.
79 Id. at 21–22.
80 Id. at 22.
81 Id. at 21.
82 Id. at 23.
83 Id. at 21.
84 Id.
85 Id. at 26–27.
86 Id. at 28.
87 Id.
88 Id.
89 Linda Rothenberg, *Crazy Is a Compliment: The Power of Zigging When Everyone Else Zags* 187–188 (Portfolio/Penguin Group) (2014).
90 Tim Worstall, "The Story of Henry Ford's $5 a Day Wages: It's Not What You Think," *Forbes* (March 4, 2012), https://www.forbes.com/sites/timworstall/2012/03/04/the-story-of-henry-fords-5-a-day-wages-its-not-what-you-think/#6e334352766d.
91 Collins, *supra* note 142 at 49.
92 Montupet, supra note 10.
93 Id.

12
ATTITUDES IN TIME

Time destroys all things.

Nigerian Proverb

How do our perceptions of time affect our businesses? Consider that in Ethiopia, the more important a decision, the more time will pass before that decision is made.[1] Serious consideration of serious matters is, no doubt, a matter of prudence. However, one of the early cross-cultural experts, Edward T. Hall, wrote in 1960 that, "this is so much the case [in Ethiopia] that low-level bureaucrats there have a way of trying to elevate the prestige of their work by taking a long time to make up their minds."[2]

In America, deadlines serve as a way to stress the importance of a task.[3] "On my desk by end of day tomorrow" is not only a boss's anxiety-inducing demand but a clear indication that you are dealing with an important, time-sensitive issue. In parts of the Middle East, by contrast, deadlines can often be viewed as "overly demanding and ... exerting undue pressure."[4] Indeed, both Middle Eastern and Latin Americans are more tied up in the present and may be expected to "sit for several hours chatting with friends of friends just to strengthen the bonds with their friends."[5] In situations like these, relationships take precedence, and managers seeking to impose deadlines may struggle to obtain results.[6]

American business persons also tend to act within strict time constraints. The "what have you done for me lately?" achievement-oriented mentality is one that demands immediate results. The Japanese and Chinese have been known to take advantage of this American impatience to gain leverage in negotiations. For example, more than one Japanese or Chinese delegation has reacted with glee upon learning that their visiting counterparts purchased return tickets home – now they know they can make their most extreme demands on that last day before departure, and, more likely than not, the Americans will give in rather than return home empty-handed.[7]

Additionally, the amount of delay permissible within a business context varies considerably among societies. In the United States, Romania and Japan, business meetings typically require punctuality, as they do in Germany.[8] In the United States and Japan, however, social occasions may come with a certain "fashionably late" component.[9] In parts of Latin America, and especially the Middle East and Africa, meeting times may be advisory only, with considerably varying times of arrival.[10] To be safe and avoid giving offense in case your host arrives on time, it is typically advisable to arrive early – just be sure to bring a magazine.

Let's now explore the ways in which time itself is perceived differently among cultures, from those who live by the clock to those who live by the sun, from those who live in the past, to those who live in the future, and all those in between.

Time Orientation: Past, Present, and Future

The GLOBE report studies past, present and future orientations.[11] The authors find that people from past-oriented and future-oriented societies behave in many similar ways, with present societies being the "odd man out."[12]

Here's how the GLOBE authors define future orientation, present orientation and past orientation[i]:

> Cultural future orientation is the degree to which a collectivity encourages and rewards future-oriented behaviors such as planning and delaying gratification (House et al. 1999).[13] ... cultures with high future orientation have a strong capability and willingness to imagine future contingencies, formulate future goal states, and seek to achieve goals and develop strategies for meeting their future aspirations.[14]

Those who look to the future may view time as a monetizable commodity. Many people, for example, speak of "saving" time in their lives – and it was Ben Franklin who famously quipped that "time is money."[15] Time is thereby made equivalent to money, and it may be for this reason that those with future time orientations exhibit a heightened urgency in their behaviors.[16]

> Cultures with low future orientation, or high present orientation, show the capability to enjoy the moment and be spontaneous. They may show incapacity or unwillingness to plan a sequence to realize their desired goals, and may not appreciate the warning signals that their current behavior negatively influences realization of their goals in the future (Keough et al. 1999).[17]

As with so many of these cultural dimensions, history helps explain why it is that people across the world differ. It may be, for example, that those living in politically or socially unstable countries react with a high present orientation.[18] In these environments, the future may be so uncertain as to confound planning. *The Lord of War*, a movie loosely based on a true story, provides one extreme illustration of this idea when a Liberian sex-worker living amid a brutal civil war says to the main character, "Why do you worry about something that can kill you in ten years? We know so many things that can kill you today."[19]

Finally, the concept of past orientation shares considerable similarities with the concept of future orientation because individuals and collectives with high past orientation also show a high capacity and willingness to correct their current behavior. Past-oriented individuals and collectives do so by recalling and showing appreciation for prior learning, memories, obligations and traditions (Keough et al. 1999). Therefore, they prefer to sustain their favorable past experiences and seek to plan for maintaining the status quo if favorable experiences dominate in their past. Similarly, they may prefer not to repeat their unfavorable past experiences, and thus make all-around efforts to develop and realize a new vision and state of the future, grounded in some ideals of the past, once the sequence of events disjoining the present from the past has transpired.[20]

Essentially, people from countries focused on the past use it as a primary resource for correcting their futures. In this way, both, past and future-oriented people share in a sense a future orientation, and for the purposes of this next chapter are therefore treated collectively.

The results of the GLOBE study show diverse geographic results. Singapore looks to the future more than any country, with Switzerland coming in second, the native African population of South Africa third, followed by the Netherlands, Malaysia, Austria, Denmark, and Canada.[21] Contrary to the hypothesis put forth by Hofstede and Bond (1998), Confucian societies do not always look to the future.[22] Instead, Japan showed just a moderate future orientation, and China was lower still.[23] Anglo-American societies with high future orientation include Canada, while the United States and United Kingdom come in just slightly lower.[24] As a general rule, countries that have taken steps to avoid uncertainty – such as Singapore, Switzerland, Netherlands, Austria, and Denmark – exhibit future-oriented thinking at both the organizational and societal level.[25]

To the extent there are regional commonalities, we see that Eastern European, Middle Eastern, and Latin American countries tend to be more oriented to the present, as do African countries though to a somewhat lesser extent, while many Northern European and Germanic European societies look toward the future.[26] The GLOBE authors plausibly speculate that the high political stability and socioeconomic status of Northern European countries explains the high future orientations, while the turbulence exhibited in the 1990s in both Eastern Europe and Latin America – and still today in the Middle East – explain and indeed make rational the decision not to plan too far ahead.[27] Additionally, they speculate that a history of reliance on governmental decision-making in Eastern Europe and other post-communist states may inhibit planning for the future.[28]

Time Orientation and Economic Success

Organizations and societies with a strong future orientation tend to outperform those that fail to look long-term.[29] It is unclear, however, what is influencing what: it may be actually that increased wealth gives people the luxury to plan for the future in a way that is not seen in poorer societies and struggling organizations. For instance, the effects of living in poverty make an orientation toward anything other than the present need to pay bills, to buy food, and generally to stay healthy unrealistic. This is indeed what Maslow speculated in his hierarchy of needs model. And as author George Orwell once said about poverty, "It annihilates the future."[30]

Unfortunately, this present orientation may result in a vicious cycle, making it difficult to break out of poverty. Indeed, future orientation may cause greater organizational income and professional success. There are many reasons for this, including a future-oriented organization's ability to react quickly to changes in the environment, the inclination of future-oriented organizations to invest in the future, and, for similar reasons, the individual benefits that accrue to the most future-oriented people. We will now explore each of these in turn.

Time Orientation and Dynamic Responsiveness

Organizations with a strong future orientation are able to respond better to changes in the environment than those with a present orientation. This may be because future oriented people, viewing time as a commodity, therefore act with urgency during times of change.[31]

However, in spite of the relatively strong future orientation of Anglo-American societies, the pressures on public organizations – including infamously impatient investors – may compel short-term organizational behavior.[32] Those organizations investing today's money for a better tomorrow may thus be penalized by the short-term oriented stock market.[33] In turn, organizations often respond – and aggravate the problem – by linking short-term stock performance to executive-level compensation schemes. The short tenure of many high-level managers also means that they tend not to have to live with the long-term consequences of their decisions, nor are they around to benefit from long-term planning.[34]

Unsurprisingly, author Daniel Pink notes that corporations myopically focused on quarterly results have inferior long-term performance: "companies pay a steep price for not extending their gaze beyond the next quarter. Several researchers have found that companies that spend the most time offering guidance on quarterly earnings deliver significantly lower long-term growth rates than companies that offer guidance less frequently. (One reason: the earnings-obsessed companies typically invest less in research and development.)

They successfully achieve their short-term goals but threaten the health of the company two or three years hence."[35]

By contrast, we can see this long-term orientation in our most visionary companies and people – from Elon Musk and Sir Richard Branson's joint ambitions to build a high-speed "hyperloop"[36] to take tourists into space,[37] to the one hundred-year (or more) plans of Chinese and Japanese companies such as Alibaba.[38] Thus, long-term thinking does the company well, though cultural mediators and compensatory policies of many public companies (focusing on short-term results) fail to incentivize along this long-term axis.

Hofstede also suggests that future orientation (or long-term orientation, as he terms it) may be *the* most important determinant of long-term economic success: "the remarkable growth of certain non-Western economies, especially in East Asia, such as South Korea and Taiwan, in the last third of the twentieth century was not due to their collectivism. What distinguished the Asian growth economies from others was their long-term orientation."[39]

All these societal and organizational benefits are, ultimately, simply derived from the combined benefits of having a number of future oriented individuals. Those with a future orientation view "time as money." They tend to act with a sense of urgency, and, consequently, they tend to be high achievers. Put differently, the GLOBE report explains that "future-oriented individuals transform future time into discrete sub goals, and thereby bring the 'future into the present.' They thus become more persistent over a period of time, resulting in high achievement motivation."[40] Conversely, the tendency to procrastinate is positively correlated with less future-oriented individuals, as immediate reward seeking tends to displace long-term goals.[41] This naturally has benefits for the organization as well as the individual.

Time Orientation and Delaying Gratification

> The idea that people have self-control problems is news to no one except economists. And once you accept the realization that we are imperfect beings, there are things you can do to help.
>
> Richard Thaler[42]
> Nobel Prize Winning Economist

Future orientation is defined to mean, in part, the ability to delay immediate gratification for future gains. Now we all know kids are bad at delaying gratification. They want what they want, and they want it *now*. Indeed, research shows that the ability to delay gratification is not fully developed until young adulthood.[43] The short-term horizon of our youth even affects legal policy, as youth are best deterred from committing crimes when the penalty follows quickly after the illegal act, while mature adults focus more on the severity of the consequences.[44] Parents may use a similar trick on their kids, as might managers with particularly impetuous employees. What the next study shows, however, is that kids have varying abilities to delay gratification, and if we want proof that future orientation is a key driver to individual success, we need look no further than marshmallows.

166   Attitudes in Time

Psychologist Walter Mischel and colleagues set out to test the ability of preschool children to delay gratification. The children were offered the choice of two treats, one with higher value than the other – for example, one marshmallow or two marshmallows. Of course any rational child – or adult – would know that two marshmallows are better than one. But here's the catch: the children had to wait a few minutes to receive the two marshmallows, but they could have the one marshmallow anytime they wished.

In the study, the experimenter would leave the room, leaving the child alone with the treats. The researcher would return, usually after about fifteen minutes. The child had a call button, however, and could call back the experimenter any time. If he did, he got the first, smaller treat, but if he waited the full fifteen minutes, then he received two marshmallows.

These studies were completed in the 1960s and 1970s and have continued relevance for many reasons, perhaps most elementally because Mischel questioned the parents of these children about ten years after the experiments took place. He made the following discovery:

> [T]hose who had waited longer in this situation at four years of age were described, more than ten years later, by their parents as adolescents who were more academically and socially competent than their peers and more able to cope with frustration and resist temptation. ... parents saw these children as more verbally fluent and able to express ideas; they used and responded to reason, were attentive, and able to concentrate, to plan, and to think ahead, and were competent and skillful. Likewise they were perceived as able to cope and deal with stress more maturely and seemed more

self-assured ... seconds of delay time in preschool also were significantly related to their scholastic aptitude test (SAT) scores when they applied to college.[45]

The ability of *four-year old* children to delay gratification thus in part predicted the social and intellectual capacity of those same children when they reached adolescence. Thanks to the diligent work of a number of researchers, the "marshmallow children" have been monitored to varying degrees for decades now, and as they've passed into their middle ages, the findings have remained consistent throughout: the ability to delay gratification pays off.[46]

The study suggests a few ways that we can all learn to be more like those patient preschoolers. Mischel found that those who did the best job waiting were able to distract themselves, for example, by "covering their eyes with their hands and resting their heads on their arms. Many children generated their own diversions: they talked quietly to themselves, sang, created games with their hands and feet, and even tried to go to sleep during the waiting time."[47]

Perhaps more importantly, the researchers were able to increase or decrease the delay of gratification in various ways. For example, when the treats were made visible and put right in front of the children, the delay dropped substantially – it was just too tempting.[48] Anyone on a diet knows this – if you don't want to eat the bonbons, keep the bonbons out of the house!

But surprisingly, when the children were asked instead to *visualize* the treat, they were able to wait much longer, even when the actual treat remained right in front of them.[49] They were even able to wait longer than children who were asked to visualize something different than the treat as a form of distraction.[50] Thus, distraction was only partially effective – visualization proved most useful.

The implications are that visualizing success – something many an inspirational speaker has suggested – has empirical roots. The next time you decide you want to quit smoking, keep the cigarettes out of the house, and imagine the smell of your smoke-free clothes, or the liberation of hopping on the treadmill without getting short of breath. If you want to save money for your child's college tuition, imagine that bank statement arriving with all those zeroes, or watching your oldest daughter throw her hat into the air at college graduation.

In recognition that we all struggle to some degree in delaying gratification, organizations increasingly are building workarounds that, in essence, give in to our irrationality. While traditional retirement plans ask employees to commit to save a certain percentage of their salary, often with a match by the organization, the Nobel prize-winning father of behavioral economics, Richard Thaler, recognized that our inability to delay gratification meant we saved less than we should. Or as Thaler put it, people don't save for retirement, "which is literally news to no one."[51]

Thaler therefore invented the "Save More Tomorrow" retirement plan. "The essence of the program is straightforward: people commit in advance to allocating a portion of their future salary increases toward retirement savings."[52] The findings were remarkable: the study looked at participants based on the number of raises they'd received during their term of employment. Those people who joined the program were on average saving 13.6 percent of their salaries by the time they'd received a fourth raise. Those who consulted a financial expert, instead of enrolling in the system, were saving 8.8 percent, while those that neither enrolled in the program nor consulted an expert were saving just 6.2 percent of their salary.[53] In the years since the study, the results have been even better: the savings rates at companies implementing the program have increased four-fold, and today a full 60 percent of companies using defined contribution pensions follow the Thaler program.[54]

While Thaler's program is broadly beneficial, the marshmallow experiment showed us that we see variation in the ability to delay gratification. Follow-up research suggests, unsurprisingly, that the ability to delay gratification is learned, not innate.[55] Studies have shown that this effect of decreasing the value of an item when there is a time delay, also called delay discounting, decreases with age but is present throughout one's life span and across cultures. That said, there are differences between people, which can be influenced by religious upbringing as well as culture.[56]

In a study done on American, Chinese and Japanese graduate students, the participants were presented with the amount of an immediate reward and a larger amount as a delayed reward, which they would receive at different delays (ranging from one month to twenty years). For each pairing, they had to choose. The American and Chinese students were very similar in their discounting, but the Japanese students showed less discounting – effectively valuing the delayed rewards more than the Americans and Chinese – and therefore, they showed a higher future orientation.[57]

Why the differences? It may be that societies provide different incentives when delaying gratification. For instance, people are more willing to delay gratification if they have confidence that the reward will be worth it. For example, if our preschool children did not fully trust that they'd receive two marshmallows after their wait, they likely would have eaten the first treat without much hesitation.[58] The children would indeed be quite wise to eat the first treat if they reasonably anticipated that the promised two marshmallows would never arrive.

This helps explain why future orientations are less common in turbulent environments where the future is, by definition, more uncertain. And this has important implications for managers. Your word is everything. If you tell your employees that by working harder now they'll get a bonus later, for instance, you ought to be sure you'll have that bonus money ready to be paid. To do otherwise sends a message to everyone that in this organization, you should take what you can get now, because nothing is guaranteed.

However, time orientation is considered one of the most "fundamental values" of a society, and an individual. This makes it difficult for managers to change the focus of this dimension.[59] Along with gratification delay training, however, managers can look for this orientation when hiring employees. For example, managers might ask prospective employees to share an experience in setting and achieving a long-term goal or to articulate a vision for the future. Even hobbies may be indicative of this – an accountant that's an accomplished piano player; a lawyer that writes popular novels on the side; a scientist that doubles as a triathlon athlete – these activities are just some of the tasks that indicate a willingness to sacrifice immediate gratification for long-term goals. Pursuing these activities also may indicate in part the power of mastery and autonomy in motivating individuals.

Finally, even if your current work force is less future-oriented than might be ideal, the good news is that in almost every culture, managers that act with a future orientation are rewarded. This is especially true in the United States – where to be a "visionary" is perhaps a leader's greatest compliment- as well as in Israel, Ireland, Canada, and the US-influenced nation of the Philippines.[60] Yet even those countries that are most present-oriented tend to prefer visionary leadership.[61] The implication is that employees of present-oriented societies may continue to live in the present, but they may be motivated by, and perform better for, managers with an eye on the future.[62]

Albert Einstein was right: time is an illusion, and this illusion is perceived differently across the world. From those with a focus on the future decidedly marked by the past, to those stuck in the present, and others that are racing to the future, our motivations, our efforts, our very way of seeing the world differs considerably from country to country and person to person. As we will see in the next chapter, communication can encourage a greater understanding of these differences, but it can also be the cause of a great many misunderstandings (Table 12.1).

TABLE 12.1 Time horizon onion diagram

Inner	Middle	Outer
Political (unstable)	Present-time horizon	Spontaneous; Enjoy the moment; take a fluid approach to life, and business schedules. Caused by, or causes, lower economic development
Political (stable)	Future-time horizon	Time sensitive – sense of urgency; willing to delay gratification; tend to show up for meetings on time
		Caused by, or causes, higher economic development; responsive to changes in environment
Economic (stock market volatility)	Present-time horizon	Lack of investment; focus on short-term earnings; short-term compensation incentives

Note

i Somewhat confusingly, the GLOBE study excludes a measurement of past orientation. However, the GLOBE definition of future orientation suggests that past orientation and future orientation are empirically linked, and result in similar behaviors. See Id. Thus, we assume that countries with a high future orientation could in fact be driven by either past or future orientations, while those with a low future orientation are present-oriented.

References

1 Edward T. Hall, "The Silent Language in Overseas Business," *Harvard Business Review* (May 1960), https://hbr.org/1960/05/the-silent-language-in-overseas-business.
2 Id.
3 Id.
4 Id.
5 Ashkanasy et al., *supra* note 60 at 323.
6 Hall, *supra* note 712.
7 Id. (referring to Americans' "terrible weakness" by Japanese businessman).
8 Larry A. Dimatteo and Lucien J. Dhooge, *International Business Law: A Transactional Approach* 18 (Thompson West) (2005).
9 Id. at 18.
10 Maralyn Hill, "Global Etiquette: Time Matters – Africa and the Middle East," *Luxe Beat* (last accessed July 29, 2018), http://luxebeatmag.com/global-etiquette-time-matters-africa-middle-east/.
11 See Ashkanasy et al., *supra* note 60 at 288. Some readers may be familiar with the Hofstede time orientation, called short-term versus long-term orientation. However, Hofstede's measurement included a focus on thrift and savings, which may be associated with elements other than one's future orientation (e.g., culturally neutral factors play a role, such as high consumption taxes, which discourages spending, and limited social benefits, which encourages saving). As a result, we consider the GLOBE studies to be more reliable indicators of time orientation.
12 See Ashkanasy et al., *supra* note 60 at 285 (defining past orientation).
13 Id. at 282.
14 Id. at 285.
15 Id. at 284.
16 Id. at 290 (noting Schneider (1989) predicted this, but "this prediction remains to be tested").
17 Id. at 285.
18 Id. at 294.
19 Lord of War Script – Dialogue Transcript, Script-O-Rama.Com (last accessed July 29, 2018) http://www.script-o-rama.com/movie_scripts/l/lord-of-war-script-transcript.html.
20 Ashkanasy et al., *supra* note 60 at 285.
21 Id. at 304.
22 Id. at 305.
23 Id.
24 Id.
25 De Luque and Javidan, *supra* note 462 at 623.
26 Ashkanasy et al., *supra* note 60 at 305, 322.
27 Id. at 305.
28 Id. at 323.
29 Id. at 315.
30 George Orwell, *Down and out in Paris and London* 20 (Mariner Books) (1972).

31 Ashkanasy et al., *supra* note 60 at 290.
32 Id. at 297.
33 Id.
34 Id.
35 Daniel Pink, *Drive: The Surprising Truth about What Motivates Us* 55 (Riverhead Books) (2011) (citing to Mei Cheng, K.R. Subramanyam, and Yuan Zhang, "Earnings Guidance and Managerial Myopia," SSRN Working Paper No. 854515, November 2005).
36 *Hyperloop*, SpaceX (last accessed July 29, 2018), http://www.spacex.com/hyperloop.
37 Tom Turuia, "Richard Branson Says He's 6 Months From Going to Space – but Mars Belongs to Elon Musk," *Business Insider* (Oct. 9, 2017) http://www.businessinsider.com/richard-branson-says-hes-going-to-space-but-mars-belongs-to-elon-musk-2017-10; see also Matt McFarland, "SpaceX to Fly Two Space Tourists around the Moon in 2018," CNNTECH (Feb. 27, 2017), http://money.cnn.com/2017/02/27/technology/spacex-moon-tourism/index.html.
38 Nastaran Tavakoli-Far, "Should Chief Executives Focus on the Next 100 Years," *BBC News* (July 12, 2013), http://www.bbc.com/news/business-23263697.
39 Hofstede, *supra* note 23 at 39.
40 Ashkanasy et al., *supra* note 60 at 293.
41 Id. at 293.
42 Richard Thaler, "Nudge, Nudge," *NPR* (Episode 803, Nov. 1, 2017).
43 See Laurence Steinberg, S. Graham, L. O'Brien, J. Woolard, E. Cauffman and M. BAnich, "Age Differences in Future Orientation and Delay Discounting," 80 *Child Development* 28–44 (2009).
44 Robert Cooter and Thomas Ulen, *Law and Economics* 472 (Pearson, 6th ed.) (2011).
45 Walter Mischel, Yuichi Shoda, and Monica L. Rodriguez, "Delay of Gratification in Children," 244 *American Association for the Advancement of Science* 933, 934 (1989).
46 See Walter Mischel, Ozlem Ayduk, Marc G. Berman et al., "'Willpower' over the Life Span: Decomposing Self-Regulation," 6 *Social Cognitive and Affective Neuroscience* 252–256 (2011).
47 Miscel et al., *supra* note 757 at 935.
48 Id.
49 Id.
50 Id.
51 Thaler, *supra* note 754.
52 Richard H. Thaler and Shlomo Benartzi, "Save More Tomorrow: Using Behavioral Economics to Increase Employee Savings," 112 *Journal of Political Economy* S164 (2004).
53 Id.
54 Sophia Grene, "'Save More Tomorrow' Gives Pensions a Boost," *Foreign Policy* (Jan. 7, 2012) https://www.ft.com/content/7cbd3ef8-36f7-11e1-96bf-00144feabdc0.
55 Celeste Kidd, Holly Palmeri, and Richard N. Aslin, "Rational Snacking: Young Children's Decision-Making on the Marshmallow Task Is Moderated by Beliefs about Environmental Reliability," 126 *Cognition* 109–114 (2013).
56 F. Paglieri, A.M. Borghi, L.S. Colzato, B. Hommel, and C. Scorolli, "Heaven Can Wait. How Religion Modulates Temporal Discounting," 77 *Psychology Research* 738–747 (2013).
57 Du et al., *supra* note 462.
58 See Kidd et al.
59 Ashkanasy et al., *supra* note 60 at 291.
60 Id. at 325.
61 Id. at 327.
62 Id. at 329.

13

COMMUNICATION IS MORE – MUCH MORE – THAN LANGUAGE

First learn the meaning of what you say, and then speak.

Epictetus

The nineteenth century Swiss philosopher Ferdinand de Saussure wrote, "In the lives of individuals and of societies, language is a factor of greater importance than any other."[1] No doubt there's some truth in this remark. However, as Bill Bryson writes in *The Mother Tongue*, a linguistic convergence is well under way that may one day make the declaration of de Saussure a thing of the past.

For the airlines of 157 nations (out of 168 in the world), [English] is the agreed international language of discourse. In India, there are more than three thousand newspapers in English. The six member nations of the European Free Trade Association conduct all their business in English, even though not one of them is an English-speaking country. When companies from four European countries – France, Italy, Germany, and Switzerland – formed a joint truck-making venture called Iveco in 1977, they chose English as their working language because, as one of the founders wryly observed, "It puts us all at an equal disadvantage." For the same reasons, when the Swiss company Brown Boveri and the Swedish company ASEA merged in 1988, they decided to make the official company language English, and when Volkswagen set up a factory in Shanghai, it found that there were too few Germans who spoke Chinese and two few Chinese who spoke German, so now Volkswagen's German engineers and Chinese managers communicate in a language that is alien to both of them, English.[2]

Language barriers are indeed falling fast through such agreements and through technological translation advances. This is especially advantageous for native English speakers, as English becomes the (dare we say) lingua franca of business. Nonetheless, language still presents a significant barrier, and it is worth noting that all of the ideas for managing internationally are of little advantage to us if they are rendered inappropriately. As the *Wall Street Journal* reports, even email exchanges between bosses and employees are a common source of conflict and miscommunication. They write: "The potential for email misfires between bosses and subordinates is mounting, as the volume of email grows and more people read it on the fly on mobile devices. Sometimes the boss is too rushed to read. Employees fuel the problems by sending poorly written emails. Deeper issues can arise if bosses' and employees' communication styles clash."[3] If we struggle so to communicate with people right down the hall, how are we doing with people across the globe? How are we doing with people who speak and think in a different language, that communicate in a different context, that express emotions more of less visibly? Judging by those living in a foreign country, not well. Internations, an organization whose core mission is to give expats a great experience around the world, conducted a study involving 12,519 expatriates representing 166 nationalities and living in 188 countries or territories. Their central finding?

> The major reasons why expats often feel unwelcome are language or accent. More than four in ten expats (42 percent) have felt unwelcome in their new country to some degree because of these factors. Expats are most likely to think that their language or accent makes them stand out in France, Austria, Denmark, the Czech Republic, and Germany. For example, 62 percent of expats in France have recently felt unwelcome due to language issues.[4]

Unsurprisingly, there is no shortage of stories in which culturally driven miscommunications result in financial loss, embarrassment and even physical harm. Nokia, for instance, introduced its Lumia phone into Latin American markets without consulting a native Spanish speaker, only to find out to their dismay that the term is a slang word for "prostitute." Additional examples abound:[5]

- Both Procter & Gamble and Rolls Royce changed the names of products prior to launch after finding they were curse words in German.[6]
- Tiz Razor, an Iranian company expanding to Qatar, belatedly learned that its name meant "passing wind" in the island nation.[7]
- When Parker Pen Company marketed a ballpoint pen in Mexico, its ads were supposed to say something akin to "Avoid embarrassing leaks." However, the company mistakenly thought the Spanish word *embarazar* meant "embarrass"; so instead, the ads said, "Avoid pregnancy."[8]
- In Italy, Schweppes Tonic Water marketed the name as "Schweppes toilet water,"[9] which is perhaps not the image the company was going for.[10,11]

Similarly, Nicholas Keuper worked first out of Germany while traveling throughout Europe, then went to Thailand, China, Hong Kong, back to Germany and then to the United States. He relates this story from his time in Thailand: "We had an Australian senior partner, and he used in the kickoff meeting an Australian expression which relates to big projects having to be approached step-by-step. He said, 'How do you eat an elephant? Slice by slice!' And of course, the core Thai executives faces just turned ashen because the elephant is a very sacred animal in Thailand. So they asked, 'But why would you eat an elephant? Do Australians eat elephants?'"[12]

These stories illustrate the ways in which communication itself presents yet another barrier to overcoming cultural differences. Words alone, however, are not the problem. Language consists not just of defined words and rules, but also informal rules regarding speaking, listening and even nonverbal body language. Let's explore these ideas by first considering a hypothetical: an emotional man named Spike and his more tranquil counterpart, Serena.

Neutral – Affective

Spike and Serena are both honest, hardworking and intelligent people, but to the outward observer they could hardly be more different. Spike shows his emotions easily. Some even say he is volatile. He's quick to flash a smile, but with the right spark, that smile can just as quickly devolve into anger or frustration. Spike is *affective*.

Serena, by contrast, keeps her emotions in check. Rarely do you see her angry. She is calm, even stoic. When she is happy, she tries to hide it from others, even stifling her laughs or putting her hand over her mouth as if embarrassed. Serena is *neutral*.[13]

Now imagine how you might perceive Spike and Serena if they were your coworkers. Let's say one day you're in a meeting where you find out the company made a costly, even dumb mistake. Spike reacts to the news by slamming his hands on the table and shouting angrily. His face is contorted in anger. Now consider your probable interpretation of this behavior. You might say, "Whatever, he always does that. It'll pass." But now imagine if Serena acted this way. For her, this is a remarkable display of anger. You might instead say, "Oh boy, this *must* be serious. Did you see how angry she was? She's never like that."

The point is that how we interpret emotions is largely driven by what we expect of the emoting person. But Spike is not just your coworker. He may be a stand-in for the highly emotive, or "affective" cultures seen in many Middle Eastern, Latin American, and Latin European countries.[14] Serena may represent the neutral cultures of the Japanese, Ethiopians, or Austrians.[15]

We judge others through interactions, so these and other differences in communication styles can lead to vastly different interpretations of people. Indeed, this is the incubator in which so many stereotypes grow strong. Neutrals traveling to an affective country full of Spikes, for example, may be tempted to say that their "blood runs hot," just as affectives in a neutral country full of Serenas may feel they're in a place full of coldhearted dullards.

But in truth, culture strongly influences an individual's affective tendencies. Suppose Spike lives in an affective society and really wants to make it known that he is angry (or happy, or sad). given how affective he and everyone around him are on a regular basis, he must be even more emotional than normal. To make any impact at all on his colleagues, he may have to scream like mad before storming out of the conference room (or laugh harder in happier circumstances, or shed tears in sadder times). He is thus enculturated, or "mentally programmed" to behave emotionally. For her part, if Serena lives in a neutral culture, she knows that even a minor expression of emotion may signal strong emotions.[16] To behave as Spike does might be truly shocking.

Although Americans are moderately affective on the whole, they tend to take a neutral approach within the business context.[17] Why the difference? The "it's not personal, it's business" mentality so often seen in American offices arises from a universalist perspective. This reinforces a rule-based approach to business in which human relations are somewhat subordinated to objective skills and general standards. This rule-based approach – in theory applicable to everyone regardless of race, gender, religion and the like – is considered "fair" and even ethical, and thus provides the justification for a relatively dispassionate approach to business.

Understanding the relative affectivity of the culture of your business partners, customers and colleagues is important: the cross-cultural businessperson seeks not to miss the note of dissatisfaction that passes ever so subtly over Serena's face; she avoids taking offense, or attributing too much significance, when Spike behaves affectively. Mutual understanding is at the heart of business relationships, but the risk of misunderstanding and the potential for mistrust is even higher in cross-cultural relationships. As the *Wall Street Journal*'s piece on emails lost in translation illustrates, communication is an imperfect art even among countrymen (Table 13.1).

Low Context – High Context

Even if we learn the same language, our style of communicating remains stubbornly connected to our cultural values. To illustrate this idea, we will introduce a Texan named Kurt. You can put Kurt in a Japanese language class, but you can't take the Texas out of his communication style. Until our Texan adapts to the ways of his new environment, he'll continue to carry on as before, and if he's like most Americans, he'll probably express himself in a direct or *low-context* way. This can be especially true in the workplace.

In low-context cultures, the meaning is on the surface. Americans tend to be assertive and competitive, a direct consequence of which is the tendency to be relatively blunt. Many Americans take pride in "saying what they mean." If everyone agrees with that version of reality, then no offense should be taken when one is communicating directly, in a low-context style. But Kurt's counterparts may be shocked by his direct nature. Low-context communicators are

TABLE 13.1 Affectivity (from passionate and outgoing to reserved and calm)[18]

1. Israel	23. Bahrain	45. South Korea
2. Argentina	24. UAE	46. Hungary
3. Brazil	25. Portugal	47. Taiwan
4. Colombia	26. India	48. Poland
5. Nigeria	27. Australia	49. Hong Kong
6. Greece	28. Ukraine	50. China
7. Spain	29. Uganda	51. Netherlands
8. Italy	30. Russia	52. Myanmar
9. Mexico	31. France	53. United Kingdom
10. Malta	32. New Zealand	54. Singapore
11. Cyprus	33. Vietnam	55. Belgium
12. South Africa	34. Chile	56. Czech Republic
13. Peru	35. Kazakhstan	57. Austria
14. Turkey	36. Kuwait	58. Luxembourg
15. Philippines	37. Qatar	59. Germany
16. United States	38. Oman	60. Denmark
17. Romania	39. Malaysia	61. Switzerland
18. Kenya	40. Indonesia	62. Japan
19. Ireland	41. Canada	63. Finland
20. Panama	42. Thailand	64. Norway
21. Ecuador	43. Cambodia	65. Sweden
22. Costa Rica	44. Saudi Arabia	

often seen as rude or uncouth – dare we say curt – in parts of the world where this level of directness is uncommon.[19]

By contrast, his Japanese counterparts will use highly contextual communication. *High context* means that there are many layers of implied meanings that are not explicitly said.[20] Between high-context communicators, much can be expressed while saying very little.[21] While little is said, even less is understood if the recipient of high-context communication is not versed in the style. For example, "lack of explicitness is a feature of Japanese [culture] … they avoid imposing a blunt yes or no."[22]

Jean Paul Montupet, the former Emerson executive vice president, refers to the "famous Japanese 'yes,' which actually means, 'Yes, I have understood your question'; it has nothing to do with their answer, which will come later. 'No' means I don't understand your question, so you have to reformulate it."[23]

Sometimes, this same Japanese team would seem to support some idea or plan brought in by Montupet's team, "but you would come back a year later and realize that none of that had happened. … I have had cases where I went back after the meeting and said, 'Okay, you have said this to us. Dave [Farr, current CEO] or Chuck [Knight, former CEO] has approved it. Now, we need to get this done.' And they responded, 'Oh, really?'"[24]

Japan is a country famous for a high-context culture that often leaves Western managers befuddled, but we can also look to France, China, and others to fit within this context as well.[25]

People from high-context cultures may express dissatisfaction through the use of questions, which serves to blunt the impact of the issue. Legal scholars Chow and Schoenbaum relay an illustrative story: "A US company had a contract from a German buyer to sell bicycles produced in China. When the first shipment was ready, there was a problem. The bikes rattled. The US buyer did not want to accept the shipment, knowing that with the rattle, they would not be acceptable to the German customer, whose high-end market niche was dominated by bikes that were whisper-quiet. What to do? In the US culture, the normal approach would be to tell the manufacturer that the rattling bikes were unacceptable and that the problem had to be fixed. In China, such a direct confrontation would be extremely rude and cause much loss of face. Knowing this, the US manager went to the Chinese plant, inspected the bicycles, rode a few, and asked about the rattle. "Is this rattle normal? Do all the bikes rattle? Do you think the German buyer will think there is something wrong with the bikes if it rattles?" Then he left. The next shipment of bikes had no rattles."[26]

In this case, the American buyer was adopting the cultural style of his host. This is a tactic that we refer to as "strategic mimicry" and is discussed further in the next chapter.

In China, moreover, rejections may be given by expressing embarrassment at the situation. For example: "I'm so embarrassed I can't meet your deadline. I promise I'll do so next time."[27] Indirect language can also be used to express rejection, such as "maybe," or "perhaps," or the use of excuses such as the need to check with one's boss.[28] Notice that none of these involve actually saying no. That sort of directness is typically reserved for lower context cultures. In China, the high context communication is used to soften a rejection or indirectly express dissatisfaction as seen in the bicycle case, which helps the recipient *save face*. Saying no is part of life, but low-context speakers should take time to learn the various ways in which higher-context cultures indirectly communicate rejections.

Saving face is, ultimately, one of the main drivers of high-context behavior. Additionally, saving face has close links with other cultural dimensions that we discuss, including collectivism and assertiveness. "Direct confrontation ... disrupts harmony, a value in collectivist cultures. Underlying the preference for indirect confrontation is a particular concern for face. Face refers to the self-image one projects to others. Respect is the currency by which face is maintained. Disrespect affronts face; respect confirms it. Although face is not unimportant to people from individualistic and egalitarian societies, it seems to be more important to people from collectivist and hierarchical cultures. Maintaining face both confirms the person's acceptance in a society (collectivism) and that person's status within society (hierarchy)."[29]

It is for this reason that "yes" may not mean "yes" in some high-context cultures, and it is expected that the recipient will know how, in a sense, to read between the lines. High-context communications, with their nuances, help others "save face" and avoid embarrassment. High-context communications are also useful when relaying bad or painful news in cultures low on assertiveness, as these cultures stress harmony and interpersonal relationships.[30] All these layers of meaning help avoid the unforgiveable: to say no directly, to cause offense or to simply hurt someone's feelings. However, Kurt, our thick-skinned Texan, may have great difficulty working through these layers of communication to understand what his counterparts really mean. He will likely wonder why they don't just say what they mean.

In many ways, the possibility for misunderstanding is the same as we saw with respect to showing emotions: we attribute meaning to the ways in which we communicate, and the words we use. Just because we share the denotation of a word by learning the dictionary definition, however, does not mean we have the same connotations. Consequently, telling a highly contextual person frankly that a business plan is flawed, or an employee's performance is lacking, might be perceived as putting someone's nose in it; after all, everyone else had the courtesy to break the news indirectly. You must be so upset that you lost your temper entirely, as Serena did – or maybe you're just a jerk. If the exchange occurs in the midst of other high context persons, the blunt message is even more painful, not unlike the feeling an American might have if the boss roundly ridicules your idea: either way it's bad, but if it's during an all-hands-on-board meeting, it's much worse.

Of course, this contextual communication has some geographic variety even within America, as we suspect that many small town or Middle Americans take a higher context, conflict-avoiding approach to communication than do the average urban East Coasters. We might needle our Long Island friends, for instance, by recalling that one-time White House communications director Anthony Scaramucci, a.k.a. "The Mooch," a "say what you mean" kind of guy if we've ever seen one, is a born and raised local (Table 13.2).

Where Context and Emotiveness Meets

> Those who know do not speak. Those who speak do not know.
>
> Laozi[31]
> *Chinese Philosopher*

East Asians tend to layer their communications in the high-context style, and this is paired with a relatively neutral style of communication in a high percentage of introverted people. The result is that they tend to say less than their

TABLE 13.2 High- and low-context regions

High-context regions	*Low-context regions*[32]
Confucian Asia	Anglo-America
Latin America	Nordic Europe
Sub-Saharan Africa	Germanic Europe
Middle East	

Western counterparts. In linguistic parlance, Westerns are more "verbal" than the average East Asian, for whom long periods of silence during conversations are not unusual. In fact, "It is a sign of respect for the other person if you take time to process the information without talking yourself."[33]

For many Westerners, however, such silence represents poor etiquette and even makes many uncomfortable – long elevator rides, indeed, are the height of discomfort for many Westerners who believe that silence should be filled. Research shows that when an uncomfortable pause extends to just four seconds, "one or more of the conversationalists will invariably blurt something – a fatuous comment on the weather, a startled cry of, 'Gosh, is that the time?' – rather than let the silence extend to a fifth second."[34]

Even within verbalizing cultures, differences may arise. For instance, it is considered polite in Anglo-Saxon cultures to use a synchronous style of communication. This means that person A speaks, person B listens without interruption, and only once finished does person B speak. By contrast, Latins are more emotive than Anglo-Saxons, so interruptions are frequent. In fact, these interruptions are a way of showing interest in the other's words – as in, "Wow, that is so interesting I cannot wait to interject with my thoughts."[35] In a similar mode, Latin societies may communicate in a more emotive way in order to signal their interest in the matter, while such emotive communication indicates a lack of seriousness in more neutral societies.[36] In many Eastern societies, "The higher the position a person holds, the lower and flatter the voice."[37]

Nonverbal Communications

Interactions are also mediated not just in words, but in body language and other nonverbal communications. Body language can in many situations signal our emotions even more strongly than words and tone,[38] and in some countries, may constitute a language of their own, alien to outsiders.[39]

For example: "Modern Greek has more than seventy common gestures, ranging from the chopping of the forearm gesture, which signifies extreme displeasure, to several highly elaborate ones, such as placing the left hand on the knee, closing one eye, looking with the other into the middle distance and wagging the free hand up and down, which means 'I don't want anything to do with it.'"[40]

Additionally, the appropriate amount of eye contact varies between cultures – some societies consider eye contact a form of aggression; others consider it instead to signal flirting between members of the opposite sex; while in Anglo societies it is a sign of interest in a conversation. American schoolteachers in some regions even note students that fail to hold eye contact and then work with these children to improve this social skill. The amount of space between speakers also varies, with many Latin societies being notably "close speakers" while Anglo-Saxons tend to prefer more distance.

So the questions arise: how sure are you that those non-verbal communications are reaching a non-native English speaker in the way you intend? How sure are you that you are correctly reading their nonverbal communications?

The Greek philosopher Epictetus said: "Nature hath given men one tongue but two ears, that we may hear from others twice as much as we speak." It is by listening – by paying attention and noting important details – that we can gather the facts on cultural dimensions and their particular manifestation in an individual or organization. Machiavelli himself argued: "[The prince] should be a very broad questioner, and then, in regard to the things he asked about, a patient listener to the truth; indeed, he should become upset when he learns that anyone has any hesitation to speak it to him."[41] Machiavelli understood well that it was of first importance for the actor to fully understand his landscape.

Listening may facilitate the learning of cultural dimensions; it can help prevent misunderstandings – we ponder whether Parker Pen's embarrassingly impregnated pen, or Schweppes' unclean drinking water, or any of the other PR disasters noted at the beginning of this chapter, were the result of marketing teams not taking the time to listen – or to even ask the question. Listening is, unquestionably, an essential characteristic of a successful leader. As Peter Drucker succinctly put it: "listen first, speak last."[42]

Building a Bridge over the Gully

What can Kurt do about all of these challenges to make himself understood, and be sure he understands and does not offend? First, he can continue to learn the Japanese language, a challenging but no doubt productive use of his time. Secondly, he can become a student of Japanese culture and behavior – taking note of verbal and nonverbal communication styles. Let's explore these points a bit more in turn.

Just as language presents a barrier to cultural differences, it can also be a bridge – in some cases, even, the strongest of bridges. English is increasingly the lingua franca of business. In China, more people are learning English than there are people in America.[43] But local languages are not going anywhere. The perfectly rational idea of the linguist Zamenhof to develop Esperanto as a global language, and its failure despite nearly 150 years of diligent effort by its proponents, is evidence of the stubborn affinity we all have for own languages.[44]

Consequently, even in cultures in which many people speak English or in which another common language is shared, making the effort to speak the local language is the ultimate show of respect. This point really cannot be overstated. Say a few words of Swedish in Stockholm, or the traditional Arabic greeting *as-salāmu ʿalaykum* in Middle Eastern nations and watch the transformation. And if you are actually able to more deeply communicate in the local language, you become an unforgettable person in the minds of those with whom you interact. Whereas before you were just another businessperson, just another foreigner or strange visitor, suddenly you become a welcome guest. Talk about a business advantage!

Additionally, to speak a language is to better understand a culture and a person. Says Hofstede: "It is almost impossible to empathize with the different ways of thinking and feeling present in another culture if one has never had to express oneself in another language."[45] Through language, we express ourselves and transmit our cultures, and when we demand of others that they communicate in our languages, all but the most fluent are able only to express themselves as a shadow of their full, emotive, humorous, intelligent selves. They may be less able to communicate subtle thoughts, less welcome to share in jokes and entertaining exchanges, and consequently less a part of the group. This is therefore a barrier not to be ignored.

Finally, in this book we have periodically referenced the ability of language to shed light on cultural dimensions. In many cultures, the respect for elders, and the embrace of hierarchy is seen in the use of words that differ based on whether one is the elder or younger member of the group. So too do many cultures hint at relative levels of gender egalitarianism and clearly assign gender roles with words and greetings that differ between men and women. *As-salāmu ʿalaykum*, for example, is a greeting in Turkish-influenced Kyrgyzstan, but only between men.

Cross-cultural negotiation scholar Jeanne M. Brett outlines some simple steps organizations can use to ensure that language is not the culprit for misunderstandings:

- Discourage jargon; make available glossaries with translations of key terms;
- Use visual aids when collecting information from group members;
- Arrange for frequent breaks where team members can discuss what was going on in the meeting in their own language. Follow breaks with a question-and-answer session; and
- Adopt a team-endorsed way to stop a meeting and ask for clarification. For example, some teams give members flags to wave when they do not understand.[46]

Along with studying the Japanese language, Kurt would also benefit from studying – through careful listening and embracing social and professional interactions – the informal rules of communication. Learning the hidden messages of diffuse cultures is often no easy task. Outsiders are said to have a particularly hard time integrating into the business culture of highly diffuse Japan and France, for example.[47] Properly interpreting neutral or emotive behaviors in a cultural context, or even the frequency of interruptions in a conversation, requires understanding not just the individual, but the culture he comes from.

Perhaps Kurt's Japanese counterparts also take the time to learn Kurt's style of communication. It would indeed be a welcome event to see a situation akin to that of President Barack Obama meeting Japan's Emperor Akihito: in the encounter, we see the president bowing before the emperor according to Japanese custom, while at the same the emperor shakes the president's hand according to Western customs.

Businesses increasingly interact with partners, customers and even employees that span multiple time zones and cross oceans and deserts. This is made possible in many ways by communication networks that allow us to speak to one another on opposite sides of the earth instantaneously. This technology, however, can also be a crutch, providing an excuse to do business from the comfort of an armchair or in front of a computer, and avoiding the frustrations of airport lines, visas, sleep deprivation and dietary changes.

Smart businesses and smart leaders don't fall prey to this trap. Time and again in interviews with the authors, the leading international executives and intellectuals returned to one core theme: the importance of face time for building international relationships and improving communication.

We noted earlier Sumitomo Chemical's Juan Ferreira using one-on-one relationships to overcome cultural differences. Emerson's Montupet noted further:

> At Emerson, the management style is one in which I will come and see you, rather than you come and tell me, so we spend an enormous amount of time traveling in the world. When I was working at Emerson, I went to Europe ten to fifteen times a year, Asia four to five times a year, the Mideast twice a year, so we spend a lot of time meeting people on the spot. And when you do that you really get a feel for what's going on. When you walk the plant with the plant manager you get the feeling for it, and you immediately know how the relationship is working. You can gather a meeting of the staff in that factory and you see exactly how it works. And that is something impossible to convey remotely.

Ultimately, nothing beats taking the time to understand the people and the culture in which you are doing business. Indeed, "researchers attribute the increased rapport in face-to-face interactions to the importance of verbal and nonverbal cues in communication (Drolet and Morris 2000; Moore et al. 1999; Thompson and Nadler 2002)."[48] These face-to-face interactions thus help build the cohesiveness discussed in Chapter 3 and to which we return in the next chapter. It even decreases unethical behavior, for the simple reason that we prefer not to take advantage of those toward whom we are favorably disposed.[49] Companies can help to force the issue by requiring that certain meetings take place face-to-face, mandating quarterly or annual visits to certain offices, or rotating certain managers between offices.

Another way to increase cohesiveness and to encourage open communication is by establishing long-term relationships. SAK's CEO Tom Kalishman works remotely, visiting the St. Louis-based headquarters twice a month. On other days, "I'm on the phone all day, every day. And that's the advantage – I'm dealing with a group of people at the executive level who I've known for a minimum of fifteen years, some up to thirty years. It's very easy to communicate. If this organization did not have that sort of history, this management style wouldn't work. I wouldn't be able to do what I'm doing."[50]

Companies have long recognized the advantage of personal relationships in business and have responded by preferring charismatic salespersons who know how to wine and dine and by establishing formal practices to ensure that long-term relationships are built not just within teams but also between transacting firms. In referring to external partnerships, Kalishman says, "that's where we tend to be much more face-to-face."[51]

Relatedly, you may prefer to interact with the same car insurance agent for your insurance issues; the same probably goes for your Realtor, dentist, hairstylist and many of your business-to-business partners. This helps to build a personal rapport between you and the agent, dentist, hairstylist and business partners that supersedes the more transactional nature of single business exchanges.

In short, be like the ideal Kurt and learn the local language – even if you can only handle four or five phrases – and don't forget the unspoken, layered and even invisible communications that accompany those words and grammar lessons. Use face-to-face interactions and foster long-term personalized relationships to help bridge the gap between cultures.

Solutions to misunderstandings, confusion, discomfort and stereotypes:

1. Listening and observing;
    a. Good listeners catch verbal cues; good observers note nonverbal cues; and
    b. Mimicry and long-term personal relationships build rapport.

References

1 *The Philosophy Book: Big Ideas Simply Explained* 223 (eds. Cecille Landau, Andrew Szuedek, and Sarah Tomley, DK London) (2011).
2 Bill Bryson, *The Mother Tongue: English and How It Got That Way* 12–13 (New York, NY: HarperCollins) (2001).

3 Dr. Nitish Singh and Thomas J. Bussen, "Why Compliance Professionals Need to Think about National Cultures," *Ethikos* (2014) (citing to Sue Shellenbarger: "Email Enigma: When the Boss's Reply Seems Cryptic," *Wall Street Journal* (Mar. 11, 2014), https://www.wsj.com/articles/when-the-bosss-reply-is-cryptic-1394578397).
4 "Expat Insider 2017: Feeling (Un)Welcome Abroad," *Internations* (last accessed July 29, 2018), https://www.internations.org/expat-insider/2017/feeling-un-welcome-abroad-39196.
5 Dave Smith, "Lost in Translation: Nokia Lumia, and the Five Worst Name Oversights," *International Business Times* (Oct. 26, 2011), http://www.ibtimes.com/lost-translation-nokia-lumia-5-worst-name-oversights-361866.
6 Adam Wooten, "International Business: Chevy Nova Tale, Other Global Marketing Myths Debunked," *Deseret News Business* (July 22, 2011), https://www.deseretnews.com/article/705388000/Chevy-Nova-tale-other-global-marketing-myths-debunked.html.
7 Id.
8 Rob Vandenberg, "These Mistakes Will Kill Your Company's Prospects When Trying to Go Global," *Business Insider* (Dec. 15, 2011), http://www.businessinsider.com/these-mistakes-will-kill-your-companys-prospects-when-trying-to-go-global-2011-12.
9 "Say What??? Campaigns That Failed to Translate," *Glantz* (Feb. 2012), https://glantz.net/blog/campaigns-that-failed-to-translate.
10 For an entertaining top-ten list of market translation fails, see Top 10 EPIC Advertising Fails, YouTube (last accessed July 29, 2018), https://www.youtube.com/watch?v=_pHWZ_XNij8.
11 It is worth noting, the classic example of the Chevrolet Nova, a sedan produced from the 1960s through 1980s and sold around the world, is enchanting but unfortunately untrue. The story goes that while the word *nova* may have a nice ring to it in English, in Spanish, *no va* of course means "no go." No va does in fact mean "no go" in Spanish, but "nova" refers to an astronomical event just as in English, and there's no evidence that Latin American consumers had any concerns or confusion about the name. "Nova Don't Go," Snopes.com (last accessed July 29, 2018), http://www.snopes.com/business/misxlate/nova.asp. (Stories of Coca Cola translating its product into Chinese characters that translated as "bite the waxed tadpole" are also inaccurate – this seems to have been more the product of local Chinese merchants in isolated markets.)
12 Keuper, *supra* note 194.
13 Trompenaars and Hampden-Turner, *supra* note 12 at 69.
14 Id. at 70.
15 Id. at 69.
16 See Id.
17 Id. at 70, 73. The partial exception to this are for those working in US service-oriented jobs, where affecting a positive attitude (and neutralizing negative emotions) is expected. See generally Brent A. Scott and Christopher M. Barnes, "A Multilevel Field Investigation of Emotional Labor, Affect, Work Withdrawal, and Gender," 54 *Academy of Management Journal* 116–136 (2011).
18 Expat Insider 2017, *Internations* 78 (last accessed July 29, 2018), https://cms-internationsgmbh.netdna-ssl.com/cdn/file/2017-09/Expat_Insider_2017_The_InterNations_Survey.pdf.
19 House and Javidan, *supra* note 8 at 5 (in particular, "directness, frankness, and being in-your-face" are offensive behaviors in many parts of the world, including Asia, Latin America, and the Nordic European countries).
20 Trompenaars and Hampden-Turner, *supra* note 12 at 90.
21 Id. (writing "much shared knowledge is taken for granted by those in conversation with each other").
22 Bryson, *supra* note 776 at 36.
23 Montupet, *supra* note 10.

24 Id.
25 Trompenaars and Hampden-Turner, *supra* note 12 at 90; see also Daniel C.K. Chow and Thomas Schoenbaum, *International Business Transactions: Problems, Cases, and Materials* (New York, NY: Wolters Kluwer) (2015).
26 Daniel C.K. Chow and Thomas Schoenbaum, *International Business Transactions: Problems, Cases, and Materials* (New York, NY: Wolters Kluwer) (2015).
27 Sean Upton-McLaughlin, "Saying 'No' in China," *China Culture Corner* (Jan. 27, 2014), https://chinaculturecorner.com/2014/01/27/saying-no-in-china/.
28 Id.
29 Brett, *supra* note 81 at 105.
30 Hartog, *supra* note 562 at 403.
31 Goodreads (last accessed Mar. 29, 2019), https://www.goodreads.com/work/quotes/100074-d-o-d-j-ng.
32 "High-Context Culture: Definition and Examples," *Study.Com* (last accessed July 29, 2018), http://study.com/academy/lesson/high-context-culture-definition-examples-quiz.html.
33 Trompenaars and Hampden-Turner, *supra* note 12 at 74.
34 Bryson, *supra* note 776 at 36.
35 Trompenaars and Hampden-Turner, *supra* note 12 at 74.
36 Id. at 75.
37 Id.
38 Philip Yaffe, "The 7% Rule Fact, Fiction, or Misunderstanding," *Ubiquity* 1 (2011) (citing to Albert Mehrabian, *Silent Messages*. Wadsorth Publishing Company, 1972).
39 Bryson, *supra* note 776 at 36.
40 Id.
41 Kellerman, *supra* note 5 at 34.
42 Drucker, *supra* note 424.
43 Bryson, *supra* note 776 at 13.
44 Esther Schor, *Bridge of Words: Esperanto and the Dream of a Universal Language* (Metropolitan Books) (2016).
45 Geert Hofstede, "Do American Theories Apply Abroad? A Reply to Goodstein and Hunt," *Organizational Dynamics* 63, 68 (1981).
46 Brett, *supra* note 81 at 146.
47 Trompenaars and Hampden-Turner, *supra* note 12 at 90.
48 Sandy D. Jap, Diana C. Robertson, Aric Rindfleisch, and Ryan Hamilton, "Low-Stakes Opportunism," 50 *Journal of Marketing Research* 216, 217 (2013) (citing to Naquin and Paulson 2003).
49 Id.
50 Kalishman, supra note 100.
51 Id.

14

ETHNOCENTRISM

> It is easy to see the faults of others, but difficult to see one's own faults. One shows the faults of others like chaff winnowed in the wind, but one conceals one's own faults as a cunning gambler conceals his dice.
>
> Gautama Buddha

Why is that which is different so threatening to so many? We'll suggest two theories: one is the need to bolster our own self-images; in essence, a need for superiority that we gain on the backs of those different from us. The other is ignorance, in which we attribute characteristics to other people that are often simplistic, if not entirely fictional. These two drivers intermingle, with ignorance fueling our sense of superiority.

Let's take the story of the Kyrgyz Republic. This small country on the periphery of the old Soviet Union has experienced multiple ethnic conflagrations over the past decades, mostly centered around the southern city of Osh. The city is beset by ethnic prejudice in which the "local" Kyrgyz community – or at least a vocal minority – historically would rampage against the Uzbek people, most of whom have been in the country for generations but elicit anger because of their status as economically prosperous outsiders. Fortunately, the situation has been calm in recent years, but southern people are sometimes still considered *bashka adam*, or "other people," by the more Russified northerners.

It's easy – and correct – to feel sympathy for the Uzbeks who are the victims of these upheavals. Sadly for the Uzbeks, returning to Uzbekistan is not a viable option either, as the country is a police state to which only the truly desperate would wish to return. But perhaps we should express, if not sympathy, at least a certain understanding, for the Kyrgyz. At the heart of the upheaval was the age-old complaint that the Uzbeks were taking jobs from the Kyrgyz people. This is the same song heard around the world, and the United States is no exception. In Osh, the sense of entitlement is heightened by the fact that the Uzbeks are economically more prosperous, so the needy locals feel a particular sense of displacement. They are not right to blame the Uzbeks, but the Kyrgyz people's struggles are nonetheless all too real.[i] Without trying to see things from their perspective, solutions are unlikely.

The French have an expression that is telling in this regard: "To know all is to forgive all."[1] This can obviously be taken too far, but the principle rings true in part: we ought not to blame, at least not until we fully understand. Only once understanding is reached can real solutions be achieved. In this way, ignorance is removed, and the space for discrimination reduced.

We must understand, however, that while it is easy to point at others as prejudiced or as aggressors, everyone to some degree stereotypes and even manifests prejudice. It is all too easy to rationalize our behavior – to cloak it in justifications – rather than to seek to acknowledge our limitations and unveil our ignorance.

In this section, we seek to uncover many of the prejudices that prevail in our and other societies, to consider what prejudices each of us may have buried deep, and to bring some of those prejudices to light, including how to deal with prejudice when it rears its ugly head in the workplace. A book about culture would be incomplete without a chapter of this sort because it is the people of "other" ethnicities, religions, and values of which we are most ignorant.

And where there is prejudice, businesses fall short. As Robert J. House writes: "All experts in international business agree that to succeed in global business, managers need the flexibility to respond positively and effectively to practices and values that may be drastically different from what they are accustomed to. This requires the ability to be open to others' ideas and opinions. Being global is not just about where you do business. It is also about how you do it."[2]

Unveiling Our Stereotypes

Much of what we have described in the above cultural dimensions involves perception: perception about how much power a leader should have as well as the proper type of leader (e.g., male or female, older or high achieving). It involves our willingness to accept what is different, as we saw with uncertainty avoidance. With collectivism, we examined an individual's relationship to in-groups, finding that the stronger the in-group, the harder it is for those outside the group to gain acceptance. These are driven by cultural attitudes, but within all these areas we have the potential for stereotyping, prejudice, and discrimination.

A stereotype is a simplified belief, good or bad, held about a certain group of people. Prejudice occurs when the stereotyped behavior is different from an individual's expectations about how people *should* behave.[3] Thus, negative stereotypes often lead to prejudice. Finally, when one takes steps that cause harm to the stereotyped person or group, discrimination occurs.

To hold a stereotype does not mean one is prejudiced. There are many positive stereotypes, in fact (though even these have the ability to cause harm or to offend). To hold a prejudice does not mean one will act in a discriminatory manner. Many people hold prejudices but are constrained – sometimes by choice, peer pressure, or organizational or legal rules – from discriminating on the basis of those prejudices. It is nonetheless accurate to say that where stereotypes are held, discrimination *often* follows closely behind.[4]

Consider the exercise first carried out in a third grade class on April 5, 1968, a day after the assassination of Martin Luther King Jr. The teacher, Jane Elliott, put her students to the test:

> "How do you think it would feel to be a Negro boy or girl?" she asked the children, who were white. "It would be hard to know, wouldn't it, unless we actually experienced discrimination ourselves. Would you like to find out?" A chorus of "yeahs" went up.
>
> That spring morning thirty-seven years ago, the blue-eyed children were set apart from the children with brown or green eyes. Elliott pulled out green construction paper armbands and asked each of the blue-eyed kids to wear one. "The brown-eyed people are the better people in this room," Elliott began. "They are cleaner and they are smarter. ... Eye color, hair color and skin color are caused by a chemical," Elliott went on, writing MELANIN on the blackboard. Melanin, she said, is what causes intelligence. The more melanin, the darker the person's eyes – and the smarter the person. "Brown-eyed people have more of that chemical in their eyes, so brown-eyed people are better than those with blue eyes," Elliott said.
>
> Elliott rattled off the rules for the day, saying blue-eyed kids had to use paper cups if they drank from the water fountain. "Why?" one girl asked. "Because we might catch something," a brown-eyed boy said. Everyone looked at Mrs. Elliott. She nodded. As the morning wore on, brown-eyed kids berated their blue-eyed classmates. "Well, what do you expect from him, Mrs. Elliott," a brown-eyed student said as a blue-eyed student got an arithmetic problem wrong. "He's a bluey!"
>
> On Monday, Elliott reversed the exercise, and the brown-eyed kids were told how shifty, dumb, and lazy they were. Later, it would occur to Elliott that the blue-eyed kids were much less nasty than the brown-eyed kids had been, perhaps because the blue-eyed kids had felt the sting of being ostracized and didn't want to inflict it on their former tormentors. When the exercise ended, some of the kids hugged, some cried.
>
> The exercise is "an inoculation against racism," [Elliott] says. "We give our children shots to inoculate them against polio and smallpox, to protect them against the realities in the future. There are risks to those inoculations too, but we determine that those risks are worth taking."[5]

The Elliott exercise shows, as Zimbardo would put it in his 1979 textbook, *Psychology and Life*, "how easily prejudiced attitudes may be formed and how arbitrary and illogical they can be."[6] It further revealed how prejudice can lead to discrimination, as quickly occurred within Elliot's classroom.

It is consequently important to reveal the stereotypes that so many of us have, and which can be so easily formed. This section, therefore, is less directed towards the overt racists, ethnocentrics and misogynists of the world; we in fact suspect those types are not reading this book in the first place. Instead, we focus this material on those that mean well and are willing to investigate whether their actions align with their values.

We know that all of us have biases to some degree. We often don't know we have these biases, but they are there, resting quietly just below the surface, invisible but ready to pollute our decisions. As Sheryl Sandberg relates, the more we deny this simple fact, the more affected we are:

> When evaluating identically described male and female candidates for the job of police chief, ***respondents who claimed to be the most impartial actually exhibited more bias in favor of male candidates.*** This is not just counterproductive but deeply dangerous. Evaluators in that same study actually shifted hiring criteria to give men an advantage. When a male applicant possessed a strong educational record, that quality was considered critical to the success of a police chief. But when a male applicant possessed a weaker educational record, that quality was rated as less important. This favoritism was not shown to female applicants. If anything, the reverse happened. When a woman possessed a particular skill, ability, or background, that quality tended to carry less weight. The infuriating takeaway from this study is that "merit" can be manipulated to justify discrimination (emphasis added).[7]

Negative Stereotype ⟶ **Prejudice** ⟶ **Discrimination** (If the prejudice is acted upon)

Traditional versus Modern Gender Ideology

Imagine you have just opened a franchise, let's say a Starbucks. What would your workforce look like if that Starbucks were opened in Copenhagen? Or Bangkok? Tokyo? Riyadh? Depending on the location, the laws may constrain your ability to hire men and women in roughly equal proportion; the education system or the cultural norms regarding career advancement may inhibit the number of women prepared to take on the senior roles. A company expecting to work with total gender parity will do so easily in some places, with difficulty in others, and in vain elsewhere. The relative gender parity for this Starbucks can be understood better by first understanding gender role ideology.

Gender role ideologies represent a given society's expectations concerning the proper role of woman and men.[8] The ideologies can be divided into the traditional and the modern views. "Traditional ideologies view men as more 'important' than women and advocate relationships in which men dominate and control women. In contrast, modern ideologies view men and women as equals and advocate egalitarian relationships between them."[9] The word "traditional" is appropriate, because, unfortunately, most human societies have for the last several thousand years valued men more highly than women.[10] Consequently, "gender is a race in which some of the runners compete only for the bronze medal."[11]

Times are, however, beginning to change, at least in some parts of the world. As the researcher Spanis notes: "More and more societies today not only give men and women equal legal status, political rights and economic opportunities, but also completely rethink their most basic conceptions of gender and sexuality. Though the gender gap is still significant, events have been moving at a breathtaking speed."[12]

The GLOBE measure of gender equality was as follows:

> The most egalitarian countries studied were Hungary, Russia, Poland, Slovenia, Denmark, Namibia, Kazakhstan, Sweden, Albania, Canada, and Singapore.[13] The US ranked approximately in the middle of the listing, while Mexico and Qatar were in the top quartile for egalitarian practices.[14] When asked whether their societies should be more egalitarian, respondents from across cultures largely agreed.[15] Qatar is the one exception, which, as we will see, results in a workplace which is largely open to women but which can nonetheless feel hostile.[16] The respondents that most aspired to greater egalitarianism were perhaps the countries we might have expected: England, Sweden, Ireland, Portugal, Canada, Denmark, the United States, and Australia.[17]

The countries that practice this the least include South Korea, Kuwait, Egypt, Morocco, Zambia, Turkey, and India. China ranked in the bottom one-third, just below Germany, Ecuador, and Austria.[18]

The four most egalitarian countries – and five of the first seven – are former Soviet satellite states (or, in the case of Slovenia, a member of communist Yugoslavia). The USSR was known for its efforts to increase female literacy and its willingness to promote women into the professional ranks. This legacy helps explain why Eastern Europe ranks as the most egalitarian region, followed by Nordic European countries. However, no society is female-oriented to the degree that women, for instance, are more likely to be represented in positions of authority or more likely than boys to be encouraged to obtain higher educational degrees.[19] The least egalitarian regions according to the survey are the Middle East, East Asia, and Germanic Europe.[20]

Gender equality relates to the likelihood that women are equally represented in the labor force and in positions of authority, as well as the contributions made by women and men with respect to child rearing and housework.[21] More egalitarian societies tend to boast more women graduates from higher educational facilities than other countries as well as a higher labor participation rate.[22] As a result, more and more countries are seeing women on the highest courts of the land, leading as presidents and prime ministers, and filling the ranks of top executive positions. Nor is this limited to traditionally liberal, Western countries: in 2010, Brazil saw its first female president in Dilma Rousseff, as have a slew of other Latin American, African, and Asian countries.[23] We are increasingly seeing women crossing the boundaries of parenthood and professional life too, with Yahoo's Marissa Mayer announcing her pregnancy in 2012 on the heels of taking up her position as CEO, and New Zealand's recently elected prime minister Jacinda Ardern likewise preparing for motherhood as she leads her country.

Another result of this female participation is that the more economically advanced a country, the more egalitarian it tends to be.[24] It is unclear whether economic growth leads to calls for greater egalitarianism, or whether egalitarianism leads to these economic advances. However, researchers Dollar and Gatti found that where a lack of gender egalitarianism leads to less education for women, those societies suffer from slower growth and lower incomes.[25]

To this point, the *Washington Post* relates the following story told by Bill Gates:

> During a meeting on the sidelines of the World Economic Forum, Gates described speaking to a segregated audience at a recent business seminar in Saudi Arabia. On one side of an auditorium sat men. On the other side of a large partition was a "sea of black," Gates said [referring to the burka-wearing woman in the audience]. A questioner asked if he thought Saudi Arabia could meet its ambitious goal of becoming one of the world's most competitive economies. … "I said, 'Well, if you're not fully utilizing half the talent in the country, you're not going to get too close to the top,'" Gates said. How did the audience react? "One side loved it," Gates quipped.[26]

In the years since Gates's visit, though human rights issues more recently have come to light that bring progress into question, Saudi women have experienced a gradual loosening on restrictions over their lives. For instance, women are now allowed to work and study in the country without the permission of a man and more recently have obtained the right to drive.[27] The order to permit women's driving was explicitly presented as an attempt to bolster economic growth. As CNN quoted Saudi ambassador to the United States Prince Khaled bin Salman as saying: "It's not religious nor a cultural issue. … We are trying to increase women's participation in the workforce. In order to change women's participation in the workforce, we need them to be able to drive to work. … We need them to move forward, *we need them to improve our economy*" (emphasis added).[28]

Despite the words of bin Salman, the deeply ingrained paternal ideology in Saudi Arabia and many traditional societies is a cultural issue, and it means that more far-reaching change may be generations away. Indeed, many see the more significant hurdle for women in Saudi Arabia as being the restrictive guardianship system whereby women are essentially forever dependent on a male relative.[29] Furthermore, it has also generally been found that men with a traditional view of their own marriages – namely, that their own wives should not work – unsurprisingly view other women unfavorably in the workforce.[30]

The negative implications of this mentality are clear given that men continue to dominate the business place in traditional societies. As long as minorities and women continue to face exclusion from the "in-groups" of business – including networking opportunities and men only social events – they will continue to be underrepresented in leadership positions.[31] Ultimately, to exclude those who are different contributes to a cycle with negative economic consequences for both the victimized and the perpetrator. This helps explain why women are less likely to participate in the workforce in traditional societies.[32]

Perhaps surprisingly, however, these traditionally minded men tend to have positive views of women – for example, that women are more moral than men – but this belief tends to be used to justify keeping women in traditional roles (e.g., taking care of the children).[33] Consequently, these traditional men are more likely to deny promotions to female employees and to believe that organizations with fewer female employees run more smoothly.[34] Perhaps most dangerously of all, often such men act in the belief that they are helping women by returning them to their "rightful places" at home.

Another way in which we see seemingly well-meaning stereotypes doing lasting damage is in the ways we speak to girls. In studies of American children, researcher Carol Dweck observed that boys were criticized eight times more often than girls for their conduct.[35] Yes, boys can be overactive and unruly, but eight times more so? Doubtful. Instead, it seems that girls are more often praised for being "cute," "helpful," and "well-behaved" due to an enculturated expectation that girls will behave better than boys.[36]

The result is that these girls grow up hearing nice things from adults, boys less so. Upon reaching maturity, however, both boys and girls strike off into a world where women may actually be held to higher standards. When these girls, now adults in university or the workplace, begin to face criticism for making the sorts of mistakes we would expect to budding professionals, they may tend to feel that criticism more than their male counterparts.[37] Men in the same position have been criticized since they were mere toddlers – they as a whole prove more able to quickly move on.[38] The result is that men tend to exhibit higher confidence than women,[39] which, in turn, may explain why men more readily apply for and take on jobs with greater responsibility.[40]

This has implications when working abroad and to better understand this, again we turn to our expatriate community. Internations surveyed expatriates around the world and found a considerable difference between the perceptions of male and female respondents.

> For 86 percent of all respondents, gender has never been a reason to feel unwelcome abroad. However, there is a difference between male and

female expats: only 79 percent of women say they've never felt unwelcome due to their gender compared to 94 percent of men. Among expat women, 11 percent state they feel unwelcome due to their gender very rarely, and another 7 percent feel less than welcome sometimes. The percentages for men are noticeably lower, 3 and 2 percent respectively.

The five countries where expat women don't feel particularly welcome are Kuwait, India, Qatar, Saudi Arabia, and Japan. In Qatar, for example, only 46 percent of female respondents have never felt unwelcome because of their gender – 33 percentage points less than the global average of 79 percent. One in eleven expat women in Kuwait even says she feels unwelcome all the time, nine times the worldwide average of just 1 percent.[41]

In reference to Qatar, the reader will recall that the country experiences quite a bit more egalitarianism than its native population would prefer, which may lead to the sort of retaliation we see here.

Gender Stereotyping

Stereotypes, including gender stereotyping, are pan-cultural and held by both men and women.[42] Indeed, "children as young as five years of age, in both Western countries such as France, Norway, and the United States as well as non-Western countries such as Malaysia, Nigeria, and Peru hold distinct stereotypes of women versus men. For example, children in these countries viewed women as weak, gentle, meek, and emotional but viewed men as aggressive, strong, and dominant. Evidence suggests that gender stereotypes only strengthen with age, with eight-year-old children holding stereotypes of women and men that are even more "sex-typed" and consistent cross-culturally."[43]

Stereotypes often harden into discrimination and thus have concrete, negative implications. As just one example of many, a study conducted using the identical resumes of prospective employees found that those with female names were less likely to receive job offers (or more likely to receive low salary offers) than people with traditionally male names. Surprisingly, both male and female participants exhibited this gender hiring bias.[44]

While the gender stereotype is always present, the way in which it manifests can vary. For example, many Western people – both men and women – perceive women as communal, and kinder and gentler than men.[45] The result is that when women are leaders, they are held to different standards than men. If they act with assertiveness, they are evaluated more negatively than men acting in the same manner.[46] Women too are more likely than men to be judged unfit for a position based on their dress style.[47] Women suffer under the same workloads as similarly situated men, but they are expected to take more time to deal with the problems and needs of their workforce.[48] As a result of these and other stereotypes, Westerners claim to espouse gender egalitarianism but often fail to follow through in practice.[49]

Americans in general view individualism more favorably than collectivism. However, American women are viewed as more communal than men, and thus Americans expect men to act with more individuality than women. As a result, the American preference for individualism and the stereotype of women as communal results in a bias against women.

Americans are of course highly individualistic. Do more collectivist cultures continue to view women as more collective, which would lead them to view women more favorably than men? In fact, still no. In some societies that highly value collectivism, it is men that are seen as the great collaborators, and women as the selfish individualists.

Consider this exhibition of mental gymnastics revealed in a study by Harvard psychologist Amy Cuddy and her colleagues:

> Korean Americans were asked to complete a survey about gender. Half the participants took the survey in Korean, thereby priming their associations with Korean cultural norms.[50] The other half completed the survey in English, thus priming American cultural associations.[51] The respondents surveyed in Korean argued that collectivism was a desired value, and that men, not women, exhibited this trait.[52] When Korean Americans completed the survey in English, however, they stated that individualism, not collectivism, was a valued trait, and that men better exhibited individualism than women.[53]

In another study carried out by Cuddy and her colleagues, Americans were told that one of two traits – either ambitiousness or sociability – was a valued trait.[54] They then read a description of a fictional student who was identical in all respects, except half were told that a female student was described and half were told it described a male.[55] When the researchers told the participants that ambitiousness was valued, they found that the fictional male was more ambitious than the female, and when told that sociability was valued, they found that the fictional male was more sociable than the female. Regardless of which trait they were told was valued, in other words, the respondents – both men and women – found that men were more likely to have that favorable trait. This pattern of attributing to men the characteristics most valued by the society is believed to occur throughout the world.[56]

As if this weren't enough, we know that the victims of prejudice might be said to be victimized twice. This is because they not only must suffer the consequences of those prejudices (and often the discrimination that follows), but their own sense of self tends to conform to these societal prejudices. We saw this in Chapter 5 through our discussion of African American golfers performing worse when told they were engaging in an exercise to measure "sports intelligence," and Caucasian golfers performing worse when told they were engaging in an exercise to test "natural athletic ability." We saw this too with the Asian

American women who performed better on a math test when primed for race and worse when primed for gender.

And perhaps the most important takeaway to all this is to understand just how deeply these stereotypes operate. Consider the incontrovertible evidence of gender stereotyping already presented, along with the inferiority of the women's position across much, if not all, of the world.[57] If we take a step back, however, we might acknowledge how astounding it is, even deflating, that gender discrimination continues to such a degree. Women, after all, are the wives, sisters, daughters, and mothers of men. Women live with men. The average woman will even have more in common with a man from her own society than with a woman from another society.[58]

But as we know, stereotypes are not only held about woman. Furthermore, unlike women, ethnic minorities tend to live in separate communities, attend different houses of worship, or be physically and emotionally far removed in general.[59] So while we can and should acknowledge the discrimination faced by women, we must also not shy away from acknowledging the ethnocentrism that drives so much of this world. Ethnocentrism is an admittedly simplistic, but nonetheless powerful, explanation for the many conflicts and misunderstandings internationally. We too often think of those beyond our borders as "other" (Table 14.1).

TABLE 14.1 Gender egalitarianism (from most to least egalitarian)[60]

1. England	21. Venezuela	41. Japan
2. Sweden	22. Bolivia	42. Zambia
3. Ireland	23. Kazakhstan	43. South Africa (black sample)
4. Portugal	24. Mexico	44. Namibia
5. Canada (English speaking)	25. Israel	45. Finland
6. Denmark	26. Switzerland	46. New Zealand
7. United States	27. El Salvador	47. South Korea
8. Australia	28. Costa Rica	48. Albania
9. Colombia	29. Hungary	49. Russia
10. Brazil	30. South Africa (white sample)	50. Thailand
11. Netherlands	31. Ecuador	51. Taiwan
12. Argentina	32. Philippines	52. Indonesia
13. Switzerland	33. Guatemala	53. Malaysia
14. Germany (East)	34. Poland	54. Iran
15. Germany (West)	35. India	55. Morocco
16. Greece	36. Singapore	56. Georgia
17. Italy	37. Turkey	57. China
18. Austria	38. Zimbabwe	58. Kuwait
19. Slovenia	39. France	59. Qatar
20. Spain	40. Hong Kong	60. Egypt

Ethnocentrism

Ethnocentrism reflects the belief that one's own culture is superior to that of another.[61] We can see ethnocentrism in Soviet Russia's race to incorporate other countries into its "superior" economic system, just as today the United States often acts on the assumption that its own culture valuing democracy and capitalism are second to none. Ethnocentrism was also a primary driver of the European colonization movement, which was underpinned by a sense that the conquerors were in point of fact saviors, bringing enlightenment to the "barbaric" peoples of faraway places. There was "a sense of cultural superiority. None of the missionaries, explorers, governors, entrepreneurs or colonial secretaries doubted for a moment that there was such a thing as a *European* culture, that it was superior to any other culture in the world or that it was capable of being adopted, to their advantage, by any people, anywhere. These were the core doctrines of the 'white man's religion.'"[62]

Recall that people often feel prejudice when others behave in a way different from what is considered "normal." Ethnocentrism, in overlaying one's own culturally driven norms atop other cultures, thus incubates prejudice. Perhaps the most archetypal example of ethnocentrism leading to deadly prejudice is the Nazi regime. The Holocaust was the result of a belief that the Aryan culture was superior and that certain other ethnicities needed to be purged from the earth.

Ethnocentrism involves using one's own culture as a lens to view other cultures. An ethnocentric European and an ethnocentric African, as just one example, are unlikely to find much that appeals to them in the other. They both, however, actually share a fair bit in common as both are in a way the victims of their own mental programming. Here's how Culbert and Schusky explain it in *Introducing Culture*:

> As one studies the many contemporary cultures, one is struck by the diversity of behavior, and the person who goes to live among another people is likely to experience a "cultural shock." Everyone begins learning at birth; much of this early learning becomes so ingrained that it is assumed to be "only natural." What one eats, wears, and believes soon becomes *the* way of eating, dressing, and believing. Therefore, it is upsetting to find other people who behave or believe differently. The easy assumption is that something is wrong with them; they will change rapidly once exposed to the "right" (our) way of doing things.[63] (Emphasis added)

It is true that when someone behaves differently, that can prove a threat to our sense of self. Furthermore, when our identity is threatened, we take offense, and we tend to lash out against the person causing that threat.[64] When the threat is initiated by cultural differences, a prejudice fueled by ethnocentrism will likely arise. In this case, we focus on the negative differences of others – or give negative meaning to differences – in order to bolster our own social identities. This gives rise to the *bashka adam*, or "other people," mentality described at the beginning of this chapter.

Ethnocentrism **197**

This aversion to that which is different can be seen in many areas. In the world of gender for example, Innovisor, a consulting firm, conducted research in twenty-nine countries and found that when men and women select a colleague to collaborate with, both were significantly more likely to choose someone of the same gender."[65]

Researchers Eagly and Chin, however, make the point that this is far from limited to gender: "Tendencies to like and associate with others who are similar to oneself *exacerbate the biases* that flow from cultural stereotypes (e.g., Byrne and Neuman 1992). Because similarity promotes liking, entree to important networks can be diminished by ingroup preference even more than by outgroup suspicion" (emphasis added).[66]

A preference for belonging and acceptance is indeed pan-cultural – social relationships are nearly at the top of the Maslow hierarchy discussed earlier. Yet in-group preferences are in many ways more extensive amongst collectivists than individualists,[67] and this takes the threat to self from an isolated, individual phenomenon to a decidedly more disruptive group phenomenon. Collectivists, for example, are most likely to show altruism toward their in-groups.[68] But they are also more likely to negatively compare out-groups to their in-groups, in an effort to improve their perception of the in-group.[69] Because collectivists derive their identities partially from their in-groups, this is an extension of the effort to "maintain and enhance a positive self-image."[70] In the Chapter 3, we provided practical solutions to increase cohesiveness, and strengthen, even create, an in-group. As we now see, this not only impacts the risk of groupthink but more deeply affects interpersonal relationships (Table 14.2).

TABLE 14.2 Feeling (un)welcome as a foreign national (from most welcome to least)[71]

1. Portugal	17. Philippines	33. Luxembourg	49. Chile
2. Bahrain	18. Taiwan	34. Czech Republic	50. Germany
3. Mexico	19. Singapore	35. Turkey	51. Sweden
4. Malta	20. Romania	36. Indonesia	52. Norway
5. Costa Rica	21. Vietnam	37. United Kingdom	53. Japan
6. Spain	22. Australia	38. Kazakhstan	54. Israel
7. New Zealand	23. Thailand	39. Brazil	55. Austria
8. Malaysia	24. Argentina	40. Italy	56. Nigeria
9. Ecuador	25. Greece	41. Peru	57. Switzerland
10. Colombia	26. Kenya	42. Ukraine	58. India
11. Cambodia	27. United States	43. Belgium	59. Myanmar
12. Cyprus	28. South Africa	44. France	60. South Korea
13. Uganda	29. United Arab Emirates	45. Hungary	61. Denmark
14. Oman	30. Hong Kong	46. Finland	62. Qatar
15. Canada	31. Netherlands	47. Russia	63. Saudi Arabia
16. Ireland	32. Panama	48. Poland	64. China
			65. Kuwait

The Rattlers and the Eagles: A Study of In-Group Coherence and Out-Group Discrimination

There are some implications for in-group/out-group relations among collectivists. That said, the following study illustrates that this tendency to form in-groups and seek to exclude out-groups is not just culture, but also a very real part of who we all are as humans.

> In the summer of 1954, Muzafar Sherif convinced twenty-two sets of working-class parents to let him take their twelve-year-old boys off their hands for three weeks. He brought the boys to a summer camp he had rented in Robbers Cave State Park, Oklahoma. Sherif brought the boys to the camp in two groups of eleven, on two consecutive days, and housed them in different parts of the park. For the first five days, each group thought it was alone. Even still, they set about marking territory and creating tribal identities. One group called themselves the Rattlers, and the other group took the name Eagles.
>
> The Rattlers discovered a good swimming hole upstream from the main camp and, after an initial swim, they made a few improvements to the site, such as laying a rock path down to the water. They then claimed the site as their own, as their special hideout, which they visited each day. The Rattlers were disturbed one day to discover paper cups at the site (which in fact they themselves had left behind); they were angry that "outsiders" had used their swimming hole.
>
> A leader emerged in each group by consensus. When the boys were deciding what to do, they all suggested ideas. But when it came time to choose one of those ideas, the leader usually made the choice. Norms, songs, rituals, and distinctive identities began to form in each group (Rattlers are tough and never cry; Eagles never curse). Even though they were there to have fun, and even though they believed they were alone in the woods, each group ended up doing the sorts of things that would have been quite useful if they were about to face a rival group that claimed the same territory. Which they were.
>
> On day six of the study, Sherif let the Rattlers get close enough to the baseball field to hear that other boys – the Eagles – were using it, even though the Rattlers had claimed it as their field. The Rattlers begged the camp counselors to let them challenge the Eagles to a baseball game. As he had planned to do from the start, Sherif then arranged a weeklong tournament of sports competitions and camping skills. From that point forward, Sherif says, "performance in all activities that might now become competitive (tent pitching, baseball, etc.) was entered into with more zest and also with more efficiency." Tribal behavior increased dramatically. Both sides created flags and hung them in contested territory. They destroyed each other's flags, raided and vandalized each other's bunks, called each other nasty names, made weapons (socks filled with rocks), and would often have come to blows had the counselors not intervened.[72]

This study effectively recreates the development of culture: the songs and rituals representing the outer layers of the onion, and the values (such as not cursing or never crying) forming the inner layers. Notice the hierarchical nature of both groups, in which leaders quickly took charge. Notice the cohesion that formed, but also the territorial defensiveness that followed. Finally, notice how quickly this all happened – over a period of eleven days a fully formed culture had taken root. It is perhaps disillusioning that these children would behave so competitively.

Author Jonathan Haidt explains that this ability to form in-groups goes back to the origins of the human species:

> [W]arfare has been a constant feature of human life since long before agriculture and private property. For millions of years, therefore, our ancestors faced the adaptive challenge of forming and maintaining coalitions that could fend off challenges and attacks from rival groups. We are the descendants of successful tribalists, not their more individualistic cousins.[73]

Men (particularly young men) are more violent than women in almost every culture and across history – so we don't know whether teenage girls would have behaved in quite the same way.[74] We do know, however, that in-group preferences form (or are already present) even in young children of all genders. When this in-group preference takes on the tinge of national or cultural preferences, ethnocentrism takes flight. Indeed, children experience "preferences between foreign nations which seem to crystallize in children earlier than the assimilation of even the simplest items of factual information about these nations. [In so doing, they] clearly showed ethnocentric attitudes."[75] We further know that this preference does not slip away as we grow older.

Before we admit defeat, we might take heart from the fact that the children were able to form a cohesive in-group – indeed an entirely new culture – so very quickly. Sharif suggests that we seem to have a natural tendency to prefer in-groups and perhaps also to exclude out-groups, but it is the rapid cohesiveness that took place that gives us the beginning of a solution to ethnocentrism.

Expanding the In-Group, Quickly

In an interview with *Washington Post* contributor Fareed Zakaria, Singapore's deputy prime minister Tharman Shanmugaratnam explains how his country forged cohesiveness out of diversity:

> "We were a nation that was not meant to be," Shanmugaratnam said. The swamp-ridden island, expelled from Malaysia in 1965, had a polyglot population of migrants with myriad religions, cultures, and belief systems. "What's interesting and unique about Singapore, more than economics, are our social strategies. We respected people's differences

yet melded a nation and made an advantage out of diversity," he said in an interview.

How did Singapore do it? By mandating ethnic diversity in all its neighborhoods. More than 80 percent of Singaporeans live in public housing (all of it is well regarded, some of it very upmarket). Every block, precinct, and enclave has ethnic quotas. [Says Shanmugaratnam] "It turns out that when you ensure every neighborhood is mixed, people do everyday things together, become comfortable with each other, and most importantly, their kids go to the same schools. When the kids grow up together, they begin to share a future together."[76]

By interacting with those of distinct backgrounds, Shanmugaratnam implies, we begin to see not just the differences but the many similarities. The similarities go indeed much deeper, and it is most often the means by which we seek to achieve commonly held goals – such as the material success and spiritual fulfillment for ourselves and our loved ones – which differ.

At the institutional level, it is American universities that are in many ways leading the transition to a more diverse America. In a similar frame to that of Singapore, Washington University in St. Louis' Chancellor Mark Wrighton says: "We are not realizing the potential of having a diverse community if people become segregated upon arrival. That applies to the domestic student body as well as the international student body."[77] Consequently, the university's transition from a regional to a nationally competitive university began with a "physical commitment to have residence halls," which would bring all students together.[78]

There is thus nothing that prevents us from seeing our in-groups in quite positive terms, as do the Chinese, Malay, Indian, and other ethnicities that are nonetheless all Singaporean today. We have to change our mental framework, and the strategy of both Singapore, as well as Washington University and many other universities, is to assume that by bringing physical closeness, emotional closeness will follow. At the level of the business, this might mean designing workspaces that encourage interactions with diverse members of the workforce, frequent business trips for employees to visit offices in dispersed parts of the world, and building working groups with an eye on these sorts of interactions.

Chancellor Wrighton would go on to relate a story that aptly demonstrates how close interactions can expand one's sense of community:

> I'm often reminded of a meeting convened by [US] Secretary of State Condoleezza Rice. She invited a large number of university and college presidents to Washington DC for a conference that was entitled "international higher education in the national interest" or something to that affect.[77]
>
> There were people from research universities like Washington University and also from community colleges and public and private universities. At this meeting, a very large number of our government leaders

spoke: the president of the United States, of course Condoleezza Rice, First Lady Laura Bush, members of the Cabinet.

The theme from each presenter was the following: "In my role, as a Secretary of State, or president, or first lady, or Secretary of Commerce, I have traveled internationally and I have encountered people who spent time in the United States on a college campus earning a degree. And these people reflect very favorably on what took place there and how rewarding it was for them." That is a real strength of the diverse higher educational system of the United States.

An expanding in-group is not a new idea, but a historic reality: in prehistoric times, humankind existed with in-groups of a few dozen members of a tribe, or at most a few hundred. In later ages, city-states developed and tens of thousands of people became assimilated, and thereafter nations have come to include millions, even billions of people. Most of these people never met and never will, but they are nonetheless bound together by a common worldview.

And today, we live again in the age of empires, but unlike previous empires this one is held together by technology and cross-national economies that ensure that teenagers from South Africa to South Korea to South Dakota often wear similar clothing, listen to similar music, and watch the same movies. If they were to meet, they would find they have much in common.

Based on the results of Sharif's study, there is no reason to doubt that even if the parents of these teenagers remain firmly rooted in their cultural preconceptions, their children can create new, more encompassing definitions of their "in-group."

Observe just how quickly a change in perspective can take place:

> Even a well-established institution like Harvard Business School (HBS) can evolve rapidly when issues are addressed head-on. Historically at HBS, American male students have academically outperformed both female and international students. When Nitin Nohria was appointed dean in 2010, he made it his mission to close this gap. He began by appointing Youngme Moon as senior associate dean of the MBA program, the first woman to hold that position in the school's century-plus history. He also created a new position for Robin Ely, an expert on gender and diversity.
>
> Associate Dean Moon, working with Professor Frances Frei, spent the first year rigorously examining the school's culture. They visited each classroom and discussed the challenges women and international students faced. Then they used that knowledge to create what Dean Nohria calls "a level of mindfulness." Without calling for major overhauls, they tackled the soft stuff – small adjustments students could make immediately, like paying more attention to the language they used in class. They laid out a new, communal definition of leadership: "Leadership is about making others better as a result of your presence and making sure that impact lasts in your absence." They held students responsible for the impact their behavior

had on others. Those who violated that principle, or even hosted an event where that principle was violated, were held accountable. The second year, HBS introduced small group projects to encourage collaboration between classmates who would not naturally work together. They also added a year-long field course, which plays to the strengths of students who are less comfortable contributing in front of large classes.

By commencement, the performance gap had virtually disappeared. Men, women, and international students were represented proportionally in the honors awarded. There was another benefit too. In a result many considered surprising, overall student satisfaction went up, not just for the female and international students but for American males as well. By creating a more equal environment, everyone was happier. And all this was accomplished in just two short years.[79]

Part of what HBS did was to expand beyond mere diversity. Diversity is the starting point, but inclusion must follow. Less oil and water, more sugar and tea. Harvard President Faust herself elaborated on this point: "simply gathering a diverse mixture of extraordinarily talented people in one place does not in itself ensure the outcome we seek. Everyone at Harvard should feel *included*, not just *represented* in this community. "I too am Harvard" must be a statement every one of us can confidently make. Diversity must become belonging."[80]

This study shows that change can happen quickly by expanding the conception of the in-group – recall that "they laid out a new, *communal* definition of leadership" – while focusing on small changes that could be implemented immediately. This communal definition ensured, in Faust's words, that everyone felt included and not just represented.

SAK's Tom Kalishman also shared his experiences in facilitating shared values. He recalls his time with Insituform, Inc., a large company undergoing a period of rapid expansion in the late 1990s. In absorbing company after company, diversity was not an option – it was being forced upon the company.

Kalishman explains that significant care was taken to ensure that the diverse companies (and people within those companies) were made to feel a part of the new whole. Kalishman's team did this by identifying key skills possessed by each new company that could be adopted by the rest of the organization.

> Everybody had something they were excellent at and could teach the other people. If you took the best of each of them, you had something that was better than any of the individuals. That's why it's so important to have best practices. They can let go of some of the components if they're recognized as being best at something. I think it's very important from a buy-in perspective that everyone feels they're part of the future direction. No one wants to be a laggard who has somebody else's means and methods forced upon them. Everyone wants to contribute to the vision of where we're going.[81]

This is advice that should resonate deeply with any cross-cultural, or deeply diverse, organization. And if the idea that we can quickly expand our in-group leaves you skeptical, know that our natural tendencies are to be positive and welcoming. Researchers have found a preference in infants six months of age and younger for friendly and helpful people rather than harmful and unhelpful people.[82] This is not mere selfishness leading to a preference for a helping hand: these children prefer people who are nice to *others* too, and stay away from those who harm others.[83]

Kindness is thus a natural state, a point South African President Nelson Mandela made when he said: "People must learn to hate, and if they can learn to hate, they can be taught to love, for love comes more naturally to the human heart than its opposite. ... Man's goodness is a flame that can be hidden but never extinguished."[84] And indeed, what we learn to hate is often based on ignorance and misconceptions. Recall that children in the above study exhibiting ethnocentrism did this before they had "even the simplest items of factual information about these nations."[85]

As noted at the beginning of this chapter, part of the solution lies in unveiling our biases and subjecting them to critical questioning. With self-recognition, we can become more honest. And as this section shows, sometimes it is as simple as giving diverse peoples the opportunity to interact, which brings understanding.

Why Diversity?

> Trade brings all mankind together and casts glory on those who venture into it.
>
> Cosimo de' Medici[86]
> *Fifteenth Century*

The crucial point for businesses is that as the conception of the in-group expands, well-being increases. In Europe, for instance, the transition from feudal towns to kingdoms saw a decline in violence of ten- to fifty-fold, and similar benefits have been experienced throughout the world.[87] This expanded identity thus contributes to country level prosperity, and it is reasonable to anticipate the same result at the organizational level.

Indeed, diverse organizations perform better on average than more homogeneous organizations,[88] and this isn't surprising. After all, we live in a diverse world, and people from different backgrounds bring ideas to the table that a homogeneous group does not. Former US Secretary of State and former Exxon Mobil CEO Rex Tillerson said as much during a 2017 speech: "I know from my long career in the private sector, my experience has been [that] the value of diversity in the workplace is [that] it enriches our work product to have individuals who come with a different cultural perspective or they come with different life experiences. That's the value. They will see things in the world that I cannot see. I did not have that life experience."[89]

Here is another way to look at this: some of the most favored foods within a culture are considered quite strange in others – venomous cobra snakes are a delicacy in Cambodia, for example, while dining on horse is living large in others. It seems fair to say, however, that taste buds are just about the same everywhere, so if one culture prefers a certain food, then it might be that they're onto something of which the rest of us are unaware. As just one example, the late chef and food writer Anthony Bourdain relates how Americans used to be unaware of the joys of certain seafood, such as squid. He notes that American restaurateurs of decades past would watch in confusion as Japanese customers would buy up these and other "unusual" items at the docks of New York, often for rock-bottom prices.[90] They in fact knew something American restaurateurs of the time didn't know, though eventually they would catch on. This story illustrates how certain ideas can at first seem unnatural, or "foreign" in a literal or figurative sense, but it's through the exposure to other ideas that the very best of these ideas filter to the top (while perhaps we will leave the venomous snakes to the dinner tables of our Cambodian friends).

We have at this point addressed numerous strategies to increase diversity, which include expanding the definition of the in-group by focusing on shared similarities. What about when the situation is reversed, and you are going into foreign territory: you are now part of the out-group and the question becomes how you can become a member of the in-group. To this end we ask: do you have any theater experience?

Strategic Mimicry and Conformance

In 1831, Charles Darwin boarded the British navy's HMS *Beagle*. The boat was small, the waves were choppy, and Darwin was continually seasick. He developed heart palpitations and felt himself dangerously ill; he became homesick as the prospect of the years-long outing set in. The other sailors sensed his unease and looked at him with misgiving. The captain was half crazy, a religious fanatic, and lost his temper easily. Darwin underwent a feeling of profound regret for the journey, but after a few weeks, on his way to discovering the evolution of species, Darwin himself evolved. He began to observe the most important details around him. He noticed that the sailors didn't complain about the food or the weather or their chores. Stoicism was valued, so he too became stoic. He noticed the captain was insecure and thus regularly asserted his status as a high-ranking navy officer. Darwin was quick to affirm his high status. He even picked up some of the sailors' mannerisms. Soon, Darwin was accepted into the daily life of the ship, and the rest, as they say, is history.[91]

Charles Darwin understood a deep truth about humans: we are attracted to – and want to spend both social and professional time with – those who are similar to us.[92] In these people, we see our own reflections. This reinforcement of our self-image is rewarding. Consequently, "over time, a mutual attraction, or group cohesiveness, develops between people whose association mediates the mutual satisfaction of reassuring self-image."[93]

The more different the cultural dimensions described above, however, the less likely it may be that someone sees his or her own reflection in you. Author Daniel Pink, in *To Sell is Human*, asserts that part of the answer may come in strategic mimicry.[94] If people naturally prefer that which is similar, then you can seek to subtly impress upon them how similar you are. Put simply, do as Charles Darwin did and be a copycat.

We in fact seem to do this naturally. Barack Obama, for instance, notably spoke in a slightly different dialect to African American majority crowds than he did to mostly Caucasian crowds during his presidency. This is known as "code switching" and is probably an example of purposeful mimicry on the part of the former president.

Bill Bryson shares this case of mimicry in *The Mother Tongue*:

> William Labov of the University of Pennsylvania ... studied the accents of New York City ... in particular he studied the sound of r's in words like more, store, and car. As recently as the 1930s, such r's were never voiced by native New Yorkers, but over the years they have come increasingly to be spoken – but only sometimes. Whether or not people voiced the r in a given instance was thought to be largely random. But Labov found that there was actually much more of a pattern to it. In a word, people were using r's as a way of signaling their social standing, rather like the flickering of fireflies. The higher one's social standing, the more often the r's were flickered, so to speak. ... most people used or disregarded r's as social circumstances demanded. He found that sales assistants in department stores tended to use many more r's when addressed by middle-class people than when speaking to lower-class customers.[95]

The salespeople were engaged in strategic mimicry much like we saw with Barack Obama and Charles Darwin. Mimicry indeed comes quite naturally to humans,[96] and we often mimic without even being aware of it. Indeed, if we try, we can probably think of a time that we caught ourselves subtly impersonating the mannerisms or expressions of close friends or family members. This is a subconscious attempt to make ourselves more likeable; perhaps it gave rise to the familiar expression that "imitation is the sincerest form of flattery."[97]

Pink cites a series of studies showing just how effective mimicry is when subtle and sincere. For example, research participants in a fictional negotiation that were asked before the negotiation to subtly mimic their counterpart obtained better results than the control group.[98] Moreover, they improved their outcomes without diminishing the negotiated outcome for the other side. Appropriately, the title of the study was "Chameleons Bake Bigger Pies and Take Bigger Pieces."

A cross-cultural component is evident as well. In a Dutch study, waitresses repeating customers' orders received 70 percent more in tips than those who did not.[99] In a French study, salespersons mimicked customers nonverbal behaviors. When they did so, customers were more likely to make a purchase.[100] The customers later stated that they were happier with the salespersons, and with the store itself, than in cases where no impersonation took place.[101] Finally, an experiment at Duke found that people were more likely to say they would buy a sports drink when mimicked.[102]

This has implications for building cohesion in order to reduce ethnocentrism and stereotyping, as well as to avoid the free-rider effect and groupthink as discussed in Chapter 3. Additionally, this strategy might be used to bridge the gap between people who communicate in different ways – for instance, you may well benefit from adopting a high context communication strategy when communicating in East Asia, just as we saw the US manager do when cautiously voicing concern about the rattling bicycles to his Chinese counterpart.

Note

i The above paragraph is the result of numerous conversations between the authors and residents, both Uzbek and Kyrgyz, of the Kyrgyz Republic.

References

1 In French: *Tout comprendre c'est tout pardonner.*
2 House and Javidan, *supra* note 8 at 5.
3 Paul R. Wilson, "Perceptual Distortion of Height as a Function of Ascribed Academic Status," 74 *Journal of Social Psychology*, 97, 99 (1968).
4 Emrich et al., *supra* note 563 at 350 (stating the Supreme Court of the United States gave legal standing to the idea that gender stereotyping tends to lead to gender discrimination).
5 Stephen G. Bloom, "Lesson of a Lifetime," *Smithsonian Magazine* (September 2005), https://www.smithsonianmag.com/science-nature/lesson-of-a-lifetime-72754306/.
6 Id.
7 Sandberg, *supra* note 301 at 139 (citing to Eric Luis Uhlmann and Geoffrey L. Cohen, "Constructed Criteria: Redefining Merit to Justify Discrimination," *Psychological Science* 16, no. 6 (2005): 474–480).
8 Emrich et al., *supra* note 563 at 379.
9 Id. at 349.
10 Harari *supra* note 66 at 170–171.
11 Id. at 171.
12 Id. at 178.
13 Emrich et al., *supra* note 563 at 365.
14 Id.
15 Id. at 366.
16 Id.
17 Id.
18 Id. at 365.
19 Id. at 362.
20 Id. at 374.

21 Id. at 350.
22 Id. at 349.
23 "The Women Presidents of Latin America," *BBC News* (Oct. 31, 2010), http://www.bbc.com/news/world-latin-america-11447598; see also List of Elected and appointed Female Heads of State and Government, Wikipedia (last accessed July 29, 2018) https://en.wikipedia.org/wiki/List_of_elected_and_appointed_female_heads_of_state_and_government.
24 Emrich et al., *supra* note 563 at 349.
25 David Dollar and Roberta Gatti, "Gender Inequality, Income, and Growth: Are Good Times Good for Women?" 3, 20 Development Research Group: The World Bank, Poverty Reduction, and Economic Management Network (1999).
26 Associated Press, "Gates: Women Key to Saudi Arabia Economy," *Washington Post* (Jan. 27, 2007), http://www.washingtonpost.com/wp-dyn/content/article/2007/01/27/AR2007012700951.html.
27 Nicole Gaouette and Elise Labott, "Saudi Arabia to Let Women Drive," CNN Politics (Sept. 27, 2017), http://edition.cnn.com/2017/09/26/politics/saudi-arabia-woman-drive/index.html.
28 Id.
29 https://www.nytimes.com/2018/06/22/world/middleeast/saudi-arabia-women-driving.html.
30 Sandberg, *supra* note 301 at 139 (citing to Eric Luis Uhlmann and Geoffrey L. Cohen, "Constructed Criteria: Redefining Merit to Justify Discrimination," *Psychological Science* 16, no. 6 (2005): 474–480).
31 Eagly and Chin, *supra* note 589 at 218 (citing to Brass 2001). (Explaining that networks are key to moving up the ranks, to gaining experience and being in the so-called right place at the right time.)
32 Emrich et al., *supra* note 563 at 349 (citing to Williams and Best, 1990b).
33 Sandberg, *supra* note 301 at 139.
34 Id.
35 Dweck, *supra* note 132 at 67.
36 Id. at 66.
37 Id. at 67.
38 Id.
39 Id.
40 Sandberg, *supra* note 301 at 61 (citing to Lloyds TSB, which "found that their female employees tended not to put themselves up for promotion despite being 8 percent more likely to meet or surpass performance standards than their male colleagues." See Desvaux, Devillard-Hoellinger, and Meaney, "A Business Case for Women," 4. Studies on gender and promotion mostly at the university level in England and Australia also find that women are hesitant to put themselves up for promotion, often because they undervalue their skills, abilities, and work experience. See Anne Ross-Smith and Colleen Chesterman, "'Girl Disease': Women Managers' Reticence and Ambivalence toward Organizational Advancement," *Journal of Management and Organization* 15, no. 5 (2009): 582–595; Liz Doherty and Simonetta Manfredi, "Women's Progression to Senior Positions in English Universities," *Employee Relations* 28, no. 6 (2006): 553–572; and Belinda Probert, "'I Just Couldn't Fit It In': Gender and Unequal Outcomes in Academic Careers," *Gender, Work, and Organization* 12, no. 1 (2005): 50–72).
41 "Expat Insider 2017: Feeling (Un)welcome Abroad," *supra* note 778.
42 Amy Cutty, Elizabeth Baily Wolf, Susan Crotty, Jihye Chong, and Peter Glick, "Men as Cultural Ideals: How Culture Shapes Gender Stereotypes," 109 *Journal of Personality and Social Psychology*, 622–635 (2015).
43 Emrich et al., *supra* note 563 at 349.
44 Sandberg, *supra* note 301 at 139 (citing to Corinne A. Moss-Racusin et al., "Science Faculty's Subtle Gender Biases Favor Male Students," *Proceedings of the National*

Academy of Sciences of the United States of America 109, no. 41 (2012): 16474–16479; Rhea E. Steinpreis, Katie A. Anders, and Dawn Ritzke, "The Impact of Gender on the Review of Curricula Vitae of Job Applicants and Tenure Candidates: A National Empirical Study," *Sex Roles* 41, nos. 7–8 (1999): 509–528).

45 Id. at 40.
46 Hartog, *supra* note 562 at 398, citing to Kelly, Kern, Kirkley, Patterson, and Keane (1980) and Crawford (1998).
47 Sandra Forsythe, Mary F. Drake, and Charles E Cox, "Influence of Applicant's Dress on Interviewer's Selection Decisions," 70 *Journal of Applied Psychology* 373, 374 (1985).
48 Sandberg, *supra* note 301 at 44 (citing to Madeline E. Heilman and Julie J. Chen, "Same Behavior, Different Consequences: Reactions to Men's and Women's Altruistic Citizenship Behaviors," *Journal of Applied Psychology* 90, no. 3 (2005): 431–441).
49 Emrich et al., *supra* note 563 at 366.
50 Cutty et al., *supra* note 868 at 628 (2015).
51 Id.
52 Id.
53 Id.
54 Cutty et al., *supra* note 868.
55 Id.
56 Id. at 622.
57 In none of the GLOBE countries studied were women found to be more advantaged in business than men. See Emrich et al., *supra* note 563 at 362.
58 See Trompenaars and Hampden-Turner, *supra* note 12 at 222.
59 Id. at 224 (noting "ethnic diversity exhibits far greater differences than gender").
60 Emrich et al., *supra* note 563 at 366.
61 Ethnocentric, Merriam-Webster (last accessed July 29, 2018), https://www.merriam-webster.com/dictionary/ethnocentric.
62 Wilson *supra* note 535 at 3475/3944 of E-book.
63 Schusky and Culbert *supra* note 3.
64 Brett, *supra* note 81 at 141, 142.
65 Sandberg, *supra* note 301 at 140 (citing to Melissa Korn, "Choice of Work Partner Splits along Gender Lines," *Wall Street Journal*, June 6, 2012, http://online.wsj.com/article/SB10001424052702303506404577448652549105934.html.
66 Eagly and Chin, *supra* note 589 at 218.
67 Id. at 219 (citing House, Hanges, Javidan, Dorfman, and Gupta, 2004).
68 Earley, *supra* note 225 at 322.
69 Id.
70 Id.
71 The Global network Internations conducted a survey asking respondents if they had felt welcome in their country of residence in the past twelve months due to nationality, culture, race, ethnicity, language or accent, age, gender, or sexual orientation. See *Expat Insider 2017*, *supra* note 798.
72 Haidt, *supra* note 98 at 11.
73 Id.
74 Steven Pinker, *The Better Angels of Our Nature* 25 (Penguin Books) (2012).
75 Henri Taiffel, "Social Psychology of Intergroup Relations," 33, *Annual Review of Psychology* 1, 9 (1982) (citing to Pushkin and Veness 1973, Milner 1975, 1981, P. Katz 1976).
76 Fareed Zakaria, "What America Can Learn from Singapore about Racial Integration," *The Washington Post* (June 25, 2015), https://www.washingtonpost.com/opinions/from-singapore-lessons-in-harmony-and-diversity/2015/06/25/86fcbfa2-1b72-11e5-93b7-5eddc056ad8a_story.html?utm_term=.bd7610e158be.

77 Wrighton, *supra* note 130.
78 Id.
79 Sandberg, *supra* note 301 at 144.
80 "History of Presidency: 2015 Remarks at Morning Prayer," *Harvard University* (Sept. 2, 2015), https://www.harvard.edu/president/speech/2015/2015-remarks-morning-prayers.
81 Kalishman, *supra* note 100.
82 Haidt, *supra* note 98 at 35–37.
83 Id.
84 Nelson Mandela, *Long Walk to Freedom: The Autobiography of Nelson Mandela* (Little, Brown and Company) (2008).
85 Taiffel, *supra* note 900 at 10.
86 Strathern, *supra* note 64 at 120.
87 Pinker, *supra* note 899 at 18.
88 Sandberg, *supra* note 301 at 140 (citing, *inter alia*, to Jessica Canning, Maryam Haque, and Yimeng Wang, "Women at the Wheel: Do Female Executives Drive Start-up Success?" *Dow Jones and Company* (Sept. 2012), http://www.dowjones.com/collateral/files/WomenPE_report_final.pdf; Cedric Herring, "Does Diversity Pay? Race, Gender, and the Business Case for Diversity," *American Sociological Review* 74, no. 2 (2009): 208–224; Elizabeth Mannix and Margaret A. Neale, "What Difference Makes a Difference? The Promise and Reality of Diverse Teams in Organizations," *Psychological Science in the Public Interest* 6, no. 2 (2005): 31–55; and Thomas Kochan et al., "The Effects of Diversity on Business Performance: Report of the Diversity Research Network," *Human Resource Management* 42, no. 1 (2003): 3–21).
89 Robbie Gramer, "As State Department Withers, So Does Diversity in Top Ranks," *Foreign Policy* (Oct. 25, 2017), http://foreignpolicy.com/2017/10/25/as-state-department-withers-so-does-diversity-in-top-ranks-diplomacy/
90 Anthony Bourdain, *Kitchen Confidential* (A&C Black) (2010).
91 Greene, *supra* note 379 at 66.
92 Earley, *supra* note 225 at 321.
93 Id.
94 Pink *supra* note 430 at 63.
95 Bryson, *supra* note 776 at 105–106.
96 Pink *supra* note 430 at 62.
97 Charles Caleb Colton, *Lacon; Or Many Things in Few Words: Addressed to Those Who Think* 114. (New York: Longman, Orme, Brown, Green, and Longmans) (1837).
98 Pink *supra* note 430 at 63 (citing to Maddux et al., "Chameleons Bake Bigger Pies," 463).
99 Id. at 63 (citing to Rick B. van Baaren, Rob W. Holland, Bregje Steenaert, and Ad van Knippenberg, "Mimicry for Money: Behavioral Consequences of Imitation," *Journal of Experimental Social Psychology* 39, no. 4 (July 2003): 393–398).
100 Id. at 65 (citing to Céline Jacob, Nicolas Guéguen, Angélique Martin, and Gaëlle Boulbry, "Retail Salespeople's Mimicry of Customers: Effects on Consumer Behavior," *Journal of Retailing and Consumer Services* 18, no. 5 (Sept. 2011): 381–388).
101 Id.
102 Id. (citing to Robin J. Tanner, Rosellina Ferraro, Tanya L. Chartrand et al., "Of Chameleons and Consumption: The Impact of Mimicry on Choice and Preferences," Journal of Consumer Research 34 (Apr. 2008): 754–766).

CONCLUSION

We have explored a wide variety of pan-cultural behaviors, beliefs and values. It is true, we assert, that humanity has much more in common than it does not. Nonetheless, it is the differences that evoke misunderstandings – that lead to war and violence on the one hand or to failed mergers, dissatisfied customers and belittled employees on the other. We have covered a wide variety of those differences – termed cultural dimensions – in this book. Now that you see the interconnected whole to which we referred in the introduction, you may better grasp in your mind's eye the parameters of culture. And while these dimensions are inextricably connected, understanding how the part makes up the whole allows one to dive deeper into those dimensions that are most confounding, most relevant or simply most interesting in any given place.

Diving in means knowing the literature, certainly, including how religions, ethnicities, social classes, ages, genders, and every other possible variety is in fact diverse. The next step, however, is something this book cannot offer: it involves getting up from that comfortable reading chair, turning off the lamp and stepping outside. It involves seeking out cultural variety, testing yourself on these dimensions and asking questions. It will be uncomfortable at times, but it is only through discomfort that professional and personal growth takes place. This study can occur during a business trip to Hong Kong, or on a vacation to Rome, but it can also be achieved in less dramatic ways: you can take note of cultural cues while attending your cousin's baptism to a faith not your own, while eating dinner at a new Thai restaurant, while watching a foreign film, or even while meeting a new friend from another part of the country. We are all – each and every one of us – diverse, so the question is not how to find diversity but how to embrace it, how to learn from it, and, ultimately, how to be a better *you* as a result.

The most important recommendation is simply to face these realities squarely – avoid taking offense at the proposition that you may have prejudice within you, and instead uphold the values you care about by looking for your own blind spots. View cultural differences not as a threat but as an opportunity for both personal and professional growth. Take pride in feeling as comfortable in Beirut as in Boston. Take comfort in forging connections with people of vastly different backgrounds. As Sheryl Sandberg once said, "We cannot change what we are not aware of, and once we are aware, we cannot help but change."[1] Enjoy the adventure.

Reference

1 Sandberg, supra note 301 at 143.

APPENDIX

Introducing Cultural Dimensions

In the first several chapters, we introduce the cultural dimensions that help to shape who we are as people, our relationships to our communities, and differences among cultures. Furthermore, and perhaps most importantly, we see how these cultural dimensions affect phenomena of behavioral psychology and, thus, how they affect cross-cultural leadership.

Beginning in the first chapter, we introduce the reader to the ideas of Hofstede, Trompenaars, and Hamden-Turner, as well as GLOBE's House and colleagues, who collectively help provide a system by which to understand culture and some of its effects upon business. While many readers may be more familiar with the work of Dr. Geert Hofstede, Hofstede himself acknowledged that his classic system only accounted for about 49 percent of cultural differences between countries.[1] Additional factors thus explain the other roughly 50 percent of a country's culture, and it is our belief that GLOBE and Trompenaars provide some of these additional factors and thus get us closer to explaining the variation among cultures. Consequently, these three sources provide us a working system, for systematically understanding culture; for understanding the effects of culture on leadership; and, finally, to peer into the world of behavioral psychology to add depth and sophistication to our analysis of cross-cultural leadership.

Chapter 2 introduces the ideas of individualism and collectivism. Individualists concern themselves primarily with their immediate families, and of course themselves. Collectivists are concerned with a wider range of relations, called an "in-group," including immediate and extended family and possibly also a community, ethnic group, religious family or even nation. Collectivists, unlike individualists, may feel obligated to share the opinions and beliefs of their in-group even when individually they are other-minded.

Chapter 3 considers the ways in which collectivism and individualism may contribute to groupthink. Groupthink is the process by which a group makes an irrational or otherwise poor decision by failing to individually consider the merits of a course of action. We'll see that ego and an unwillingness to dissent drives groupthink, and that individualists' need for uniqueness makes excess ego a particular threat. We'll see both individualists and collectivists are prone to obey those in authority to a fault, that conformity with group decisions leads individuals across cultures (but especially in collectivist cultures) to believe even faced with overwhelming countervailing evidence. Finally, we'll draw on the strategies of societies with particularly strong institutional cultures to identify the remedies to these problems.

Chapter 4 continues the group work theme by considering free-riding, or social loafing – an event in which some members of a group work less than they would if working alone, riding sometimes even shamelessly on the coattails of others. We'll see that collectivists are less prone to social loafing, but only if paired with like-minded teammates. Individualists, by contrast, will only discontinue their loafing if the incentives are reworked to compel them to.

Chapter 5 discusses achievement versus ascription societies. In achievement societies, status is earned based on one's accomplishments, while in ascription societies, status is granted based on one's natural or inherited properties. What qualifies as an accomplishment in achievement societies or is favorably ascribed in ascription societies varies. Common achievements may include profession, material wealth or education level. Common ascription factors include gender, age or kinship. By observing waiters retaliating against rude customers by, among other things, spitting in their customers' dishes, we'll see that when status is diminished, people have a tendency to act out. We'll also explore the common need for achievement, some of the negative implications of the long work hours characteristic of the highest achievers, and propose an alternative that seeks to balance efficiency and productivity.

Chapter 6 discusses power distance, or the degree to which a society is hierarchical versus egalitarian. All cultures have differences in status. But in hierarchical cultures, the distance between a person at the top of society or an organization and a person at the bottom is very large. In egalitarian societies, distance is narrow. In hierarchical societies, this large power distance means that the person at the top has much more power over his or her subordinates than a comparable status person in an egalitarian society. We'll see how the twenty-first century's Information Age is flattening organizations, but how hierarchies can also bring about some surprising organizational benefits, not least of which is loyalty.

Chapter 7 discusses power, its addictiveness, and the tendency for power to corrupt. We show through a simple experiment how power makes us less able to empathize with others, and we look to a classic and troubling experiment involving Stanford undergraduates to show how quickly empowered people can use their authority to dehumanize, humiliate and harm others. With a mixed exploration of the !Kung people of the Kalahari, Dutch schoolchildren and US accounting scandals, we devise a strategy to reduce the corrupting influences of power.

Chapter 8 introduces the cultural dimension of uncertainty avoidance. In countries with high uncertainty avoidance, the uncertain future is a thing to fear, and attempts to minimize the uncertainty are likely to follow. In low uncertainty avoidance countries, the uncertain future is embraced, and may be cause for excitement. We'll see how our birth order – and our governments – affect our willingness to take chances such as opening a new business or embarking on a new profession. In places with high uncertainty avoidance, the society may seek to minimize risk by embracing (1) the latest technology, (2) a strong legal system, (3) a religion or ideology, (4) or by working long work hours. In so doing, we'll see how the very perception of what is right and moral can differ between countries, from those that consider universal fairness to be the height of morality to those that carry the burden to help those closest even at the expense of others.

Chapter 9 introduces the related concepts of loss and risk aversion, which cause us to value what we already have more than we should and fear loss more than gain. As a result, we fail to make the sacrifices necessary to conclude mutually beneficial agreements, we hold on to jobs we no longer want, pursue degrees and even careers simply because we have started them, and thus miss opportunities to grow ourselves and our businesses.

Chapter 10 introduces the idea of assertive societies (sometimes termed "masculine"), in which people are motivated to achieve material success and may exhibit greater aggressiveness or a tendency to show off, whereas less assertive societies (sometimes termed "feminine") exhibit modesty, respect for relationships and favor a work-life balance. We'll see the close connection between assertiveness and charisma, as well as charisma and narcissism, and see that while most leaders are charismatic, the characteristic we should most value is humility.

Chapter 11 builds on the concepts introduced in Chapter 10 by discussing motivation. We'll see the surprising ways in which people everywhere can be intrinsically motivated by social relationships, autonomy and the ability to gain mastery. We'll also see that extrinsic rewards and intrinsic motivation can be a powerful, but dangerous, combination.

Chapter 12 discusses attitudes to time. This includes those societies that look toward the future, and those that either focus on the present or the past. We will discuss how future and past orientations tend to be of benefit to a society's economic welfare, and how a four-year-old's ability to delay snack time predicts his future personal and career success. We'll also see that while time orientation varies, people everywhere are of the belief that the best managers are future-oriented types.

Chapter 13 introduces various forms of communication styles. We'll see why people from certain cultures are more willing to express their emotions – sometimes quite loudly – while others seem rather cold and disinterested. This chapter also shows how some communicate directly and frankly, often inadvertently offending those that layer their communications more deeply; while those speaking with great nuance and caution often perplex and confuse the direct communicator. We conclude by helping bridge the gap between these and other communication styles.

In Chapter 14, we look at the Rattlers and the Eagles, two groups of twelve-year-old boys on summer break, to see just how quickly factions and even profound animus are created. We see how this tendency to exclude is not just a moral concern but a drag on the performance of diverse organizations. We will also see, however, the rapidity with which in-groups can be formed and transformed and propose strategies for organizations to better bind together their diverse members. We therefore conclude in Chapter 14 with a review of the most common forms of stereotyping and ethnocentrism affecting organizations and provide specific action items that leaders can take to stamp out this malady.

Throughout these chapters, we discuss the impact of the cultural dimensions on organizational culture and structure. Though many factors affect organizational culture – including economic conditions, the type of business and the number and type of competitors[2] – a "wealth of literature" demonstrates a strong correlation between country culture and organizational culture.[3]

The reader should note that in analyzing the cultural dimensions, societies (and individuals within societies) fall on a scale somewhere between the two extremes that we now present. For example, we will note that Americans are perhaps the most individualistic and that Filipinos may be the most collectivist, but many countries blur some individualism with some collectivism elements. Additionally, even the most extreme cultures still are prone to exhibit traits reflective of the opposite sides of the spectrum – for example, although Americans are considered the most individualistic in the world, Americans, like all humans, exhibit what researcher Jonathan Haidt calls a "hivish" nature that compels certain collective activities with respect to close acquaintances.

In discussing these ideas, we reference the degree to which certain countries and regions exhibit these dimensions. For consistency, we will use the GLOBE's geographic "clusters." Although in some cases the regions are vast and dissimilar in certain ways, the clusters represent regions that have more cultural similarities with one another than with any other region.[4]

For reference, these clusters are as follows:

1. The "Anglo" region or cluster includes the United Kingdom, Australia, South Africans of European descent, Canada, New Zealand, Ireland, and the United States.[5]
2. The "Latin Europe" region or cluster includes Italy, Portugal, Spain, France, Switzerland (French speaking), and Israel.[6]
3. The "Nordic Europe" region or cluster includes Finland, Sweden, and Denmark.[7] Not studied by GLOBE but also part of this region are Norway and Iceland.
4. The "Germanic Europe" region or cluster includes the Netherlands, Austria, Switzerland, and Germany.[8]

5. The "Eastern Europe" region or cluster includes Balkan, Central European, Eastern European, and Central Asian nations.[9] Those studied by GLOBE are Hungary, Russia, Kazakhstan, Albania, Poland, Greece, Slovenia, and Georgia.[10]
6. The "Latin America" region or cluster includes Western hemisphere countries with a Spanish or Portuguese colonial history. Those studied by GLOBE are Costa Rica, Venezuela, Ecuador, Mexico, El Salvador, Columbia, Guatemala, Bolivia, Brazil, and Argentina.[11]
7. The "Middle East" region or cluster includes Northern African and Western Asian countries of Arab descent or influence. Those studied by GLOBE are Qatar, Morocco, Turkey, Egypt, and Kuwait.[12]
8. The "Sub-Saharan Africa" region or cluster includes the entirety of the African continent. Those studied by GLOBE are Namibia, Zambia, Zimbabwe, Nigeria, and South Africans native to the land.[13] A more detailed analysis of Sub-Saharan Africa would be preferable and generalizations about the continent as a whole are to be resisted.
9. The "Southern Asia" region or cluster includes Iran, India, Indonesia, Philippines, Malaysia, and Thailand.[14]
10. The East Asia region or cluster (termed "Confucian Asia" by the GLOBE authors) includes countries influenced by China or Confucius. Those studied by GLOBE are Taiwan, Singapore, Hong Kong, South Korea, China, and Japan.[15]

Cultural Dimensions: What's the Use?

Many discussions of culture, while technically correct, risk taking too narrow of a perspective by focusing on singular manifestations of culture. For instance, showing respect by accepting the business card of a Japanese acquaintance with both hands and actively reading the card is an oft trotted out (and of itself perfectly acceptable) recommendation. But this sort of one-off inquiry leaves us scratching our heads: how does that tidbit on business cards help me deal with anything else in Japan? And what can I learn from that information about doing business in other countries?

For that, we need to examine culture as a whole, as a "system with many mutually interdependent parts."[16] We need to understand first that hierarchies, collectivism and ascribed status are valued in many Eastern cultures. Then, we might understand why that business card is of symbolic importance; we might be able to predict what other cultures take a similar approach (those with similarly hierarchical, collectivist, ascription-oriented cultures), and we might be able to ponder how those values may manifest in other ways within Japan (such as a preference for group decision-making and promotions based on seniority).

Additionally, we want to look beyond the expected dimensions within Japan. While those are instructive, they don't explain the cultural values of every

Japanese. Some Japanese may be highly individualistic, others traditionally collectivist; some may be extroverted, rather contrary to the introverted type we may imagine. Consequently, it is incumbent on us to know how to identify where individuals as well as societies as a whole fall on the spectrum of cultural dimensions.

Let's consider a hypothetical to see how we might use our understanding of cultural dimensions to better understand the behavioral and motivational drivers of a person: if an American believes that the US Constitution is the most important document in US history, what does this tell you about Americans? Without knowing whether most Americans would agree with *this* American, it doesn't tell us much. What does it tell us about *this* American, then?

At the very outset, it suggests that he is a universalist – he puts his faith in a set of rules that apply to everyone. We could then inspect the Constitution itself to learn more. There, we would see clauses such as the right to freely exercise any religion, the right to freedom of speech, the right to bear arms – in short, it is a cornucopia of individual, rather than collective rights. It is reasonable to assume then that proponents of this document will tend to be individualistic and thus believe in a right to behave in most any way that does not cause harm to others. The prohibition of alcohol appears as a curiosity – a decidedly collectivist idea in limiting the rights of individuals for the benefit of the group – but its subsequent repeal just fourteen years later highlights this as the exception that proves the rule.

Additionally, the focus on human rights such as freedom of religion, the prohibition of slavery and the right of all persons to vote regardless of race, religion or gender suggests the person holds relatively egalitarian values, though the fact that these provisions were not in the original document suggests some caution in this analysis. At the very least, we know that such values have not always been held within America.

Subsequently, cross-cultural students might add credence to these assumptions by looking up all of these dimensions for American society. They would find that America is indeed highly individualistic, egalitarian as a society (though less so at the organizational level), and with a modest level of gender egalitarianism in practice but aspiring for greater equality. As noted above, this man is unlikely to perfectly fit the American cultural stereotype, but he is likely to share many of the values and so the substantive overlap strengthens our predictions.

Finally, we go one last step and apply the lessons set forth in this book connecting the cultural dimensions to the business organization and the business leader. If our hypothetical man is universalistic as hypothesized, he is unlikely to give special treatment to employees, and we might expect him to be a stickler for the rules. However, because he is not only universalistic but also egalitarian and presumably holds gender equality in high regard, we can also expect him to extend fair treatment to all employees based on objective characteristics. We can guess from the constitutional preferences for equality between all people that he would be willing to promote based on performance, not status or gender, and because he is universalistic, based on objective indicators and not just subjective preferences.

These are, however, hypotheses and may or may not accurately describe the person before us.

The point is that by focusing on these important characteristics of people's lives and integrating these facts with known cultural dimensions, we can extrapolate much about individual beliefs. The bigger the belief or the stronger the impact on one's life, the more powerful the predictions. But even small observations, when cobbled together, may add up to something insightful. See a Norwegian waiting patiently at a deserted streetlight for the light to turn in her favor? You have the first indications of a universalist. Walk with her for a moment and overhear her phone conversation, in which she says, "Boss, I think that's a really bad idea," and it would not be unreasonable to suspect someone unafraid of power differentials. Observe her hang up the phone, put in her headphones and begin jogging, and it's worth wondering whether she is future-oriented as she keeps an eye on her long-term health.

Let's now return to these dimensions in detail and review the tools to make such analyses.

References

1 Hofstede, *supra* note 4 at 89.
2 Marcus W. Dickson, Renee S. BeShears, and Vipin Gupta, "The Impact of Societal Culture and Industry on Organizational Culture: Theoretical Explanations," in *Culture, Leadership, and Organizations: The GLOBE Study of 62 Societies* 75 (eds. Robert House, Paul J. Hanges, Mansour Javidan, Peter W. Dorfman, and Vipin Gupta, SAGE Publications) (2004).
3 Id. at 76.
4 Vipin Gupta and Paul J. Hanges, "Regional and Climate Clustering of Societal Cultures," in *Culture, Leadership, and Organizations: The GLOBE Study of 62 Societies,* 190–192 (eds. Robert House, Paul J. Hanges, Mansour Javidan, Peter W. Dorfman, and Vipin Gupta, SAGE Publications) (2004).
5 Id. at 183.
6 Id. at 184.
7 Id.
8 Id. at 185.
9 Id. at 186.
10 Id.
11 Id.
12 Id. at 187.
13 Id. at 188.
14 Id. at 188.
15 Id. at 189.
16 Schusky and Culbert, supra note 3.

INDEX

Note: Page numbers in italic and bold refer to figures and tables, respectively.

accountability 57, 151
achievement-ascription: meritocracy and ascription societies 65–6, **67**; "need for achievement" 68–73; onion diagram **67**; self-fulfilling prophecy 64–5; status 67–8
achievement-orientation: attributions 62; societies 62–3, 65–6
achievement-oriented mentality 161
active-leisure activities 6
agentic state 37
agricultural revolution and collectivism 17
altruistic punishment 58
Altruistic Punishment in Humans (article) 58
ambassador-related commissions 152
ambition 70, 73, 135
ambitious-types 135, 137, 165
American culture 3–4, 11
Anglo-American societies 163–4
Anglo-Saxon cultures 179
antisocial punishment 58–9
Ariely, Dan 31, 127, 154
arrogance 100
Asch, Solomon 41–3
Asch experiment 42
ascribe status 62
ascription-based society 63
ascription-orientation 63
ascription-oriented audience 66

assertiveness: authoritative leaders and 135; behavior 138; charisma and narcissism 137–42; consultative and agreeable leaders 135–6; countries 136; cultural dimensions 134–5; defined 134; extrovert and 136; gender egalitarianism 134; GLOBE study 136; humility 138; individualistic 135; introversion-extroversion 139–42; leadership 138; "masculine" dimension 135–7; onion diagram **139**; practicing **137**; societies 135; unassertive people 135
attribution societies 92
authentic devils 47
authoritarian leadership 94
authoritative leaders and assertiveness 135
autocratic leadership 93–5
autonomy 12, 76, 96, 145–6, 148, 150–1; and mastery 146
autonomy-undermining scenario 152
availability heuristic 126

backhanded compliments 152
balanced lifestyle 71
Bay of Pigs and humility 33–6, 43
behavior 8
behavioral economics 3
behavioral psychology 8

belief systems and institutions 7
benevolent autocrat 95
Berns, Gregory 44
Bickman, Leonard 103–4
"bitter factional infighting" 60
blind obedience to authority, discouraging 38–41
Booth, Mac 35
Branson, Richard 165
Brett, Jeanne M. 38, 87, 181
bridge to cultural barrier 180–3
Bryson, Bill 172, 205
Buddhism 62, 83
Buffett, Warren 106
bureaucracies 91
bureaucratic organization 91

Cain, Susan 139
Cameron, Kim 90–1
careers and contributions 105
caste system 82
chaebols 63
chain of command 87
child-bearing 13
Chinese human rights activists 66
Churchill, Winston 41
class-conscious people 66
cognition 8
cognitive bias 126–7
cognitive dissonance 44, 149
coherence and diversity 48–51
collective thinking 33
collectivism 16, 31–3, 87, 187; consensus and 22; and hierarchy 23; type 12
collectivists 20–2, 59–60; cultures 21–2, 32; and hierarchical societies 22–3; societies 11, 15–17, 69
Collins, Jim 36, 38, 156
communication 105, 153, 172–4; bridge to cultural barrier 180–3; context and emotiveness 178–9; low context, high context 175–8; networks 90; neutral, affective 174–5; nonverbal communications 179–80
community bonding 15
compensation 151; packages representative 20
competence 68–9
confirmation bias 46
conformity: at business environments 32; encourage dissent and avoid 51; in workplace 41–5

confrontational approach 40
Confucianism 17, 62, 69, 81, 83; hierarchical relationships 83
Confucian societies 163
conglomerates 63
connectedness 49
consensus and collectivism 22
consultative and agreeable leaders 135–6
context and emotiveness 178–9
Cook, Tim 48
critical thinking 37, 96
cross-cultural actors 116
cross-cultural applicability 155
cross-cultural businesspeople 85, 175
cross-cultural conflict 51
cross-cultural management 3
cross-cultural managers 138
cross-cultural negotiation 20, 87, 181
cross-cultural organizations 156
cross-cultural studies 43
cross-cultural tactic 39
cultural affinity 6
cultural differences 16
cultural dimensions 213–19
cultural future orientation 162
cultural imperialism 5
culturally driven miscommunications 173
cultural variability 89–90
culture 1–2; absolute presupposition about life 5; defined 4–8; economic, political and religious 5–7; human nature *vs* 8–9; lag 5; with low future orientation 162; onion diagram **7**; pancultural **9**; survival mechanism 7–8
customers 2
cyberattack 66

Darwin, Charles 204
death from overwork 70–1
decision-making process 34
defiance 37
degree of egalitarianism 77
degree of universalism 8
dehumanization 103
delay discounting 168
delaying gratification 165–9
delegative leadership 93–4
DeLisle, Tracy 152
Deming, W.E. 39
democratic leadership 93–4
differences of opinion 14

direct confrontation 177
dirty industries 49
discomfort and ascription-achievement hybrid 66
discouraging conformity 45–8
diversity: and cohesion 49; ethnocentrism 203–4
dominant religion of society 6
Drucker, Peter 100
Dweck, Carol 34–5
dynamic responsiveness 164–5

Earley, P. Christopher 59
Ebbers, Bernard 102
economic indicators 80
economic productivity 91
economic prosperity 25–6, 70
economic revolution in *Sapiens* 18
economic success 164
The Economist 5
educational systems, China 96
egalitarian culture 92
egalitarianism 82, 85, 94
egalitarian managers 93
egalitarian organizational cultures 93
egalitarian societies and organizations 94
ego 34, 100; assertiveness cultural dimension 35
egotistical leaders 100–10
elixir of power: avoiding *106*; combating 104–6; egotistical leadership 101; power corrupts 101
Elliott, Jane 188
emotions and behaviors 21
employees 2; autonomy 91; empowerment 90; honesty 68; loyalty 22–3; performance 96; satisfaction 68, 96; social relationships 22–3
employer-employee relationships 23
employment: for life 2; termination 105
enculturation 14, 18
Enlightenment Era 18
Epictetus 180
Equatorial Guinea 79–80
E-test 105
ethnocentrism 113, 186–7, 196–7; diversity 203–4; gender ideology 189–93; gender stereotyping 193–5; in-group coherence 198–203; out-group discrimination 198–9; stereotypes 187–9; strategic mimicry and conformance 204–6

European individualism 18
extrinsic motivations 146–8
extroverts 139–42; countries **141**; Europeans and Americans 140; migrants' 140; onion diagram **142**; people feature's 139; sex partners 140–1

face-to-face interactions 50
fairness 66
familiarity heuristic 126
fan fiction 150
fear and anxiety 130
feelings of self-confidence 145
Ferreira, Juan 50
fictional negotiation 105
Five-Factor Model of Personality 8
flexible work practices 73
Ford, Henry 156
"the framing effect" 130
Franklin, Ben 162
freedom 17; of expression 85; of information 66
free-riding effect 56–9; in collectivist cultures 59–60; for individualists and collectivists 60; in-groups 59–60; out-groups 59–60
future-oriented individuals 165

Galinsky, Adam 101–2, 105
Gates, Bill 90
gender egalitarianism 12, 134, **195**
gender ideology 189–93
gender stereotyping 193–5
"genius to folly syndrome" 102–3
German business culture 115
Gini coefficients 85
Gini index 79
global competitiveness 25–6
GLOBE 73, 213, 217; measure of gender equality 190; report 162
GLOBE Study of 62 Societies 3
"goldilocks" principle 120
good father 95
Good to Great (book) 36, 106
Google 66, 92
governance 84–5, **86**
governmental decision-making 164
governmental spending and tax incentives 18
Grant, Adam 130; affirmation of cohesion 48
gravediggers 49
green sheet process 36

gross domestic product per capita (GDP/capita) 78–9
group bonus scheme 21
group dynamics 33
group praise and rewards 20
groupthink: Bay of Pigs and humility 33–6; blind obedience to authority, discouraging 38–41; coherence and diversity 48–51; conformity in workplace 41–5; defined 33–4, 51; discouraging conformity 45–8; individualist and collectivist biases 31–3; obedience to authority 36–8; overcoming 33, 41–5, 51; prevention *51*

Haidt, Jonathan 18, 49
Hall, Edward T. 161
happiness 146
hard work 70
harmony-seeking organizations 39
heuristics 126, **132**
hierarchical cultures 37
hierarchical organizations 93
hierarchical society 38–9
hierarchical *vs* egalitarian: autonomy 76; degree of egalitarianism 77; governance 84–5, **86**; leadership styles and power distance 93–6; paternalism and Gini coefficient 78–81; power 76; power distance 77, 87–90; professional freedom 76; religion 82–4; success in velocipedic age 90–3
hierarchical work environments 95
hierarchy and stability 81
hierarchy of needs 144–6, *145*
high-context communicators 176
high-context culture 176–7
high-level employees 156
high standards 70
high status people 68
Hindu religion and caste system 82
Hofstede, Geert 3, 165
Holocaust 37
honesty 66, 105
House, Robert J. 187
How Google Works (book) 92
human happiness 144–6, *145*
humanity 81, 103; lack of 34
human nature *vs* culture 8–9
humility 36, 138
Hyundai 63

illiberal democracies 85
Indian caste system 63
indicator of merit 64
individualism 11–12, 130; collectivism 16, 31–3; collectivists in workplace 20–2; employee loyalty and social relationships 22–3; in-group 12–17; institutional collectivism 25–7; societal and religious drivers 17–20; transformational leadership, loyalty through 23–5
individualistics and egalitarian cultures 22–3
individualists 59–60; teams 21
industrialization and individualism 18
inferiority 67–8
Information Age 90
informational advantage 90
in-group collectivism 12; collectivists in workplace 20–2; and economic conditions 12–17; societal and religious drivers 17–20
in-groups 59–60; *see also* out-groups; coherence 198–203; collectivists 20, 25; as in collectivist societies 78; competition 49; individualism 12, **13**
institutional collectivism 25–7, **26**; collectivism onion **27**; personal individualism 27; in personal lives 26
intellectual property 88
intelligence 68–9
International Herald Tribune 90
intolerance 113
intrinsic motivation 146–9, 151, 157
introversion-extroversion 139–42
introverts 139–42; in Asia 140; countries **141**; Finland 140; onion diagram **142**; people feature's 139
"irrational decisions" 130
Iveco 172

Japan 176
Japanese custom 181–2
Jobs, Steve 146
job satisfaction 73, 95

Kalishman, Tom 49, 202
karma 82
karoshi 70–1
Keuper, Nicholas 33
King Jr., Martin Luther 188

kleptocratic dictators 101
Knight, Chuck 40
"know-it-all" manager 92
Kraut, R.E. 153
Kurt 181
Kyrgyz Republic 186–7

laissez-faire leadership 93–4
Land, Edwin 35
language barrier 173; *see also* communication
Lay, Kenneth 35
layered culture 4–5
leaders, behavior 103
leadership 1; of conglomerates 63; consensus and collaborative behaviors 139; styles and power distance 93–6
Lee, Richard Borshay 100
Liberian sex-worker 163
liberty 145
listening and observing 183
Lord of War, The (movie) 163
loss of humility 101
low-context cultures 175
lower-income economies 16
low-skilled workers 148
low-status people 68
loyalty: and interconnectedness 25; and teamwork 93; through transformational leadership 23–5

managers: and opinion surveys 105; self-orientation 105–6
market-driven logic 156
marsh-mallow children 167
"masculine" dimension, assertiveness 135–7
Maslow, Abraham 144
Maslow's pyramid (hierarchy) 144–6, *145*
mastery 146, 148
Mayo, Margarita 138
McDonnell, John 33, 36
McDougall, Christopher 8
Medina, Carmen 67
mental programming 5, 16, 93
meritocracy 64; and ascription societies 65–6, **67**
middle-class consumer goods 79–80
Milgram, Stanley 37, 41, 45, 68, 103
mindless automatons 18
Mischel, Walter 166
modeling collective commitment 24
Montupet, Jean Paul 1–2, 40, 176
moral responsibility 22

Morita, Akio 35
Mother Tongue, The (book) 172, 205
motivation 8, 151, **158**
motivational leaders 101
multiplicity of interactions 88
Musk, Elon 165
Muslim community 84
Muslim religion 84
mutual interdependencies 49
mutuality 23

natural athletic ability 65
Natural Born Heroes (book) 8
"natural" inclination 101–2
negotiations 129
Nemeth, Charlan 47
New York Times 90, 106
noncontingent rewards 151
nonfinancial extrinsic rewards 152
nontrivial challenges 147
nonverbal communications 179–80
non-violence 66
non-Western economies 165
"no risk, no reward" perspective 69
Nowak, Tim 87–8

obedience experiments 37
obedience to authority 36–8; discouraging **41**
one-size-fits-all solution 93
onion diagram: achievement-ascription **67**; assertiveness **139**; culture **7**; extroverts **142**; introverts **142**; time horizon **168**; uncertainty avoidance (UA) **122**
opinion surveys 105
organizational loyalty 23
organizational resilience 91
organizations, as regulators and lawmakers 105
Originals (book) 67
out-groups 59–60; *see also* in-groups; discrimination 198–9
overconfident personalities 140
over-justification hypothesis 150
oxytocin, pleasure-inducing chemical 19

pancultural 7, **9**, 66, 73, 96
pan-cultural application 154
pan-cultural behaviors 211
pan-cultural motivation 144–6; cross-cultural implications 146–8; extrinsic rewards 148–54; motivation **158**; task performance 154–7

participative leadership 93–4
particularism 23, 117
past-oriented individuals 163
paternalism 22, 78–81, 83, 93; governance 84–5, **86**; religion 82–4
paternalistic management culture 78
pawnbrokers 49
"pay-for-performance" incentives 20
performance: and expectations 64; improvement 70; orientation 25–6
Performance without Compromise (book) 40
"person-environment fit" 141
Peruvian culture 3–4
Pink, Daniel 164
Poehler, Amy 111
Polish and Czech managers 94–5
political systems 6
Powell, Colin 71
power 76; as static 102; and status 67
power distance 77, 87–90; and business decisions 87–90; culture 81; and leadership styles 93–6; organizational 94; within organizations 77; political structure 84; productivity and 77; relative income equality 83; satisfaction and 77; South Asian and East Asian societies 83
Predictably Irrational (book) 31, 127
Pre-Information Age 90
problem-solving skills 155
professional freedom 76
prostitutes 49
protestant 82
protestantism 69, 82
"Protestant work ethic" 69
psychological health 70
psychology 3
public institutions and economic prosperity 25–6
public recognition 21
push-pull tension 49
pyramidal power scheme 81

Quiet: The Power of Introverts in a World That Can't Stop Talking (book) 44, 139
Quran 84

Rand, Ayn 35
regional commonalities 163
relationship-oriented particularist cultures 121
relative paternalism 79

religion 82–4; and culture 6–7; and governance 81
Renaissance 18
representativeness heuristic 126
respect and family **63**
reward group participants 21
Riding the Waves of Culture (book) 3
right to privacy 66
risk-averse countries 114–15
risk aversion 109–10
risk-aversion bias: in Americans 129; Asian participants 129; and behavior 129–30; and business 130–2; cognitive bias 126–7; difference in offers 128–9; heuristics 126, **132**; negotiations 129; rational perspective 128; self-criticism 129
risk-taking behavior 111
risk tolerance 111–12
Rosenberg, Jonathan 92
rugged individualism 12
rule-based approach to business 175
rule-based orientation 119
rule of law 118

sacrifices 20
Samsung 63
Sandberg, Sheryl 71, 129
Sapiens: A Brief History of Mankind (book) 82
satisfaction surveys 31–2
satisfaction to employees 22
Save More Tomorrow retirement plan 167
Schmidt, Eric 92
scholastic aptitude test (SAT) 167
self-acclaimed reputation, manager 92
self-actualization 112
self-aggrandizement 81
self-criticism 129
self-determination 146
self-fulfilling prophecy 64–5, 92, 122
self-help mechanisms 110
self-identification 18
self-interest 24
self-oriented 102
self-policing 60
self-reliance 12, 17
self-sacrifice 24
self-serving bias 36
self-serving incentive 57
seniority 64; and competence 92
sense of fairness 58
sense of loyalty 14
sense of reciprocity 22
sense of satisfaction 96

sense of self 14
sense of societal well-being 17
sense of urgency 69
shared organizational values 104–5
shareholders 2
Singaporeans and uncertainty 112
social and economic inequality 84
social anxiety 21
social bonds 15
social connectedness 157
social contract 14, 16, 81; theory 95
social hierarchy 83
social loafing 56
social pressure 56
social relationships 146, 148
societal earnings 15
societies, benefits 70
sociopolitical differences 82
stable organization 73
statistical office 41
status and power 67
"status endowment effect" 68
stereotypes 64–5, 187–9
stereotyping 65
Stone Age 17
strategic mimicry and conformance 204–6
strikes 3
structural constraints 105
struggling elders 13
Sulloway, Frank 110–11
supporting partner 46
Suriewicki, James 33

tax incentives 18
team performance 58
teamwork 55–6
temporal and spiritual realms of society 84
Thaler program 168
Thiel, Peter 35
thinking, loss aversion 130
time commitment 22
time horizon onion diagram **168**
time orientation 162–4; delaying gratification 165–9; dynamic responsiveness 164–5; economic success 164
trade-off theory 140
traditional economic reliance 16
transactional leadership 23–5
transformational leadership, loyalty through 23–5
tried-and-true management techniques 46
trust 88, 94; uncertainty avoidance (UA) 120–2

trustworthiness 122
turnover 23; intentions 73
tyranny 81

UA *see* uncertainty avoidance (UA)
"Ultimatum Game" 57
unassertive people 135
uncertainty avoidance (UA): high societal 112–13; and less-developed countries 112; low individual 112–13; onion diagram **122**; practicing **113**; question often, judge slowly 117–20; religion and ideologies 116; risk aversion 109–10; risk reduction 114; risk-taking behavior 111; risk tolerance 111–12; rule of law, technology and science 110; self-help mechanisms 110; technology 114–15; trust 120–2; universalism, contractual/legal implications 120–2; universalism *vs* particularism 116–17
uniqueness, need for 32, 43
unity and societal harmony 17
universalism 117; contractual/legal implications 120–2; *vs* particularism 116–17
"unremitting guerilla warfare" 60
unskilled laborers 147
Upside of Irrationality, The (book) 154

velocipedic age 90–3; success in 90–3
vision of leadership 71

Weber, Max 69
WEIRD (western, educated, industrialized, rich and democratic) 1, 11, 36, 58–9, 62
The Weirdest People in the World? (book) 8
"What Makes an Effective Executive" 100
Wisdom of Crowds, The (book) 33
worker bees 18
work-group dynamics 21
WorldCom 102
World War Z 46
Wrighton, Mark 91

yes-man culture 38
YouTube 150

Zakaria, Fareed 85
Zamenhof 180
Zimbardo, Philip 103, 189
Zuckerberg, Mark 106
Zweigenhaft, Richard 110–11